11/04/2022

For Friendship's sake,

Dr

Dan

THE DUST OF

OLD DOLE ROAD

THE DUST OF
OLD DOLE ROAD

FROM POVERTY TO PEACE

DAN OLIVER

Tate Publishing & *Enterprises*

Published by Tate Publishing & Enterprises, LLC
127 E. Trade Center Terrace | Mustang, Oklahoma 73064 USA
1.888.361.9473 | www.tatepublishing.com

Tate Publishing is committed to excellence in the publishing industry. The company reflects the philosophy established by the founders, based on Psalm 68:11,
"The Lord gave the word and great was the company of those who published it."

Cover design by Rebekah Garibay
Interior design by Christina Hicks

Published in the United States of America

ISBN: 978-1-61777-103-3
1. Religion / Christian Life / Personal Growth
2. Biography & Autobiography / Personal Memoirs
11.02.09

Photo Gallery

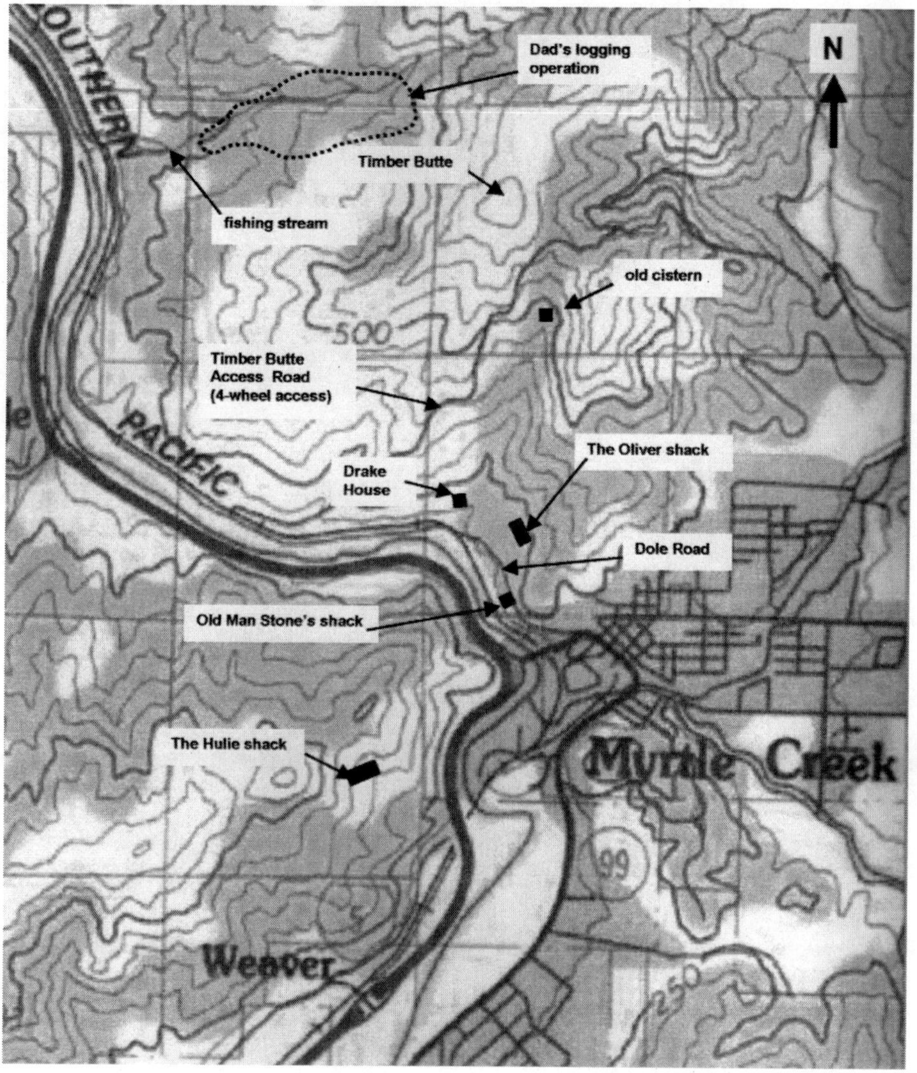

Myrtle Creek, Oregon, typography showing locations referenced in book.

U.S. Highway 99 bridge over the South Umpqua River, at north entrance to Myrtle Creek. View is from the conglomerate bluff off Dole Road, as it was in 1960, with the ever-present sawmill haze.

The Shack, 1950. Mom is in the doorway. Patsy, my oldest sister, is standing beside her. The women in front are Aunt Helen Thackery and Aunt Edna Sjorgren. Note the canvas "siding" on the lower right side of the shack. The dog is Saddy.

A Monarch cooking range. Just like the one Mom cooked on.

Old Maytag washing machine, converted from gasoline engine to electric motor.

Dad and Mom, wedding day, May 1941

Family photo, Summer 1951 at Grandpa and Grandma Backlund's.
Kids left to right: Carol, Ellen, me, Patsy. (Linda yet to be born.)

Cousins in Uncle Paul's old 1928 Chevy (bathtub model), 1950. Left to right: Denny Sjorgren, Rey Ellen Walker, Gary Walker, Dan Oliver, Carol Oliver, Karen Thackery, Marilyn Thackery, Ellen Oliver, and Patsy Oliver. Cousins missing: Dick Sjorgren and Linda Oliver (Linda yet to be born). This picture was taken at Grandpa and Grandma Backlunds, just a few weeks before the Hubbard Creek fire destroyed their home. Note the old fruit jar and the Golden West Coffee can under the car.

Dad's "logging cat." Early Fordson, steel-wheeled farm tractor; otherwise, known as "The Thing."

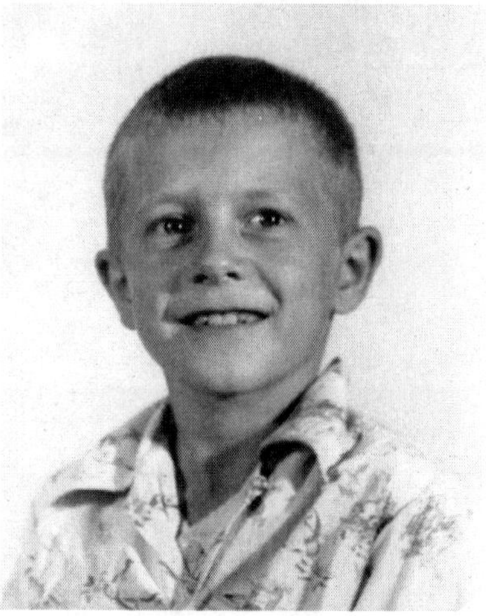

My third grade photo.

Mr. Stone, 1963. Dole Road on left of photo. Myrtle Creek just over the rise behind him. Note the character: stogie, bib overalls, pocket watch outlined in front pocket, garter on left bicep, big ears, no teeth, hair slicked back. Yet, presentable. Gosh, I loved that old man.

Recreation in the "pick'n field," 1960. Me playing guitar. Sisters left to right: Ellen and Carol. Linda standing.

Sitting around in the Schumacher fruit pickers' camp. Mom is second from right

Dad and Mom with "Uncle Joe,"
Schumacher camp boss in 1960.

My first car, 1952 Ford.

Howard Gallios's 1950 Mercury.

Entrance to Gallios boys' broom handle mill. Note slab wood cart and Howard's 1950 Mercury in the background.

Saw table and motor. Stack of cut broom handle "cants" in background.

Back Row, left to right: Harold Gallios, Ada Gallios, Grant Olds, Eldora Olds, May Plum, Howard Gallios, Linda Olds, Carol Gallios, and Grandpa Plum. Kneeling: George Gallios, with younger Old's children. Photo taken just before I enlisted in 1963 at the Plum's Ranch off South Myrtle Road, scene of the infamous "Pistol Pack'n Mama."

George McNaughton and son, Chris in 1963.

My friend Richard Sowersbery, died from Leukemia at age 21, 1963.

My father, Walter "Tiny" Oliver, 1963.

My mother, Dorthy "Dot" Oliver, 1963.

Me just before enlistment in the Air Force in 1963.

My sisters (left to right); Patsy Walton, Ellen Gould, and Linda Bott, 2010.

My sister Carol and husband Richard Smith, 2010.

Myrtle Creek Dairy Queen as it is today. Author's Subaru Forester parked beside restored 1949 Ford pickup—the new and the old.

Me today, at peace.

Dedication

In loving memory of Mom who accepted her lot in life, bearing all with patient endurance and with the expectation that better times are coming.

To my sisters, Patsy, Ellen, Carol, and Linda for their unfeigned love and devotion as they tirelessly ministered to Mom on her deathbed, witnessing to all that she was a loved and precious child of the heavenly Father. May their example be indelibly written in the books of heaven's library to be read by all.

And to Dad, who in spite of the weakness of the flesh, was an instrument of the heavenly Father used by Him to form me into an instrument of His eternal peace.

In Loving Appreciation

To my darling wife, Chloe, whose kind disregard for the sensitivity of my toes allowed her to make the type of edits and critiques the draft copy needed.

Table of Contents

Introduction	25
The Dust of Ol' Dole Road	29
The Trek	31
The Canvas-Sided Shack	45
The Early Years	65
Logging and Attempted Murder	85
Survival 101	101
Survival 201	113
The "Chittim" Years	129
We Called It Fun	149
Friends on the Hill	175
Goodbye Canvas-Sided Shack	197
Fruit-Picker	205
The Good Dole	229
Good Influences (Reasons Why I Will Never Live Like This)	253
Peace	267

Introduction

This book was eight years in the making. I began the first chapter some weeks after my hike around the old home place off Dole Road in December 1999. I cannot recall the exact reasons for the journey, other than a stirring in my aging heart to which I responded. So vivid were the memories that erupted from my subconscious as I trekked Timber Butte that warm winter day, I could hear the echoes of the .22 rifle off the canyon walls where, as a pre-teen, I hunted rabbits, gray squirrel, and deer.

I completed the first chapter in a single evening, after which the project lay dormant, gathering moths in my mind for several years.

Who's going to want to read a stupid story about my life, I mused.

I set it aside. One day in the fall of 2005, I was speaking with my wife, Chloe, of a nagging desire to complete a memoir of my years on Dole Road for my children and grandchildren. She read the draft in its unfinished state and believed that it was more than a simple narration of events and circumstances.

"There's something here that others will want to read; that they need to read," she said. And thus, she gently began to encourage me to complete the project. Off and on, over the next several years, I responded to my wife's kind goads until finally the story is somewhat complete.

My original intent was to leave a simple record of my life during those trying years, when fear and tears were the companions that rocked my sisters and me to sleep. At least to me, it seemed that only in sleep could I escape the cries, the whimpers, and the sodden sounds of flesh hitting flesh as Dad, in drunken rages would curse and verbally and physically abuse Mom until he either grew tired or passed into unconsciousness.

The situations and circumstances were not all bad, but memories of the drunken rages and beatings flavored life with hopelessness and despair. Like I stated, originally I intended to write a simple story of survival, to explain that even in the most difficult and brutal environment, a child can emerge from the chaos and be somewhat adjusted and productive. In telling the story I felt compelled to point out that it was not because of my own inner strength and character that I emerged the person I am today, but to acknowledge the parts played by others who came into and out of my life in that period of time; a critical time that my heavenly Father used to form and shape me. The story also illustrates, in a narrative way, that it is the decisions we make, regardless of our circumstances at any given time that form the person we become.

As the story developed, and especially into the latter chapters, I began to see a thread weaving its way through the narrative. It was no longer a simple description of events; it was becoming something bigger.

You see, in one sense, we are all alike. None of us choose our parents. A baby does not choose where it lives, nor can a child control who its parents are or what they do. The axiom applies to all. While we cannot control our circumstances, we make decisions, and in that sense form who we become as adults. Yes, we each are the biological fruit of a man and a woman, our parents. We then become tempered and shaped by their parenting, our environment, our education, and life's experiences—both good and bad. But it is not only our immediate environment. We must also consider the roles played by acquaintances and friends, and by others who weave their way into and out of our life. I could have been born in a yurt in Mongolia. Or, I could have been born the son of a European aristocrat. In each scenario, the story would be different. And so, my story is indeed "my story." It is unique to me.

For many of my adult years, I struggled to understand the situations and circumstances in Dad's childhood and life's experiences that made him who he was. He was an enigma, two different people. When sober, he was kind and seemed to deal quite well with the trials and pressures of providing for the needs of a wife and five children. But on the other hand, when the level of alcohol reached the required percentage in his bloodstream, a different character emerged. In my attempts to understand why he was the way he was and why he did the things he did that were so hurtful and terrorizing, I would come to a dead end. Perplexed and confused, there never seemed to be reasons for his drunken rages. His actions seemed without rational cause, and thus were beyond the finite capabilities of my experiences and education to comprehend or understand.

While unique to me, my experiences are not unlike those of others. Others have endured far worse than I. For those who have similar experiences, this story may probably stir chords of empathy. My deeper purpose and hope is that it helps you see that in all life's experiences, both good and bad, God weaves the threads in our lives and in our relationships. While we might eventually come to know that His will and purpose is to save us, how He chooses to work with each of His creations is a mystery. Our lives are too often filled with hopelessness and despair, and peace is far from us as we grope like blind men for direction and purpose from what we experience and endure. I have come to see that God has a grand purpose in all He allows. Thus, I draw strength and peace from the wellspring of knowing He is working out all in all for His ultimate praise and glory.

It was not about me, but was becoming the story of how a loving, heavenly Father worked to form the foundation of grace in which I now stand. May the end result of this work be a joint fellowship and worship of the One who works all things for the good of those who love Him.

The Dust of Ol' Dole Road

I walked the cold hills in the late December chill,
Fifty years removed from the time.
Memories came clear, in my mind I could hear,
Daddy cursing and dear Momma crying.

In my mind I looked back, and saw a canvas-sided shack,
Shadows flickered from lamps of kerosene.
Kids praying in fear for Momma so dear,
From the beatings by a man drunk and mean.

Dear Momma don't cry, God will hear by and by,
Oh, dear God, please lighten our load.
Give us peace, Dear Lord, from the pain and discord,
In the shack by that dusty Dole Road.

In the light of day, we'd work and we'd play,
In the shadow of a mean, drunken brute.
And by late afternoon, or by the light of the moon,
We'd be praying in the brush of Timber Butte.

In life day-to-day and at night as we lay,
It seemed our prayers never were heard.
For eight long years, in our struggles and tears,
Five kids prayed these sad, haunting words.

Dear Momma don't cry, God will hear by and by,
Oh, dear God, please lighten our load.

Give us peace, Dear Lord, from the pain and discord,
In the shack by that dusty Dole Road.

As life's pages turned, there were lessons we learned,
Of faith, love, and joy complete.
In pain and loss, we learned of the cross,
And in all, our daily needs did meet.

Though in life we were tried, God's grace was not denied,
Yes, in pain, love and joy were sowed.
And in time God's hand, according to plan,
Moved us from the dust of old Dole Road.

Yes, God heard by and by, and our tears He did dry,
Oh, dear God, you have taken our load.
Peace at last, Dear Lord, from the pain and discord,
We left that shack by the dusty Dole Road

The Trek

I took the north exit off Interstate 5 into Myrtle Creek. Taking an almost immediate left-hand turn onto the narrow bridge, I crossed over the South Umpqua River. Strange, I had never thought how unusual this bridge was. It wasn't that long; a hundred and fifty yards, maybe, and it was lower on the west end than the east end by at least forty feet. The water, tinted like weak coffee with a tinge of milk, flowed centered between the footings of the arch that carried the road on its back. I traversed the river, the engine straining slightly as the old Subaru climbed the bridge grade from west to east. Immediately upon exiting the bridge, I entered Myrtle Creek. I had lived in this town for most of my childhood, and crossed that bridge many times since moving away in 1961, but had never thought much about the strange characteristics of the bridge. It was part of old U.S. Highway 99 and had probably been built in the '20s. I had always thought it a beautiful bridge, a graceful, concrete structure, with one main arch supporting the roadway from underneath.

Crossing the east end of the bridge, and with Old Highway 99 still continuing to climb slightly, I entered Myrtle Creek at the point where Dole Road, dropping steeply from an outcropping of eon's old conglomerate, intersected the highway at a tangent on my left.

The town still wasn't much to look at. It had grown some since I had left, but not much. All the old sawmills had long since become silent and were torn down. Nothing remained to remind one of their prior existence and the role they played in people's lives. The town had once resounded to the twenty-four hour-a-day shrill, whine, and clatter of the timber industry. It now lay silent in this late December morning of 1999. I had decided to come down from my home in Amity to walk the steep hills one more time. A twinge of nostalgia, I guess. Something was unsettled in my mind. I couldn't put a finger on it, but I was soon to know the trek I was about to take was the preamble for the story that follows.

I took the first street to my right at the north end of town and drove a couple blocks further to what is now the city park. Some creative citizens had decided the old mill property and log pond would make a nice community park. They were correct. I had stopped at the park several times over the years and had admired the way the space was used. Where once I had gigged bullfrogs, the pond had been drained, cleaned, and planted with grass. There was a nice flat, five-acre or so, saucer with steep sides. Its bottom had a well-kept ball diamond and space for a soccer field with lots of room left over for spectators and other activities. On the side closest to the river, seven or eight RV sites were created. Showers and toilets were up on the old berm that had once been the west side of the millpond. The old Southern Pacific rail spur ran between the RV site and the river, and if you walked the tracks north for a hundred yards or so, you passed under the east end of the Highway 99 bridge I had crossed just moments before. Yep, it was a nice place. The town folks had done well.

I coasted my old beater Subaru into a parking area. I stretched the old back muscles to remove the ever-present kinks and in the process noticed a small veteran's memorial. Crossing the parking lot, I climbed the half dozen or so steps to read the names. Didn't recognize any. I guess I was subconsciously looking for old friends and classmates. None were found. There were a good number of names on the brass plaque. Must've represented all the men in Douglas County who'd died in all the big and little wars over the years. I spent six years between 1963 and 1969 stateside with Uncle Sam in the Air Force, all during the hottest part of the Vietnam War. There were some Vietnam veterans on the plaque for sure. I felt a lump in my throat. I tried to swallow, but choked. Tears made it difficult to read. It's funny how those things grip one's heart and sort of squeeze your chest. But by this time in my life, I had reached the point in my relationship with my heavenly Father where I had turned all such matters over to Him. I swallowed the lump in my throat, dabbed at the tears with my shirtsleeve, and turned away.

It was close to 9:00 a.m., still fairly early. It was going to be a nice day, especially for late December, and I was getting an early start on what I planned to do. The sun was going to win the battle over the light fog.

Clear sky by noon, I thought.

I returned to the car and opened the rear hatch to get the canvas ankle-high hiking boots I had bought the night before at the Roseburg Wal-Mart. Nice boots, even if they were a trifle large. A couple pair of thick socks took care of the fit problem. We take things so much for granted today. I couldn't help but think what I paid for shoes growing up as a kid. I had to buy my own clothes. I thought about this as I put those boots on. If my memory was any good, it seemed I paid a whole heck of a lot more for necessities back then than I do now. Technology has its benefits. Cheap overseas labor helps, too.

Retrieving a fanny pack with its two water bottles and a "snack" pouch from the car, I locked up and belted on. Clomping from the park, I crossed Main Street (Highway 99) and started my trek up Dole Road. It was paved now, but the grade had not changed, just pavement over the old road surface.

Hmm, I thought, *still as steep as it was back then. Seems to me the Douglas Country road crews could have worked on the grade over the years. Some things never change.*

I worked my fanny off trying to peddle my old tank of a bike up that road without having to get off and push it over the top. That bike must've weighed fifty pounds!

Halfway up that steep pitch of Dole Road, I began looking for a slight trace off to my right. It was still there, though only recognizable by one who knew where to look and what to look for. I wondered how many people living in this town knew that this barely discernible depression coming steeply off the crown and then down the shoulder of the rocky hillside to intersect with Dole Road is a token reminder of the Applegate Trail. I'll bet most of Dole Road was part of the Applegate Trail at one time.

Jesse Applegate and several of his brothers thought there had to be a safer route than the last leg of the Oregon Trail, which involved a dangerous raft trip in the rapids of the Columbia River, at present-day Cascade Locks, Oregon. One of Jesse's sons, a nephew, and an uncle drowned when one of the party's rafts capsized. After setting up a homestead west of present-day Salem, Oregon, he and other family members were determined to locate and open a safer route. The Applegate Trail was the fruit of their efforts. At the time of my trek, the trail he scouted and opened in 1846 was 153 years old. The trail began close to present-day Winnemucca, Nevada, and ended in present-day Dallas, Oregon. While originally it was a rough and often dry trail, it stood the test of time, and for the most part, Oregon Highway 166, U.S Highway 99, and present day Interstate 5 pretty much overlay the original route.

Yep, the Applegates built their trail right past the place where I was destined to live as a kid. I wouldn't have known about this piece of history if Mr. Stone hadn't mentioned it in one of our conversations. Mr. Stone had built a tar-papered squatter's cabin just over the top where Dole road crowned the hill and no more than fifteen feet off the road. If there was a person who fit the definition of "friend," it was that old man. He told me he had come from Missouri in the early 1900s with a team of mules, a covered wagon, and his wife.

Hmm, I wonder if Mr. Stone drove his team of mules over the old Applegate Trail when he made his trek into this part of Oregon.

Thoughts like these played bumper pool in my head as I veered off Dole Road and stepped onto the faint trace of the Applegate Trail.

The trail pitched upward at an ever-increasing angle away from Dole Road. As a kid, I remember faint traces of wheel ruts that yet remained in the soft conglomerate. The trace was only visible for about fifty yards, which took me to the point where it crowned out on the shoulder of the rock outcropping then disappeared completely into a faint foot trail that merged with Dole Road.

At one point I stopped and turned, looking back down that old immigrant trace. I was up sufficient in elevation to see the graceful bridge I crossed less than a half-hour earlier. Turning, I looked up at a hogback rising steeply between the town on the south and Timber Butte to the north. I stepped off the barely visible trace of the Applegate Trail and began my climb. The boots seemed to be working okay.

Not bad for less than twenty bucks, I thought.

The hillside was thick with scrub oak, madrone, and poison oak. As a kid, I had seemingly developed a strong resistance to poison oak, even able to handle it with no harsh consequences. After all these years, I was hoping I still retained immunity to its evil oils. Just to be safe, I carefully picked my way around the stuff (I wasn't raised to be stupid) as I worked my way up the hillside. After a quarter mile or so, I reached a small saddle on the ridge and looked down the steep slope to the north into the small basin where the old shack once stood. It was this very ridge that separated our home from town. Of course, the shack's not there anymore. Douglas County put the property to better use back in the '70s, constructing a local sanitary transfer station. Further down, about a half mile away, and looking north, was the

South Umpqua River and the rail line hugging the bottom edge of Timber Butte. Dole Road lay between the rail line and the river. Everything seemed so much larger from a child's eyes. A scrub oak was a tree; a hill was a mountain.

I had a good view of Myrtle Creek to the south. The mills were long gone. There was not a single mill in that town. They used to have four or five mills with their wigwam burners spewing thick white smoke, which on mornings like this would have simply hung heavy, blanketing the town with soot, grit, and grim. They were the way of life back then. You can get used to anything if you don't know there are alternatives. Back then, we didn't give those burners a second thought. I couldn't help but think how things had changed in the past forty or so years. Now it seems you can't even burn a twig in your backyard without having to get a permit, and God forbid if you don't.

At this point, I was probably three or four hundred feet above the Main Street area, looking down on top of the water reservoir, a large round metal cylinder about a quarter mile directly below me. The main water source for the town, in much earlier times, was taken from a cistern built in the bottom of the small canyon that came off Timber Butte that was now looming off to my left. A six-inch cast iron pipe carried water from the cistern into town. I knew where every foot of that pipe was buried. Dirt had compacted into the trench, leaving a depression for most of its length. It made a nice even-graded trail through the woods.

I continued my climb, keeping to the ridge. Two hours or so of huff'n and puff'n brought me to the crown of Timber Butte. My feet and ankles were now disagreeing with my decision to purchase cheap hiking boots. The boots provided little ankle and instep support as I traversed the steep slopes. Not really a hiking boot. More like a cheap "tennis" shoe with cleat soles.

Red Mountain lay a short distance off to the northeast, with the overlaid and serrated ridges of the Cascade Range disappearing into the lingering morning haze to the east. Timber Butte wasn't that high in the sky, around 2,500 feet. There are no big mountains in that area of the South Umpqua, just valleys separated by steep ridges. Back then it was my "mountain."

Wood smoke from dozens of homes spread tendrils of fleecy lace threading into cracks and crevices of the rough topography. I gazed increasingly eastward into the layered foothills of the Cascades. Forty or fifty miles further east, hidden behind the deepening layers of smoke, blue haze, and the high Cascade ridges, lay Diamond and Crater Lakes.

It was all as I remembered. Oh, there had been small logging operations on several of the slopes over the years, with a couple of new skid roads here and there. Timber Butte was well named. The only timber was on the top of the butte itself. The rest of the mountainside was relatively free of timber, with ranchers continuing to use its open, grassy slopes as sheep graze.

The South Umpqua River was west and about two thousand feet lower in elevation from where I sat on a pitchy stump at the top of the Butte. The calling card of that stump is probably still on the driver's seat of that old Subaru, if the old beater hadn't been recycled into metal. Off to my left was the head of the canyon, where about two-thirds down was the old water cistern. I decided to see if I could find it.

Should be fairly easy to locate, I thought, as it was placed directly in the streambed.

I drank some water from my canteen, ate a candy bar, and began my descent off Timber Butte. I crossed a small clearing that ended in a saddle nestled between Myrtle Creek and the butte, and hit the old access road.

Sometime in the early '50s, a road had been punched from the river up the south shoulder of the Butte into the saddle.

As I turned to my right onto the dirt road, I thought, *Sure a better road now than it was then. Any four-wheel drive rig could make it to the top, even under the somewhat damp conditions of the day.*

By now, the fog had burned off from the lower elevations, and it had warmed a bit.

Wasn't a bad day after all, I thought, as I smiled at my good fortune in choosing this particular day to make the trek.

The road pitched steeply down as I moved off the saddle. I rounded a corner and stopped. A jackrabbit had jumped onto the road from the down slope berm. The little critter was facing me about fifty feet away and didn't seem at all agitated by my presence. I was close enough to see the twitching of its nose; his long ears stood straight up, facing forward. He seemed to be trying to figure me out. I took a couple steps forward; he still didn't move, so I raised my left arm, pointed my forefinger at him and said, nice and loud, "Bang! You're dead!" Darn if the little fellow didn't wobble on his haunches, and plop over on his side! *What in the—?*

That's strange, I thought. *A trickster rabbit. Surely I'm seeing things.*

But as I approached, it didn't move, lying right where it teetered over. I stood over it. It was lying on its left side with its right eye staring up at me already glazing over in death. While it was a skinny thing, it had been eating. It had a couple blades of green grass protruding from the corner of its mouth. I gently touched it with my foot, still not wanting to believe what I was seeing.

Maybe it's a possum rabbit and just acting naturally. But it was nothing more than a jackrabbit that decided to die the moment I pointed my finger at him and said, "Bang."

Yep, I scared him to death. I left him in the road. *I don't know, I didn't check. Maybe he was a her.* The rabbit was still lying there when I rounded the next corner and disappeared from view. *What in the world? Strange.*

When the meat supply was low, there was always a jackrabbit within rifle shot. The part that bothered me about the rabbit that died from my finger bullet was that many times I killed rabbits full of boils. They were diseased! It's a wonder we survived. I still wondered what was wrong with the rabbit back up the road.

The memories came. Suddenly they were there, from the subconscious to the conscious. Scenes long buried in dusty archives of the mind, stimulated by sights, sounds, and smells. Scenes now being displayed in conscious reality. The .22 rifle, jack rabbits everywhere, buzzards drifting on invisible canyon currents, distant sounds of mills and highway traffic, a lamb mewing on some hillside, my dog barking.

I had two good dogs, Saddy and Sandy. Both were sandy colored and of medium build, and both were squirrel-treeing dogs. Saddy was the first dog; Sandy the last, both would chase jack rabbits. Of the two, Sandy had actually caught a rabbit. I had watched her bust up a steep slope chasing the rabbit as it had darted in and out of the greasewood that covered the hillsides. She had carried her kill back to me, laying it at my feet. She had looked up at me with her soft brown eyes and tilting her head as if to say, "Bet you can't do that?"

Shoot, more tears.

Either dog would keep a squirrel treed, barking until Mom or I would grab the .22 and plunk it from its perch. We ate the squirrels too. I never did care for the taste. They were generally fat little critters, as one of their staples was Myrtle nuts. Many of the gullies, washes, and canyons in that country were full of Myrtle trees. They bore a nut about the size of a Macadamia nut. They are a bitter nut, and full of oil. The squirrels liked them, and the nuts made them fat; probably what gave their meat that strong, gamey taste I didn't care for. I didn't see one squirrel this day.

Must've all died off, I said to myself. The Myrtle trees were still there, so the food supply had not disappeared. Oh well, things go in cycles. Another mystery.

Shaking my head to clear the fog bank of memories, I became aware that I had traversed about a half-mile of the slope in a somewhat unconscious state. You know, like when you're on a long road trip and your mind drifts and you can't remember anything about the last hundred miles or so. Anyway, I decided this was a good place to turn left, jump off the road, and head for the bottom of the canyon. I'd then turn downstream and follow the watercourse until I ran into the old cistern.

I had to watch my step. The grass was damp and slick. In places, the slope was greater than forty-five degrees. I stopped to gather my bearings, and in looking around, I realized that I was on a bench where the family had spent part of one summer peeling cascara bark.

I hit the bottom of the canyon after fighting my way through a thick stand of scrub oak and turned right to follow the watercourse to the cistern.

Couldn't help but thinking, *Here it was, the end of December, and there was no water.*

'99 must have been a dry year. As I continued down the bottom of the canyon, a trickle appeared.

I stepped out of the creek bottom onto an old game trail that appeared just above the watercourse on the side of the canyon to my right. It headed in the right direction. Downhill.

At one point I paused and looked at an area I recognized on the opposite side of the stream (still nothing more than a trickle). It wasn't more than fifty or sixty feet away. It was the place I had killed two white-tailed spikes with my Marlin .22 late one summer afternoon. Hunting season was always open for us. When we needed meat, I went hunting. There was always a doe somewhere in the canyon, in some grove of timber, on some bench, or on the slopes of the canyon walls. If I shot, I rarely missed. Dad taught me never to shoot at a moving target, and never to shoot if I did not have a clear shot. I think back on those times and the number of deer I killed to provide meat for the family. The weapon of choice was always the .22 rifle and nothing more, and all before my thirteenth birthday.

Yep, for sure this was the place I killed the two spikes. They were probably brothers, still hanging around together and neither knowing what was to happen. I saw the first one, downed it, then seeing more movement, waited; spotting the second, I downed it too. I knew that what I was doing was illegal. However, my conscience never bothered me. All in the family justified our action. We needed to eat, and it was a simple necessity. There wasn't any right or wrong about it. I look back now at what I did, killing my first deer before my tenth birthday, and dozens more thereafter. Dad taught me to field dress, telling me, "You had better do it right, or the meat will be ruined." I did it right. Even though a white tail isn't the biggest of the deer family, I recall several of the barren does being a little bit more than I could handle as a pre-teen. I always seemed to manage to get them home without bruising too much meat. Most of the meat I bruised was my own anyway.

The cistern was lower in the canyon than I remember, but it was still there. I was surprised to find that it had been enlarged with new sides and a new roof. It was probably fifteen by fifteen feet, and even had a relatively new padlock on the door. There was no glass in the door, but there was an opening covered with a galvanized wire mesh. I saw water in the bottom. Somebody was still using the old city cistern. Couldn't imagine it being the city, but you never know; probably the property owners who now lived on what was then the Old Drake place. They were not using the cast iron pipe, but a two-inch plastic hose. The hose was laid parallel to the rusty cast iron pipe.

I followed the pipe and plastic hose, paralleling one another, both exposed in the creek bottom. In a few more minutes of walking, I came to the place where the exposed cast iron left the creek bottom and became buried in a trench on the hillside. That point marked the beginning of the old "pipe" trail through the woods. The plastic pipe continued down the streambed. It was now obvious that the homeowner lower in the canyon and closer to Dole Road was using the old cistern as a water source.

I stepped out of the creek bottom onto the still faint trail over the pipe trench and followed it until it reached a point a few hundred feet above where the old canvas-sided shack once stood.

Breaking off the trail through the thick stands of scrub madrone, I stepped into a clearing. Instead of our old shack, I was looking at the local Douglas County sanitary transfer station. I had completed a circle from where, a few hours earlier, I had gazed down from the hogback now directly south of me. Across the parking and unloading area, the county had placed several large bins in which the locals could dump their garbage and refuse from elevated concrete platforms.

Man, was this ironic or what? I thought. *This seemed to be a fitting replacement for the "dump" in which we used to live.*

The road into the station followed the general line of our old driveway, which I followed until it met with Dole Road. Crossing over Dole Road, I continued moving down toward the South Umpqua and the railroad tracks. In a short time I hit the tracks, turned left, and followed them into town, passing under the east end of the bridge I had crossed just a few hours before. A hundred yards from the bridge, I stepped off the railroad grade and into Mill Site Park.

As I stood beside the old Subaru, looking around at how things had changed over the years, I thought about the trek I had just completed around an area that defined my existence from 1949 to 1961. There was a stark realism to that period. Terror, too!

The memories were still creating images and sounds in my mind as I started the Subaru and exited the city park. I pulled onto Main Street, heading north back to Mom's home in Winston. At the north end of town, I suddenly pulled the wheel slightly to the right and drove onto Dole Road. I immediately passed the Cornutt home on my right, still standing and looking far better than it did in 1960. We had moved into that rental after Dad was released from his final stint in the Douglas County Jail in late 1959.

As I drove past the house I thought, *Well, at least there were a couple of good years in which living alongside Dole Road wasn't so bad.*

About a half mile further, I drove past the driveway to the old shack off Dole Road (now the entrance to the refuse transfer station).

As I drove, I couldn't stop the stirring in my soul. I began to lose myself in memories of those years when seven people lived in a canvas-sided shack on the outskirts of Myrtle Creek, Oregon. No electricity, no running water, no stable source of income. We lived and existed in the dark shadow of a man who in his drunken stupor blamed everybody but himself for the hand he felt God dealt him, and in his uncontrolled drunken rages directed his anger on the person who loved him most...Mom. How did she endure those years? How did she survive those years of abuse and remain a relatively adjusted, normal person? Shoot, for that matter, how did any of us manage to remain sane and functional? For it was in the despair, in the hopelessness, in the suffering, in the deepest, darkest moments of our circumstances, that all I wanted to do was take the .22 rifle and blow Dad's brains out.

The Canvas-Sided Shack

My memories are like images shrouded in fog. Something triggers them. The winds in my mind blow, and a formless shape is transformed into something recognizable. Such are the memories of those years prior to my sixth birthday. I see a shack on Tisch Creek, a small feeder stream for South Myrtle Creek. I see another home on a hillside next to Clark's Branch road. It's four or five miles upstream from where Clark's Branch Road intersects Dole Road a mile or so from the Round Prairie Lumber Mill. We rented this home from old Mrs. Jennings. Her ranch was another half mile or so further up Clark's Branch. The house we rented burned. I don't remember the fire. Mom lost her wedding ring. We moved into the Golden rental next to Highway 99 on the west side of the South Umpqua about a mile north of Myrtle Creek. We drove back to the burned home to look for Mom's wedding band. We didn't find it. We're back at the Golden place. I can see Dole Road across the river from the house. When it's dry, there's lots of dust from the cars.

I see my oldest sister, Patsy, catching the school bus in the morning and getting off the bus in the evening. It's morning, and it's still dark. A man comes to the door. The man is bleeding from cuts to his face and head. He rolled his car over the bank off Highway 99. His car is on its side almost in our yard. Dad's not home. He's logging and left for work well before sunrise. Mom is scared, says she can't help. She closes the door. The man leaves and comes back with some other men. He has bandages on his cuts. The men roll the car back on its wheels. Somehow they start the car. They are gone.

In another memory, Dad has a workshop in the garage up the driveway by the highway. It's my fifth birthday, and he surprises me with a present. It's a toy truck with wheels. It's blue. I put my knee on the flat bed, and push with my other leg. I can "ride" the truck on the linoleum in the living room.

And still another memory. I'm crying. I'm putting on my socks. Mom asks what's wrong. I tell her, "I don't know which one's the left sock and which one's the right sock." She laughs. She tells Dad when he comes home from work. They both laugh.

It's 1949. We are moving again.

....

There were six of us when we moved onto the Rice place. The Rice place consisted of about forty hillside acres off Dole Road less than a mile north of Myrtle Creek. Dole Road is on the east side of the South Umpqua River. It begins where it intersects Highway 99 at the north end of Myrtle Creek and ends where it intersects Highway 99 again, about six miles north of town across the South Umpqua from what at that time was the Round Prairie Lumber Company.

Dad was older than Mom by about fourteen years, and at the time we moved to the Rice place, he was around forty or forty-one. Everybody called him "Tiny" because he was short. He stood five-foot-four and weighed 140 pounds. There wasn't an ounce of fat on him. He grew up in Riddle with a mean-spirited dad and eleven or twelve living brothers and sisters. Grandma Mabel died in 1918, having contracted a severe case of the "Spanish Flu," and of complications delivering her fifteenth child. Grandpa Frank died in 1936.

Dad was born in 1908 in a covered wagon in Talent, Oregon, when my grandpa was in the process of moving my grandma, and ten or so other kids, from Klamath Falls to Riddle, Oregon. Can you imagine that? I find it difficult at times to get my mind wrapped around that concept. It's not so difficult when I realize that Grandpa was born in 1863 during the Civil War! Both Grandpa and Dad married in their early thirties; and so because of their late marriages, it was like skipping a generation, leaving me with the interesting fact that I am only one generation removed from the Civil War.

Dad had black curly hair and green eyes. Though his dad was Irish, his mom was Dutch. He said he was black Irish. He had a quick temper, becoming extremely temperamental and violent when drinking passed a certain point. Not that in this statement I am disparaging any black Irish who are of even temperament. I only echo some of the words Dad used to excuse his behavior. Somewhere prior to his marriage to Mom, he had nurtured alcoholism. He had just turned thirty-three when he married and had about fifteen years of bachelorhood under his belt in which to cultivate bad habits.

He had an eighth grade education, which was typical of people of his time. He was quite intelligent and had a gifted ability to make do with just about anything at hand. Must have been the way he was raised. I know little of his early years and the events and circumstances that formed and shaped him into the person he was. He wasn't a constant drunk; probably what we label a binge drinker. He would get to drinking, and in the early stages before he turned mean and ugly, he was social and talkative. He would tell us stories about prospecting on Cow Creek, or working in the potato and alfalfa fields in eastern Oregon, or driving long-haul trucks from Roseburg to Portland for his brother-in-law, Elmer Landers. He'd often state that, in his youth, he and his older brother, Archie, were decent boxers and used to go at it, with or without gloves, especially when their drinking reached a certain stage. He mentioned on several occasions about being a golden glove's boxer, but I didn't put much stock in that—just booze talk. But who knows? Like I said, I really didn't know that much about his life prior to his marrying Mom.

Mom's name was Dorothy, but everybody called her "Dot." She was nineteen when she married, and immediately began to have kids, four of the five between 1941 and 1946. First there was Pat in July, 1941; me in November, 1943; Ellen in February, 1945; Carol in October, 1946. Linda came along in January, 1951, a year or so after we moved onto the Rice place on Dole Road.

Mom was a gentle spirit, inheriting all the patience of Job from her dad and mom. Grandpa Carl Backlund was an immigrant Swede, Grandma Mabel, an orphaned Norwegian. There must have been something in this mix of genes that gave Mom her gentle spirit. I never saw Mom get mad or angry with anybody, even with cause, nor to gossip or slander.

There was an interesting piece of family history that came to the fore when Grandma went to apply for Social Security. Seems there were no records of Grandpa Carl being a U.S. citizen! He was an illegal! As the story goes, Grandpa Carl and his brother Oscar left Sweden and ended up in eastern Canada. They walked across Canada following the Trans Canadian Railroad, and ended up "immigrating" into the United States through the panhandle country of Idaho. They worked in the woods for a time, eventually hearing about a community of Swedes and Norwegians in the Roseburg, Oregon area. So exchanging logging boots for walking shoes, they continued west, settling in the Elgarose community west of Roseburg up against the east slope of the Coast Range.

Grandpa Backlund immigrated from Sweden to Elgarose. Well, the Olivers "immigrated" from the west side to the east side of the South Umpqua. I don't know why we moved to the Rice place, other than the fact it didn't cost Dad one red cent. That must have been an appealing benefit for Dad. Free rent was good. Mrs. Rice owned the property. The Rice family were early settlers in Douglas County. She, or her family, also owned the Rice Furniture store in town. She needed somebody to "keep an eye" on her forty-acre place, as there were folks using her property for a garbage dump. Dad told me later that she also wanted to keep the woodcutters away. So they had their agreement. Stay as long as you want. Just stop the dumping and woodcutting on those forty hillside acres. I was six years old, or close to it.

There was an old shack, but the roof was bad. We could not live in the house until the roof was fixed. There was no electricity, no running water, no indoor plumbing, and obviously, no outdoor plumbing.

We lived in a tent through most of the first winter! It was an old World War II army surplus tent, square with a metal-protected hole for a stovepipe. Mom's Monarch range was our heat and cooking surface. I don't remember much else. Mom said it was absolutely miserable—cold, wet, drafty—and the tent sat at an angle, as no level ground was available to pitch it on. Everything in the tent sort of sloped downhill. All of us kids got sick, and both Dad and Mom were certain one of us was going to die from some damp winter malady. We all had constant, severe colds. The experience tempered our constitutions though; made us tough.

So there we were: a poor family of six—rag-tagged, bedraggled, and sick. Four kids ranging from three to eight in age, living in a tent in the middle of a wet, cold, Oregon winter. I look back on that miserable time and ask myself if the emigrants didn't have it easier moving up the Applegate Trail in covered wagons?

Dad dug a hole and installed the outdoor "plumbing." He dug another hole in the streambed to catch run-off water and called it a well. Yes, we drank the stuff. No filters, no modern way to get at the water but to dip a bucket into the hole and carry this "potable" brew 150 feet to the house. It was that way until we moved off the place in 1958. Oh, we dug a well, put a hand pump on the well cover, but we still had to hand-carry water to the house. That barely potable brew must have been another source that tempered our constitutions. Heaven knows the forms of microbes we ingested from mice, bugs, slugs, and worms sliding off the dank dirt sides to stew in the shallow pool at the bottom.

I must have been a tough little bugger in the physical sense, too, as the water-hauling chore ended up my responsibility. I detested washing day, as all the bath water and water for washing clothes had to be hand-carried with dozens of trips. Even as a six and seven-year-old child, I remember carrying three-gallon buckets, one in each hand Though pretty much taxing my strength, it was my way of reducing the number of trips. Dad jokingly said I was lazy, that what I was really doing was cutting down my work time.

Yeah, so what, Pop; besides, two buckets provide balance.

One bucket made me twist to the side and so, indeed, two buckets were more comfortable than one bucket.

We moved into the shack out of desperation. The tent wasn't working—too cold, too drafty. The shack was no larger than a small singlewide mobile home. It was fifteen-by-thirty feet. Four hundred and fifty square feet of living space for a family of seven!

Ah, the memories of the Monarch range. It had warming ovens above the cooking plate and a big baking oven with the temperature gauge on the outside of the door. Mom loved that stove, and she could make it sing to the tune of her cooking. With the right amount of wood in the firebox and with the right settings on the dampers, she could get the heat adjusted for any kind of cooking or baking. This was the stove she had in the Golden place, and for the remainder of that first winter, it was our only source of heat. That shack used and abused heat. It had holes everywhere. At first, even the tent wasn't as drafty. Cracks in the floor, no inner walls, only the outside walls with knot holes plugged with tops of tin cans and then covered with newspaper and cardboard. The spaces where the roof trusses rested were open, and we stuffed anything and everything we could find into those gaps to stop the mad rush of heat from the house. Dad ripped the almost non-existing doors from their frames, built "new" ones from scrapes of lumber, and that's how we lived the remainder of that first winter and spring. In the eight years we lived in that shack, Dad never built new doors. I can still see the Z-bracing on the inside of the doors.

The tent no longer existed. It morphed into a roof of sorts. Dad cut and layered strips of canvas over what little roof existed to seal the major holes. While the roof still leaked, it wasn't too bad. A few pots, pans, and empty coffee cans took care of the problem until a more permanent roof was built. With the major holes in roof and walls sealed, and the floor covered with strips of heavy tarpaper and linoleum, the shack was transformed into a domicile that was definitely better than the tent.

In the two years that followed our move into the shack, Dad worked between binges to improve the "house." If there had originally been windows in the house, I don't quite remember. I remember the windows Dad made. He used whatever he could find. What he found were windows from old abandoned cars. He took a flat windshield, or a side door window, framed it, and then placed the framed window into a piece of plywood about three-by-four feet. He hinged the piece of plywood at the top and fastened this co-mingled piece of wood and glass to an opening he cut and framed in the side of the shack. The hinges allowed the window to open up and out from the bottom. We'd prop it open with a stick Dad cut for that purpose. In this way, we were able to ventilate the house from time to time. This heat exchange method provided a cooling draft in the summers; it also provided an open invitation for every mosquito, gnat, fly, yellow jacket, and occasional feather-winged creature within flying range to stop in for a visit. Skunk smell easily permeated its porous walls. The insects didn't do exposed food any good, especially in the summertime. We'd have to inspect and pick fly "blows" (eggs) from various types of food before we ate it. Flies seem to really like meat.

In that two-year period, Dad replaced the temporary roof with new corrugated aluminum roofing. That took care of the leaks, but with no ceiling or insulation, the aluminum roof functioned like a reverse heat exchanger. It extracted heat from the inside to the outside in the winter; in the summer, it pulled heat in from the outside. Dad wasted nothing. He took the canvas from the roof, tacking it to the outside of the house to provide additional seal. Shoot, we were probably the only house in that part of the country that had canvas siding!

You have to get your mind wrapped around what this shack looked like. A fifteen-by-thirty rectangle with an aluminum roof, recycled car parts for windows, and leftover tent canvas for siding. The outside was the good-looking side. Inside: no ceiling (just the aluminum roofing), no inside walls, just the inside of the outside walls covered with cardboard, ends of tin cans over knot holes, decorated with a single hung picture of a logger chasing a bear over a fallen and bucked log. There were two small bedrooms; the larger one, for the girls, didn't have a door. Neither of the rooms had a ceiling. When you looked up, you saw aluminum—no matter where you stood inside. When you looked down, you saw rolled tarpaper roofing on most of the floor, with linoleum only in the kitchen. Whether tarpaper or linoleum, all was pockmarked by Dad's calked logging boots.

With the inside space somewhat separated by walls, there was some modicum of privacy for the girls and for Dad and Mom. Nobody walked around in their underwear, and all dressed and undressed in the privacy offered by the walls, or with "lights out."

Neither Dad nor Mom openly displayed affection for one another, but at times, when lights were out, and after they assumed all kids were asleep, one could hear sounds of intimacy. There was simply no way not to. As we kids matured, though, Dad and Mom would "sneak" off for a couple of hours for time alone, usually in the warmth of a summer evening with a blanket and beer somewhere on the banks of the South Umpqua close to home.

Dad bought one of those blue-tin, belly-type heater stoves; probably in the hope that its often-glowing red sides would ignite the tinderbox we came to name "the shack." The stove had an oval shape that fit quite well in the corner opposite the cooking stove at the other end of the house. As long as the outside temperature didn't drop below freezing, we could keep the inside fairly warm, but we had to keep a fire burning in both stoves all the time. Man, how those stoves consumed wood, and anything else that would burn. One winter, Dad located dozens of diesel truck oil filters in the "community" dump at the point our driveway intersected Dole Road. On an especially cold night, he'd toss one of the canisters into the stove, damper it down, and we'd all head for bed in the knowing our "oil stove" would keep its fire burning all night. Caution! Do not attempt to heat your home in this fashion. There is no adequate way to dampen ten pounds of oil left to burn by itself in this manner.

Work was such a way of life for me that I took it for granted. Not life…work; not that I liked doing any chore. Whether or not work appealed to me was not part of the equation. The chores had to be done, regardless. Like breathing, work was just a part of my life. I did whatever I was told, and then some.

The thought I was being worked hard as a pre-teen never entered my mind. When I was told to do something, I did it. I neither shirked my responsibilities nor pawned them on my sisters. Of course, they might have a different view of what passes for my reality. They each had their own assigned chores around the house. They helped Mom as much as they were capable, and of course that was age-dependent. Their chores consisted of washing and breaking dishes, setting the table, and breaking dishes, and cleaning up afterwards, and breaking more dishes. They helped with the clothes washing and house cleaning, canning, and so on. As you can imagine from my description of the house, there wasn't a whole lot of housecleaning to do. Because there were four of them and only one of me, they would occasionally help with the woodcutting and water-hauling chores. These were the basic domestic chores that had to be done in addition to the "other work" we were expected to do.

It was my job to cut the firewood…when we didn't have a source of oil filters. The job was made lighter when Dad could afford to buy a truckload of mill ends or "pond lilies." The mill ends were the ends of finished lumber that were removed in the resaws when the lumber was cut to length. I loved those. Generally, they could be used as delivered in the heater stove, having only to be split once or twice for use in the cook stove.

I did not like the pond lilies then, and I don't like them today. They require work to turn them into burnable pieces. Pond lilies were cut from the butt end of logs before the mill debarked the log and sent it through the head saw. Pond lilies would vary from a few inches to two feet in length and would be the diameter of the log, whatever that happened to be. Splitting difficulty grew exponentially with length, width, knots, grain, time of day, weather, and my general attitude toward them at any given time. Pitchy pieces were set aside for kindling and starter. The type of pitch varied from clear, runny and sticky, to darkly transparent that would almost be a controlled explosion when touched by flame. One could create and hold any type of fire depending on the mix of wood placed in a firebox. A family wanted to obtain, split, and stack the wood during warm weather to allow time to cure before using. Any who have attempted to burn green, uncured sapwood in the middle of a damp Oregon winter knows what I'm talking about. Draft wide open, white smoke from the chimney, no heat from the fire, but plenty of smoke in the house.

Dad would quip, "Heap big smoke but no fire." Every family who heated their homes by wood had that rustic wood smoke smell to their clothes, too often accentuated by tobacco smoke. Secondhand smoke? Yeah, I know what it is.

But even so, for the most part the pond lilies made good firewood, and anybody who heated with wood generally had the remains of a truckload or two somewhere in their front yard, or along the side of their house.

Even as a seven-year-old, there weren't many of those pond lilies I couldn't chop into submission. By that I mean, cut into designated pieces for the stoves. Generally, there were three categories we split—heater stove wood, cook stove wood, and kindling wood for starter. If the block wouldn't split down the middle (which pretty much assured I could make nice wedges from the block), then I would "slab" it off. "Slabbing" is where you chop a few inches in from the outside and twist the blade of the ax outward just as it penetrates the sapwood. I got pretty good at this. If the grain in the block was too tight or twisted, then the next tool was the wedge. I'd use a lightweight sledge or the flat backside of the pole ax blade to drive the wedge into the block until the wood eventually split. After that, it was fairly easy to finish off. If it was simply too tough or knotted, then I left if for Dad to chew on.

I've got one scene stuck in my memory where I attacked a particularly cantankerous piece with grain so tight the ax blade would bounce off the block. Literally, it was like trying to chop a piece of rubber. Oh, how I'd swing the ax at such a stubborn block. You know, the kind of swing where you've got both hands on the handle, circle the ax as far back behind you as possible, and bring it back over your head. The weight of the ax head broke the sound barrier as it passed over my head; and as I brought the ax down, my feet left the ground in the hopes that this was the blow that hits with sufficient force to create a crack…any crack…in the piece of rubber. *Boing!* With hands still on the ax, it literally bounced back over my head. My frustration eventually brought forth a stream of finely tuned swearing with every swing that would have brought shame to the most profane of loggers, let alone a seven-year-old. Exhausted, I took my frustration out by dropping the ax and rolling the worthless piece of you-know-what down the hill into a tangle of wild rose bushes. I looked toward the house to see that Mom and Dad were witness to my vocal tirade and "pond-lily banning to rose bush hell."

Dad would leave me to myself when he thought I was capable of doing the job. As was often the case, I simply could not split the tougher pieces. He sure could.

In the times we couldn't afford a truckload of mill ends (which was most of the time), I'd roam the hills in search of standing dead trees or dead suckers from the sides of the madrone tree clumps. One of the characteristics of a madrone tree is that, when you cut one down and leave a high enough stump, the roots will send out shoots all around the stump. In time, a dominant shoot would take over and the weaker shoots die off. This natural process left good, dry firewood in the form of dead shoots up to four inches in diameter just waiting to be burned. Only problem is you had to work at it. So I'd chop, or, using a bow saw, remove the dead shoots from the stump, limb them, and drag them to the house where I'd place them in a sawbuck and saw them into stove-length pieces. Not a very efficient wood cutting operation, but it kept me thin and fit, and Mom supplied with wood for the Monarch range.

It was hard work keeping warm, but in the process I became quite skilled and efficient using a pole ax and bow saw. I suffered no serious cuts or injuries; other than the time in my early teens I dropped a crosscut saw on my right leg, leaving three puncture scars I carry today. I'd work at least one full day each weekend to cut sufficient stove-length wood to last the coming week. If there was one thing I hated, it was to come home from school and cut firewood after dark. We had no outside light, and so it made working outside a little difficult.

Occasionally, Dad would locate a dead fir that we'd fall and then buck into stove-lengths using a crosscut saw. By experience, I know why they call that type of saw a "misery whip." It not only brings great discomfort to untested muscles, but can also damage soft flesh, as I briefly mentioned earlier.

So there I was, probably only ten years old. Dad's teaching me how to work the opposite end of the "misery whip." We got quite good at it, and though that kind of work quickly tired me, I always felt good after the wood was sawed, split, and stacked beside the house under the eaves for some protection from the wet weather. Man, how those two stoves went through the firewood in the winter. The job was never done.

We didn't have refrigeration. It's a wonder we all didn't die of ptomaine, or dysentery, or typhoid (what with the water we drank), or contract polio or some other terminal illness or disease. We didn't have any way to store food other than by canning, which Mom managed to do when fruits and vegetables were in season. Early in our stay in the shack, Dad brought home an "icebox" in which he could place a store-bought block of ice. And thus, during the hottest months of the year, we had a way to keep meat from spoiling. Generally, if I shot a barren doe, we'd put the meat in pillowcases or flour sacks and hang the meat in the well. If we couldn't keep it cool, Mom would can the meat. She had a good pressure cooker, and we'd eat canned meat when nothing else was available. She was extremely careful regarding the possibility of the meat being spoiled, due to a poor seal on the jars. If she did not hear a healthy "hiss" when she lifted the seal lid, she'd take no risks and would go bury the meat. She didn't even want the dog or cat to get at it.

Though poor and penniless, we were not without cleanliness. There were no piles of junk accumulating inside the shack or outside. Trash and paper were not allowed to collect in the yard. As needed, Dad would order a "police action," where all us kids would be "ordered" to pick up all bits of paper, cans, bottles, lids, whatever, that may have accumulated around the house and its immediate environs. Anything that could be burned would be tossed into the fifty-five gallon burn barrel; cans and bottles would be tossed into our own version of a landfill, a small pit Dad had dug away from the house into which such could be discarded—out of sight, out of mind, so to speak. Mom kept the house fairly clean, sweeping and mopping floors on a regular basis. The occasional infestation of lice and bedbugs would be resolved with a good fumigation of DDT. That's right; once a year after the weather turned warm, all bedding would be taken outside and sprayed with DDT using a canister-type pump sprayer. The house would be closed up (all food taken out), fumigated, and then closed for the rest of the day. We'd open the house late in the evening for airing, sleep outside, and put everything back the next day.

Linda, my youngest sister, was born in 1951. I have no memory of Mom being pregnant, but I do remember Dad taking her to the hospital, and the two youngest, Ellen and Carol, being farmed out to Grandma and Grandpa Backlund. Because Patsy and I were in school, we stayed home with Dad until Mom and Linda were released from the hospital. Dad was working in the woods then and "Pat" and I were left to fend for ourselves before and after school. We were quite independent for our age. True early "latchkey" kids. Well, we had a latch on the door, but never locked it.

Seems back then they kept the mother and baby in the hospital for a number of days. I think Mom was in the hospital for at least a week. Dad had a conniption fit when he got the bill. He ranted, raved, and cussed; thought it totally outrageous that a simple few days' hospital stay could cost eighty bucks. It didn't make any difference to him that it also included the doctor's bill. He never did pay it. Now that I think of it, I believe he never paid for the aluminum roofing either. He thought that bill too high also. Not that Dad was a thief, mind you. It was the principle of the thing.

Sometime shortly after their marriage, Dad bought Mom a brand new Singer treadle sewing machine. Like the old Monarch range, it was one of her few treasures. She wasn't much of a seamstress, but she put it to use, repairing what clothes we had and occasionally would make one of the girls a new "calico" dress from a flour sack. Yep, that's right. You could still buy flour in fifty-pound sacks. The cloth of the flour sack was of sufficient quality that one could use it to make a small dress, or a shirt, or a bunch of handkerchiefs. Wasn't a whole lot of good looks to anything you could make from it, but at least the finished article had some utility.

When Dad wasn't working at a "regular" job, I would help him cut and sell fire wood and fence posts. In season, we would pick prunes, walnuts, filberts, beans, and strawberries—anything to make a few dollars to put food on the table. We would peel cascara bark; one winter we picked wild rose hips. Yes, there was a market for them. I can't remember where we sold them, but there was a buyer who purchased them and re-sold to some pharmaceutical company who then extracted the vitamin C for a health supplement.

More than one time, we would work as a family picking up beer and pop bottles along Highway 99 or some well-traveled county road. You have to get your mind wrapped around this image. Dad would park the car in a wide spot and send a couple kids with gunny sacks down one side of the road to the rear, with crews of two on each side working forward. The ones sent to the rear (sometimes this would include Dad), would work back to the point where the "picking" had stopped, then work back up the opposite side of the road back to the car. Dad would hop in the car, drive up the road, and pull over at some point in front of the "crew" working up the road. Using this method, we'd hop, skip, and jump our way down the road until we ran out of road, time, or the car trunk and backseat area became full. Imagine, four kids sitting on top of stinking beer and pop bottles as we drove to the little store on the south side of Myrtle Creek to redeem what we "mined" from the road. We were scavengers in the true sense of the word, yet performing our duty for the environment. Little of that thought entered our mind back then; we were simply working to make a few bucks for food, beer, and incidentals—oh yeah, soda pop and candy, too.

A good point about Dad's character was that when he was home (not in jail), there was always food on the table. In spite of his many faults and weaknesses, Dad possessed sufficient self-respect to ensure there was something for his family to eat. And oh, could Mom cook fried chicken, bake bread, cinnamon rolls, cookies and the like. We weren't fat, but neither did we starve, except for that one time. That time was when Dad spent six months in jail on attempted murder charges filed against him by his sister Blanche. I'll get to that story in a later chapter.

I'm telling you all this to paint a picture for you of what life was like day-in-and-day-out on the hillside. We called it a hillside, even though we didn't actually live on a hillside. It was sort of like living in a three-sided bowl, with the house at the bottom, the entry (driveway) side open with a slope toward Dole Road, then the railroad tracks, and then the South Umpqua with U.S. Highway 99 (not yet Interstate 5) on the opposite side of the river. The river was less than a half-mile from the house.

We lived about a mile and a half from the set of buildings that comprised the Myrtle Creek grade school (grades one through four), elementary school (grades five through eight), and high school (grades nine through twelve). In the first couple of years, I rode the school bus; but in the fourth grade, I took to walking to and from school, as riding the bus took too much time. For morning pick-up, the Oliver stop was first on the bus route and thus we had to ride the bus for about an hour before we got to school. In the evening, for some reason, the school reversed the route and the Oliver house was the last stop on the route. *Enough of that wasted time*, I thought. So I walked. It really was uphill both ways.

While some of my friends had TV in the mid-'50s, we didn't even have a radio; except for a brief time when we had a who-knows-what-brand-of-battery-powered-tube-radio. Dad strung a piece of wire from the antenna connection on the back of the radio, out through a hole in the side of the house, then across the yard, where he anchored the other end to an insulator high in a madrone tree. At certain times in the morning and evening when the "skip" of the ionosphere was right, we could pick up stations as far away as Mexico. I remember on some mornings waking to the Breakfast Gang out of Chicago, and some evenings we could listen to the Grand Ol' Opry being broadcast from some mid-west 50,000 watt station. Of course there was KRNR in Roseburg, and some other local AM stations we could receive in the "bowl" in which we lived. With no such thing as energy efficient transistor radios back then, it didn't take long for those vacuum-powered tube radios to drain the large dry-cell batteries. They were simply too expensive to replace, so we only had a radio when Dad was flush with cash. That only happened a few times.

Both Dad and Mom could have been early country music artists. Shoot, together they sounded better than Johnny Cash and June Carter ever did. They were good. Dad had a great voice. Could have been a serious country star with a little work and promotion. He played both guitar and harmonica, but he sang what I thought were old songs at the time. Funny how that goes, isn't it? He was singing old country and hillbilly songs from the thirties and forties, some no more than fifteen or twenty years old at the time, and of course, me being in the single digits in years, I thought they were old. Here I am today, singing the same songs I learned from Dad, and I think the songs are great!

Mom also played the harmonica. When the mood would strike them (usually after a six pack or two), Dad would pick up his old guitar (have no idea what make it was), and he'd start playing; they'd both start singing. They would sing country and the old gospel songs. In that environment, I learned to sing, play the harmonica, and eventually, play the guitar. My sisters all sang. Good, too. We could all harmonize. I think if we'd had some training and the right kind of exposure, and reasonably adjusted parents…well, who knows, maybe we'd have made it to Nashville.

A couple of years after we moved into the shack, Dad bought Great Aunt Lilly's custom-made parlor guitar. Aunt Lilly married Mom's uncle, Oscar Backlund. Aunt Lily's hands were pretty well deformed from rheumatism, and it was too painful and difficult for her to play. From what the kin say, she was a Flamenco guitarist. She had the guitar and a lady bug-style mandolin custom made for her in Chicago around the turn of the twentieth century. The guitar was a gorgeous piece of work, with wood and mother-of-pearl inlay, light as a feather and with exceptional tone. Dad taught me a few chords when I was nine, and within a few weeks I was playing and singing *Jack the Lonely Cowboy*. After a couple of years, Dad turned all the social guitar playing over to me. Whenever friends or family visited, he would tell me to go get the old guitar and play a few tunes for the folks. He'd join in with the harmonica, and we'd have a good time until the alcohol began to take effect. Then I'd excuse myself and head outdoors 'cause I knew the fireworks were about to start. And these were not the kind of fireworks one enjoyed watching, especially after any company left.

Dad sure abused that beautiful guitar though. Drunk and angry one night, he kicked it, cracking the face, and losing some of the mother-of-pearl. I think he took a kick at Mom but missed and put his foot into the guitar. When he sobered up, he patched it using some new glue on the market called Elmer's Glue-All. That guitar has held together until this day.

Hmm, I should probably contact the Elmer Glue Company and see if they will have me do a commercial extolling the durability of their glue.

I eventually quit playing this particular guitar in the early '90s. Tension from the steel strings was pulling up the lower bridge, causing the face of the guitar to pull outward.

I eventually had the instrument repaired by a luthier in Newburg, Oregon, but I have basically retired the instrument. I hope its tone or playability was not damaged by the fact I'm not playing it. Even so, the fact that it is still playable at 115 years of age is a wonderful testimony to the skill of its creator, a Swede named Almcrantz.

....

We read a lot. During those quiet times between drinking binges, the whole family took advantage of the town library. In addition to music, reading by kerosene lamp around the dinner table was one thing we did to pass the dark winter nights. We'd read wherever the lamp happened to be. In the winter, it was fairly close to one of the stoves, for until we slipped into bed under the mounds of homemade blankets, it was quite cool away from the stoves.

There were friends and family visits on both sides of the family, and the things that typically make for social occasions and events. Church too, as Mom had a leaning toward Pentecostalism, but now that I think back, it was probably a way for her to get away from the day-to-day drudgery. There were uncles and aunts and lots of cousins on both sides, too. So it wasn't as if we were totally isolated and cut off from the world. It was far from that. What hurt was the knowing that we were never up to "par" with the rest of our friends and family. We knew the rumors and gossip. *Too poor to have a pot to piss in*, was the phrase I think I heard more than once. I'm certain there was some ostracizing, but now that I look back, many of my schoolmates were probably not much better off. Who knows the domestic issues going on behind closed doors in other homes.

We were not alone in the travails and trials of alcoholism. Sometime in the late '50s, there was a high school senior who killed his abusive father using a shotgun. As I wrote in my introduction, during Dad's drunken abusive spells, I would sometimes lie in my bed and fantasize about killing him, or hoping that he would die in a car wreck. Such thoughts are probably not uncommon for those exposed to such verbal abuse and violence.

There we were, a family of seven living in a little fifteen-by-thirty foot shack clinging to a sloped basin on a hillside. No electricity, no running water, no indoor facilities, living like we just stepped from a covered wagon, using whatever we could find at hand to build a home and have some form of stability. Reading by kerosene (Dad still called it "coal oil") lamps. We were less than a mile from town, but because of the way the hills were formed, we could just as well have been 50 miles into the wilderness for all the good living that close to town did us.

Still there was that matter about my dad's brains…when the fear and anger from the increasing violence and abuse toward Mom would reach a point where I thought we'd all be better off with him dead! Yes, I prayed that if there was a God in heaven that in one of Dad's drunken binges, God would have mercy on Mom and us kids and drive him off the opening in that cliff that overlooked the Highway 99 bridge crossing the South Umpqua River. I was to learn the meaning of mercy and grace later in life, and I thank God He did not answer my prayer. God knows how I hated those times and how I willed myself to sleep in spite of the vile curses, the slaps, the mushy sounds of fist against flesh, along with the cries and whimpers of pain.

The Early Years

No one knows when or why it started. Isn't that the way it is with those who abuse others? Something happened. Some event, or word, or gesture, or situation triggers an explosive response of uncontrolled anger and hatred directed toward the target of the abuser. There are probably as many reasons as there are persons who fit the profile.

When sober, Dad was in control. Only when under the influence of the alcohol demon did he lose control. So I tend to think that it was the drug that released the violent side of his character. Without the alcohol, Dad was loving and caring, gentle and patient. At least this is how I saw him. There was nothing I feared about him when he was cognizant and coherent. He adored me as his only son, and would often use the phrase, "This is my intelligent son in whom I am well-pleased." He introduced me to his friends in this fashion. He gave me much freedom to do as I pleased, with only reasonable restraint on where I went or what I did. And yet he was very concerned about who I was with and when I would return. He taught me to tell the truth and to never lie.

I know now that Dad was a binge drinker. Usually, Dad would drink himself into unconsciousness, wake the next day, have coffee, something to eat, and then, feeling better, start the cycle again. I can see the struggle so clearly now. First, just a few beers, or other mediums of alcohol; then, when it took effect, a few more. Often, his drinking buddy was his brother, Arch, or occasionally he'd have some other friend drinking with him. As long as some third party was around, there was no violence. In retrospect I believe that, even when drunk, Dad knew that his violent nature was something to be controlled in the presence of others, and thus under such conditions we could relax. Only when we were alone as a family did he release himself to his violent nature, when at some point a threshold was reached and the loud acrimonious accusations would begin. He would accuse Mom of being unfaithful, of being the lowest, most worthless person alive. He would accuse her of being the reason for his many failures, telling her that if she just would work a little harder, "do this" or "do that" a little better, understand him a little more, that he then wouldn't do the things he did. He blamed her for his drinking, and he blamed her for the cause of her abuse. According to him, she was no good and she deserved what she received. Simply by being who she was gave Dad sufficient reason to beat her.

Following the accusations and denigration might come the grabbing and twisting of an arm, or grabbing the hair and pulling the head back; then a slap or two, and as the drinking continued the violence would escalate to hitting, hitting anywhere, and kicking, too. Like a dumb, docile sheep, Mom would take it, but with plaintive cries, "Stop, you're hurting me!" And, "Honey, don't. I'm bleeding!" Or, "I think you broke my nose!"

The marks would be present the next morning: bruised and swollen lips, a black eye (maybe two black eyes), and evident soreness in various parts of her body.

Mom was not guiltless in this, not that she ever did anything that I could see that would provoke the violence. "Guilty," meaning that she too would drink. Maybe this was the only defense she had, for alcohol numbs pain. She was able to endure the abuse only in her own drunkenness.

But what a saint she was. No matter how physically abused the night before, she was up the next morning, building a fire in the Monarch range and cooking breakfast for us kids; Dad included if he was up to eating something. But then the drinking would continue.

And such was the cycle for nine years—in jail, in the hospital, then home; followed by a period of peace as Dad worked in the woods, or at whatever he could find to do to put food on the table until the alcohol demon called once again.

....

From the first day on the hillside, there was work. Woodcutting and water hauling were my chief chores—morning, evening, whenever.

Dad had worked through the late winter and spring to make the house livable, partitioning off a couple of small bedrooms for the girls and adding a hall closet. My bed was an old metal army cot with a thin cotton mattress. The bed sagged in the middle, but it wasn't that uncomfortable. I didn't have a bedroom. My bed was placed in the hallway running along one side of the house, between the kitchen and the so-called "living room" on the opposite end that served double duty as Dad's and Mom's "bedroom." Not a whole lot of privacy, but somehow we each had our space.

In the late spring of our first year, after the weather had warmed, we spent time outside. Dad got the idea to raise rabbits, not only for us to eat, but to sell. I guess his entrepreneurial side was kicking in.

We got a buck and a couple of does, and pretty soon we had lots of baby rabbits. However, Dad lost interest, probably because he'd neglected the marketing side of the business. No sales equals no money. Shoot, we all lost interest, so we ate the assets. The empty hutches stood in silent testimony to the idiom that *the best laid plans of mice and men oft go astray.* We eventually tore the hutches down; we probably needed firewood.

Dad had a logging job or two during the first year in the shack. If one was involved in the logging industry, it generally was referred to as "working in the woods." Dad was a faller, and thus worked ahead of those who limbed, bucked the trees, set chokers, and yarded the logs from the woods. As a faller, Dad worked by himself, falling ahead of the other crews; obviously a whole lot safer that way, for the other crews, that is.

Even as a six-year old, Dad would "invite" me to keep him company in the woods. Shoot, it wasn't just for the company; he wanted somebody to carry all the small stuff. I would work hard to keep up and be of some use, while generally staying out of the way to avoid becoming a victim of some unwise action on my part. I would carry the pole ax, gas, oilcans, and the lunch. Dad would carry the heavy stuff like the power saw, wedges, ax, and so on.

Our lunches were always an experience in camp cookery. If it were sufficiently damp that a fire could be built without setting the woods on fire, Dad would locate some pitchy wood and get a small fire going to toast sandwiches. Sandwiches consisted of either sliced corned or roast beef. It was the canned type. He'd cut a couple of forked limbs and in the "Y" of the limb place a sandwich, and we'd toast the bread over the fire. Caution. Never toast your sandwiches over a pitchy fire. White bread quickly turns into black bread, and the whole sandwich tastes like turpentine. There would be some coffee from a thermos jar to wash down some homemade cookies, then back to work. Such is the substance of my early memories of "logging" with Dad.

There is another memory, Dad's last attempt to teach Mom to drive. At this time, she was into her late twenties and had never learned this useful skill.

It was the summer following our move, and watermelons were in season. Mom was four months pregnant with Linda. The wreck spelled disaster, but only for the watermelon.

We were heading down Clark's Branch Road in a '36 Dodge. Dad decided it was time Mom learned to drive. He parked the car on a wide shoulder, and they traded places. He sat in the passenger seat, holding Carol. Pat, Ellen, and I were in the back seat, and Mom was in the driver's seat. She got the car rolling. That must've been something to witness: Mom working the clutch, three-speed floor shift lever, throttle, and all that, while at the same time trying to keep the car on that narrow gravel road. She didn't. The car took an early exit off the road, over a bank, rolling a few times to lie on its side in a narrow pasture between Clark's Branch Creek and the gravel road. The front bumper was pointed directly at a fence, right at the point where Richardson Road branches off Clark's Branch.

Nobody was hurt. Mom was the only one in the front seat. Dad was in the back seat with all the kids, still holding Carol. A spare tire was somewhere in the mix of bodies, arms, and legs. I had a small scratch on the back of my neck, which was the extent of injuries, except for the damage to Mom's pride and the watermelon. There was nothing we could do but crawl from the car, jump down into the pasture, and scramble up the bank over the flattened blackberry vines to the road.

There we all were, sitting on the shoulder of the road, each contemplating their own navel, when Dad cusses, remembering the watermelon in the trunk. "Ah, for blinkety-blank-blank," he said. He scrambled down to the car, opened the trunk, and started cussing some more. The watermelon was in pieces. He seemed to be more upset about the busted watermelon than he was about the car…and six people with no way home. He scrambled back up the bank over the flattened blackberry bushes cradling the larger pieces of melon in his arms, and the six of us had an impromptu picnic sitting in the dust and gravel of Clark's Branch Road.

Some good Samaritan passing by stopped his car and asked, "What happened?" Stupid question. We're having a picnic. After Dad explained it was all Mom's fault, the good Samaritan offered to take Mom and us kids home. Dad stayed behind. In a few hours, he came driving up the driveway with the car. Other than a few additional dents and scratches from the blackberry vines, the car was fine. Seems that Dad was able to enlist the aid of some other Clark's Branch travelers to help him get the car back on its wheels. With their help he got it started and then drove it home.

Mom never tried to drive or take "driving lessons" again as long as she was married to Dad. Nobody questioned the wisdom of her decision.

An interesting fact is that Mom eventually passed her driving test following Dad's death in 1974. She had remarried, and her second husband, Jack Hogg, also attempted to teach her how to drive. She first bent the front bumper of his treasured '65 Rambler around a telephone pole in a sloping parking lot in Winston, and then over the next couple of years failed her driving test six times, proving to all that she really wanted her driver's license. I told her to quit taking driver's lessons from her husband and take lessons from a professional instructor. She took my advice and passed her driver's test the first opportunity following. She loved to drive.

Now you have to get your thinking cap on here and your imagination working a little bit because most people to whom I tell this have a hard time believing that there were people living in the 1950s that did not have a home with electricity and running water. So if your imagination is working you have to ask, "Well, when did you take a bath, and when and how did you wash your clothes?" I suppose the other question does not have to be asked regarding where we went to the bathroom because that obviously was done in an outhouse, usually with magazines or newspaper for wiping purposes. One summer, when corn came in season, we saved the cobs, dried them in the sun, and used them; but not for long, too rough. We went back to the paper.

Now with seven in the family, it took a fairly big hole to hold all that stuff, but even then, we didn't have to "move" the "house" all that often. Nature did a good service in the composting department and would keep the stuff working in the pit with the liquid leeching off into the surrounding soil. Occasionally, we'd have to dig a new hole and move the outhouse to the new spot. I say "we," but if my memory serves me right, I was the one digging the hole.

Now early in our first year or so on the hill, Dad had it in his mind to build us a good outhouse. "Good" is a misnomer. I know by experience there is no such thing as a "good" outhouse. By "good," I mean not just a plain ol' two-holer, but an enhanced four-holer. It was made better than "good" because Dad decided to build one using peeler cores. Peeler cores were the "cores" that remained after a veneer mill completed "peeling" veneer from a peeler log.

What Dad had in mind was to buy a few dozen of these peeler cores and make a "log cabin" type outhouse.

When completed, it was a good-looking outhouse. But, before Dad could build it, a hole had to be dug. Again I say "we," but I was the one who dug the hole. I remember it quite well, *Thank you, Dad*. It was late summer, and the ground was hard. I used that experience as the gauge, whereby I judge the hardness of soil to this day. That ground was stage nine. Stage ten is concrete.

Dad staked out the plot, handed me the pick and shovel, and said, "Dig until I say you can quit." I was only seven or eight, so I have justification in stating that the job bordered on child abuse. After about a week, Dad had mercy on me and finished the job. While it was hard work, I learned from it. Plus, it built strength and stamina into my skinny little frame. As a result, I am better off for it. It taught me that children can do a whole lot more than they think they can.

Even though I did not burden my own children with such physical labors, it was because of the way I was raised that I expected more from my own kids than most parents of my generation. I don't think Dad was lazy, I just think he raised me as he was raised. I could be wrong. I soon learned that if he could have me do the work, he had time to sit under a shade tree with Mom drinking beer until he passed out or became mean enough to begin beating on her. Usually that was the way it was. It just became a way of life.

When Dad finished that four-holer, it was a beauty. It had three nice holes at adult level and a lower, smaller hole at a 90-degree angle to the three larger holes. That was for Linda, the baby. She was probably potty-trained by this time, and that seat was tailor made for her small butt. My sisters were the only ones who ever took advantage of the multi-hole feature and was probably why Dad built a four-holer.

A few events are imprinted in my memory about this outhouse. First, it was decent looking. Second, it was so well constructed that it could easily have done duty as a bomb shelter. These were the hot days of the Cold War, and maybe that's what Dad had in mind when he built it. Ha!

Not only was the new outhouse decent looking, but it also had an appetite for things other than that which came from the human body. One night, it digested a flashlight. If the light had batteries, its use was required after dark, meaning there was no moonlight. Without a light, we'd have to sort of "feel" our way down the unlit path, around an elbow of scrub oak and madrone, and keep going until we bumped into the door. On this particular dark and dank night, Dad happened to have live batteries in his flashlight.

"Go ahead, take it," he said. "Save the batteries. Don't leave the light on when you're sitting."

I sat, placing the light on the bench between two holes. The bench wasn't level. It was dark. I did not switch the light off.

Hmm, strange, I thought. *Is the yellow orb on the inside of the closed door really moving?* Before I could grab the light, it rolled into the blackness of the hole to my left. I watched the dusty-yellow light as it was slowly swallowed by the soft, watery puree in the hole. It was late summer, and those little microbes, maggots, and whatever were doing a really good job turning that "stuff" into something other than what it started out as. My thoughts at the time were that I was going to get my hide tanned.

Gosh, I thought, *that's Dad's only working flashlight, and there it is sinking out of sight. Must be kind of like the lights of the Titanic, it just sort of slid beneath the waves. All hands and passengers were lost. Batteries included. Shoot, now I'm going to get it!*

I was conjuring up all sorts of explanations and excuses as I sashayed my way back to the house, not afraid of the dark anymore, but more afraid of what Dad was going to do to me. Even so, I told the truth. He didn't say much of anything; he just rolled his eyes, shook his head, and went back to reading his comic book. This was a good example of how we can conjure up things in our mind and become paralyzed by the unknown. I sure did not want to go into that house, but Dad was in one of his sober times and, as I said, when sober, he was a pretty nice guy.

Then there was the time Dad was sitting on the "throne," and he had his wallet out counting his money. Like my incident with the flashlight, he must have placed some of the money on the space between the seats. Of course this is all speculation on my part, as I really only know what followed.

He was in a hurry as he went past the uphill side of the house to the small workshop. Dad returned, carrying the garden rake, cussing under his breath as he made his way past the house back to the toilet. In a few minutes, he came to the back door of the house, calling Mom outside. He held the rake out at arms' length between them. On the tines was this smelly mess mixed with paper. Dad's nose was really bent out of shape and wrinkled. I can't imagine what Mom was thinking.

He told Mom, "Take this, Dot. There's a $20 dollar bill in that mess someplace. Clean it."

Mom cleaned it.

Well, $20 dollars was $20 dollars. I can't imagine what a store clerk may have thought if that bill spent any time in the cash register; or, someone who received it in an exchange, wondering about that strange odor in their wallet or purse.

The great outhouse was not long for this world. Aunt Peggy made sure of that.

Aunt Peggy, Dad's eldest sister, and her husband, Uncle Dave, traveled by Greyhound to Myrtle Creek to visit for several weeks. I have no idea where Mom and Dad found room to put up guests because beds were in short supply in our home. They must have slept in the girls' bed and the girls slept on the floor. Peggy was closing in on sixty; she was the eldest of Dad's siblings, being born in 1895.

Uncle Dave had one of those kind, gentle personalities—a compassionate soul. He'd help me collect and cut firewood, haul water from the well, and do whatever he was able. As a World War I veteran, he had served in France. Motorized vehicles were being used in the war, but so were horses and mules. Uncle Dave was a muleskinner, hauling freight in wagons to the front lines. "Over there," he had received a dose of mustard gas, not sufficient to kill him; but sufficient to scar his lungs to the point where he was almost totally disabled. While he could work somewhat, he quickly became short of breath, having no stamina. He also suffered greatly from rheumatism. Knuckles on both his hands were swollen and painful, but he never complained. He would drown his pain in beer, whether store-bought beer or home brew; he liked both. So did Dad and Mom.

Aunt Peggy was coldblooded. Not in a mean-spirited way, but by the simple fact she was skinnier'n a scarecrow; she must've had thin blood. She'd get out of bed in the morning after the fires were built and head for the wood range. She'd place a kitchen chair in front of the stove, open the oven, stick her feet in, and sit there for hours drinking coffee, smoking cigarettes and roasting her feet, never so much as lifting a finger to do anything. She loved music, though. When Dad brought out the guitar, Mom or I would be blowing on the harmonica, and with all the girls singing, Peggy'd sit there in her chair with her boney shoulders alternating up and down like a steam engine, keeping impeccable time with the music. She looked like a scarecrow in a dress doing double duty as a human metronome.

Aunt Peggy was a heavy smoker, and as is often the case with smokers, they'd have a smoke while sitting on the throne. Both Dad and Peggy were smokers, and with two smokers in the house, it reeked of tobacco smoke. Nobody seemed to mind. It was just the way things were.

The new outhouse was completed in the late summer of our second year on the hill. It was a particularly dry year, and being late summer, things were about as dry as they could get in that country. On that day, all but Aunt Peggy were out picking pole beans. As we drove up the driveway leading to the house after work, we notice a pall of smoke kind of hanging low in all the brush between the house and the well. Looking off to our right where the smoke was thickest, we noted a blackened, torched area. And no toilet! Alas, where once stood the palatial outhouse amongst the madrone and scrub oak, all that remained was a smoldering, somewhat stinky hole.

Aunt Peggy was a real trooper, though. She attempted to fulfill her duties as designated fire fighter, using a single bucket of drinking water from the house. She poured the water on the path in front of the outhouse. All that remained was a faint damp spot in the trail, never getting closer than twenty-five feet to the fire.

The miracle of the incident was that no major forest conflagration was ignited by her carelessness. For some reason, after scorching an area not more than twenty or thirty feet across, it extinguished itself! There were plenty of dry leaves and brush. Dad couldn't explain it either. Must've been a miracle.

Not much else to say about our burned-out toilet, other than the fact that we had to have one. Dad built a new one; he said the hole was getting full anyway. It was not nearly as nice as "the Castle," just a typical two-holer that provided faithful service for the remainder of our stay on the hill.

Summers were hot and dry, and one of our duties was to clear a firebreak around the house. Living in brush and timber, the shack would have no resistance to the flames. So, more work! We'd use hoes and grub-axes to clear all brush and grass; and in this way, we created a fire break four to five feet wide, and in a radius of a hundred feet or so around the house.

It was later in that same year of '51, following our loss of the four-holer, that disaster struck west of Roseburg, Oregon. Days, weeks, months without rain, then the Hubbard Creek fire. It was perfect fire-season weather, dry and somewhat breezy with an east wind; humidity so low, you couldn't find it. All that was needed was a spark. The spark was provided by logging equipment. The fire seemed to rage for weeks, but I'm certain it was no more than a week to ten days. It seemed longer as we waited for news, as the Elgarose and Melrose areas, up against the east side of the Callahan, were in its southward-burning path. It was not looking good for homes in the old Swedish settlements where Grandpa and Grandma lived.

The effects of the conflagration could be seen in the sky northwest of Myrtle Creek. Each succeeding day, the smoky haze thickened, creating a particularly ominous appearance. The sun, as it sank lower in the sky toward evening, would change from yellow to orange, and then red to brown. Just before setting, you could look at the sun with a naked eye, as it became almost obliterated by the ever-thickening smoke hanging on the horizon. Light filtered through, creating a surreal appearance to the countryside—like looking through lenses of dark, orange-brown sunglasses.

The fire burned southward, along the eastern slopes of Callahan Ridge, in some places burning into the timber over the crest of the Callahan, but ever southward along the steep eastern slope; burning a home here, a barn there. It destroyed Grandpa's and Grandma's home; it destroyed my Aunt Edna and Uncle Stanley Sjorgren's home. It destroyed Stanley's brother's home. It was a bad one. The Hubbard Creek Fire destroyed a significant number of homes in the Elgarose area, homes that had been built on the heights and benches that ascended toward the Callahan Ridge. The fire's southward progress was halted in that area, as the country roads helped provide natural firebreaks for the fire fighting crews.

I cannot recall visiting my grandpa and grandma again until after their new home had been built. Grandpa and Grandma had a small insurance settlement, and the Red Cross helped with some building supplies. With my Uncle Tub (Edgar) Walker (Tub married Mom's youngest sister, Alice) acting as a foreman and all-around carpenter, a small single-bedroom bungalow was completed within a short span of time.

Grandma and Grandpa were able to save or salvage some of their belongings; one of them being Grandma's beloved wood range. This range was installed at one end of her new small but functional kitchen, and from the range she continued to bake her wonderful tasty, homemade white and brown breads, cinnamon rolls, and coffee cakes. My uncle Paul still has this old range sitting in his workshop. How we cousins loved to visit and take advantage of our Grandma's good nature by always eating more than our share of her fresh-baked pastries. Anyone who has tasted a cinnamon roll or coffee cake made the Scandinavian way knows what I'm talking about. They were wonderful, and so was she.

....

It was our habit to take a bath once a week, whether we needed one or not. I'm certain our sense of smell was somewhat conditioned to our hygiene-challenged circumstances. In the summer during "swimming" weather, we'd take soap with us and bathe right in the river. Why not? It was convenient, and I didn't have to haul water. Otherwise, bathing took place right in the house in a galvanized washing tub.

The job would start with me hauling water from the well and dumping it into kettles and other large metal containers placed on the surface of the cooking range. When the water was heated, it was poured into the tub, mixed with cold water; when the temperature was right, I'd disrobe and bath first.

That's the order. I got to bathe first, then my sisters. Patsy bathed in my water, then the others in descending age order. Now, I'm certain that Mom made an attempt to freshen the bath by mixing in hot and cold water. Thinking about this method of hygiene kind of makes my skin crawl.

Some years prior to this time, Little Jimmy Dickens, an early country singer, wrote a song titled *Galvanized Washing Tub*. This song is a fitting description to that form of bathing. Anyone who has taken a bath in this manner, in a tub filled with hot water in an otherwise cold room, can understand why one would "*...squeal like a fresh-stuck hog...*" when their back touched that cold galvanized metal. And how, after climbing out of the tub to dry standing next to the stove, one side would be "*...burn'n and a-bak'n...*" while "*...the other side was shivr'n and a-shak'n...*"

Take my word for it. You don't ever want to wash clothes like we washed clothes. At best, it was a family affair, but the worst was that it took all day. It was work, work, and more work.

We started with water, lots of water. Water pulled from the well hand-over-hand in a bucket tied to a rope. It all had to be carried in pails from the well to the "laundry" area. Now all of this work took place, rain or shine, outside.

Buckets of water were poured into the heating tub that was placed on a ¼ inch sheet of steel over a fire pit built into a bank of earth on the backside of the house. A fire was built in the pit, and water was heated. Heated water was dipped from the "hot tub" and dumped into a washtub (all round, galvanized tubs), set on a bench about two feet high. Next to the washtub was a rinse tub. Oh yeah, the rinse tub had to be filled with more buckets of water. Mom would mix cold water with hot water to get the correct temperature, and then begin "washing" clothes using an old-fashioned scrub board. She often used lye soap. These were hard, uneven chunks of soap that you could still buy, usually from the feed store.

Occasionally, after saving a sufficient amount of rendered fat, Mom might make up a batch of lye soap. For a couple weeks or so, ashes from the stoves would be dumped into the trash-burning barrel. The barrel would be placed on some blocks about six-inches off the ground, and after sufficient ashes were accumulated, water would be poured over the ashes. The water would leech through the ashes and drain from a hole in the bottom of the barrel into a glass container. This would be the lye "extract." Mom knew how to mix the right amount of tallow and lye, and let the liquid harden. It could then be broken into chunks of a desired size. That's my memory of how lye soap is made the old fashioned way.

Hmm? I used to think when I observed this process. *This whole thing is kinda' spooky. Let's see if I have this right. Mom mixes fat with lye made from ashes, stirs it all up, then lets it sit to harden into soap that is then used to remove grease, fat, and dirt from our clothes.*

Soap making is a true alchemy.

She would soak the clothes for a short time, then reach into the tub, pull out an article, lay it over the scrub board, rub the chunk of lye soap on it to coat it good, then begin scrubbing. She would scrub until all the dirt and stains that could be removed were removed. She would then "wring" the clothes by hand to remove as much of the cleaning water and soap as possible, and then throw the scrubbed article into the rinse water. The clothing would then be dipped up and down in the rinse water several times to rinse out as much soapy water as possible, wrung out again, then placed in a basket for hanging on the clothes line. She didn't use gloves either. The lye soap could actually burn one's skin if exposed too long. Her hands were always red and sore after a washing job.

When the wash and rinse water became too soiled, it was dumped, and I had to haul more buckets of water.

Rain or shine, the clothes were hung outside on clothes lines to "dry." If it was raining, or otherwise too wet or cloudy to dry, she'd simply take what clothing was needed for immediate use into the house and place the wet articles on one of those folding clothes racks or on lines strung over the stoves. In this manner, they would dry in no time. In the wintertime, this was the normal activity and scene around and inside the house on Saturdays.

My job was to keep the tubs supplied with water for heating and rinsing. As hard as my job was, Mom's was harder. All that work made her tough. I was well into my early teens before I could out-grip or out-arm wrestle her. It was something special when I did.

Then there was the ironing. Like I said, we had no electricity, and while electric irons had been invented way back in the early days of electricity, we obviously couldn't use one. Mom used the old heavy "flat irons" that were shaped like an inverted flat-bottomed boat. Even at that time, they were probably classified as antiques.

The irons were handled using a thin iron sleeve with a wooden handled clip. In one position, the clip fastened the sleeve to the flat iron; in the other position, it would release the iron. Several of these flat irons would be placed on the surface of the wood cooking range, and after a bit of time were deemed sufficiently warm with which to iron. Mom always sampled their temperature by placing a bit of spit on the end of her finger. Then, placing the sleeve over the iron and "clipping" them together, she'd pick the iron off the surface of the stove and test the bottom with her wet finger. If it "phizzed," she'd start to iron with the article of clothing she'd placed on the ironing board situated close to the stove.

She'd sprinkle the clothes using either a pop bottle or beer bottle with a sprinkler-type adapter corked into the end. When an iron cooled, she'd place it back on the stove and replace it with a fresh hot one. Thus the process would repeat until the job was done. Think about the labor involved in this. First you had to have some firewood, a fire had to be kindled, the stove surface warmed up, the irons warmed up, and then you ironed. In this way, our cleaned "Sunday best" were ironed and ready for wearing.

This "manual" form of washing went on for several years until somewhere, somehow Dad located a gasoline-powered Maytag washing machine. *Hmm?* Come to think of it, I cannot recall a single time that Dad ever helped Mom with the washing, other than to dig the fire pit for heating the water and to build the wash bench on which the tubs were placed. I never thought anything about it at the time. Nor can I recall if Dad was even home on those days we washed clothes. He must have been though, but I cannot remember him ever helping with this chore.

When Dad had a job and the income was pretty steady, he sometimes would drink at the taverns in town, coming home drunk. But, he was up the next morning ready for work. However, some time after school started the second year in the shack, he lost his job, and he was without work pretty much throughout our second winter. This was the winter Linda was born. She was born January 30, 1951.

Not only was Dad out of work, but also the Dodge Mom rolled off Clark's Branch road a few months earlier had quit running.

Dad was without a usable vehicle, and Mom was about to give birth for the fifth and final time. Uncle Glen Thackery (married to Mom's eldest sister, Helen) loaned Dad an old '36 Ford two-door coupe. Dad owned this car a year or so later.

When Mom's time was close, Dad drove us all to Grandma and Grandpa Backlund's, supposedly to stay until after Mom would be released from the hospital. I was looking forward to the stay until Mom told me that Patsy and I had to go back home with Dad. Carol and Ellen were the two who got to stay. I had forgotten that Patsy and I were in school. Dad was going to take care of the two oldest, while Grandma and Grandpa took care of Carol and Ellen. So we headed back to Roseburg. Dad had Mom admitted to the hospital and then drove back home. We obviously survived. Dad knew how to take care of kids when Mom wasn't around.

Anyway, I think Mom was in the hospital at Roseburg for at least a week, following which we were all united, once again, back home at the shack.

It was the middle of winter again, but now there were seven people in the shack. I have vague memories of Linda as a baby, Mom changing her diaper, and feeding her Pablum. After Mom quit breastfeeding, she fed Linda milk from a beer bottle to which she fastened a disposable rubber nipple. Her milk formula was a combination of Sego® canned milk diluted with water, into which a few tablespoons of corn syrup or sugar were mixed. This was all heated on the wood range, poured into the warmed beer bottle, and then given to Linda. All of us kids must have been raised on the same formula, but for some reason, Linda ended up being the runt of the bunch. She weighed thirty-six pounds when she started first grade! A puff of wind would knock her over.

Patsy was born with a harelip. While her palate was not cleft, her deformity was sufficiently severe that when Dad first saw her as a newborn, he cried. Prior to Pat's sixth birthday, she'd had six surgeries at Dorenbecker's Hospital in Portland to correct the defect. Dad and Mom scheduled her final and seventh surgery immediately after school was out the spring of 1951. Patsy had just finished the fourth grade, and I the first grade.

After school was out, Dad and Mom made arrangements for Patsy and I to travel alone by Greyhound Bus to Portland. We would be staying with Mom's Aunt Rey and Uncle Victor. Mom and Dad put us on the bus in Myrtle Creek, and away we went. Dad and Mom followed the bus to Roseburg, checked on us at the Roseburg depot, decided we would be okay, and off we headed for Portland.

This was several years before any construction on I-5 started. We traveled Highway 99 to Junction City; then onto 99E through Albany, Salem, Woodburn, Canby, Oregon City, into

Portland. Just before Oregon City, I caught my first glimpse of the Willamette River. It was the biggest river I had ever laid eyes on. I remember thinking to myself, *Man, you can't throw a rock across this one.*

Aunt Rey and Uncle Victor picked us up at the Portland Greyhound Bus Depot, and we stayed with them in their home in east Portland for a week or so. They had no children, and thus our visit, while special to me, must have been equally special for them. They treated us with kindness and love. Patsy had her operation, and I went with Uncle Victor to watch the Rose Parade from his office somewhere in downtown Portland. He worked as either an architect or a draftsman. We were several floors up and had a great view. That was the only Rose Parade I have seen in person.

In a few days, we were back on the bus and headed home. Patsy recovered quite quickly from her surgery. Dad and Mom were pleased with the results.

For the rest of the summer between my first and second grades, Dad worked on the house to better prepare it for the coming winter. He was working in the woods, and he took me with him a few times. In the fall of '51, I entered the second grade.

It was during second grade that I learned to play the harmonica. One day, I stuffed a harmonica in my pocket and took it to school. I was playing *The Wreck of the Old* '97 during recess for the other kids, while my teacher, Mrs. Tilche, listened and asked me to play for the entire class. For some reason, as shy as I was, I did as she asked. Mrs. Tilche was sufficiently impressed to ask me to play for an upcoming PTA meeting, which I did. The music gave me an outlet and some notoriety "on campus."

It was also during the second grade that I met Gordon Simmons. We would pal around at school and became best friends. We had much in common, primarily being shy and skinny. Gordon lived just a few blocks from the grade school, and lunch break was sufficiently long enough for him to walk home, gulp down a sandwich and soup, and walk back in time for the first afternoon class. He invited me to his home several times to have lunch with him. It sure beat baking powder biscuits with homemade jam, which my lunch almost always consisted of. While Gordon was not as capable as I in the wood cutting skills, or general all-around independence, we found a mutual liking and respect for one another. I led, and he followed. Our friendship lasted the years of our stay in Myrtle Creek.

During our stay in the shack, Mom attended church at the Myrtle Creek Assembly of God, and with us kids tagging along, we were introduced to God and religion. On most Sundays, we would attend the Sunday morning services with us kids in Sunday school class, depending on our age. More often than not, we also attended the evening service.

We became established in the shack off Dole Road.

Logging and Attempted Murder

In the summer of '51, Dad worked as a faller on a small logging operation a few miles up South Myrtle Creek. I remember the place well. One day, well into summer, Dad took me with him; again to carry axes, gas and oilcans, the Thermos®, and the lunch pail. We trudged up through the brush. I was working my little legs like crazy to keep up with Dad, all the time telling me to "hurry up," "watch out for yellow jacket nests," rattlesnakes, and things like that. At the same time, I was watching to avoid getting slapped across the face by a vine maple or Pacific Yew branch he'd pushed aside and then let go. Those limbs could really put your eye out. We stopped next to a fairly large old growth Douglas Fir that was leaning backward into the hillside. I remember the butt of that tree looking as big as the side of a barn. For some reason, Dad had fought our way through the brush and limbs to get to this specific tree, the first tree he was to fall that day; and the operation was something to watch.

Dad had it in his mind for that tree to fall downhill, like all fallen trees were supposed to. No way was he going to let that tree lie opposite to all the others that he had previously fallen on the hillside. He set my skinny little seven-year-old butt aside, and then walked around and around the tree. He held his single-blade pole-ax in his right hand, pointed upward, and sighting along the ax handle into the crown of that tree. I figured this was a religious ritual all the good fallers went through to ascertain the "fall-ability" of a tree with a particular bad "lean" to it. Anyway, Dad went this way and that way around the butt of the tree, stopping every now and then to sight along the edge of the ax handle into the branches. Yep, this had something to do with tree-faller sacraments, some religious ritual for sure.

Finally satisfied, he told me where to stand, and not to move. He then got the chain saw started and warmed up. By this time, I had determined that this "circle-a-tree-with-occasional-sightings-along-the-handle-of-a-pole-ax" ritual was necessary to determine how and where the undercut was going to be placed, and just how the back cut would be made in order to "steer" the fall of the tree in the direction Dad wanted. Shoot, I wasn't so dumb. Even a seven-year-old could tell that tree was leaning so far back up-slope it would only fall one way…backwards, up slope; or at best cantered to one side and laying across previously fallen trees, all busted to pieces and good for nothing but firewood.

Dad had bought a brand new, single-man, blue Homelite® chainsaw. Even so, compared to the lightweight powerful saws one can buy in any hardware store today, this thing that Dad bought was a toy. It was the best that technology had to offer at the time. It still took time to make the undercut, and when finished, I could see that it was totally out of place. The undercut wasn't pointing downhill but was off at a tangent. Dad seemed to know what he was doing and after knocking the undercut block from the trunk with the end of the pole ax handle, he started the back cut right next to the uphill side of the edge of the under cut, and worked the saw back around to the opposite side. The engine was screaming, sawdust was flying, and the blue-white, two-cycle exhaust smoke was hanging heavy around the base of the tree. This part of the falling operation took some doing, as the bar was not sufficiently long to reach across the butt of the tree; so he had to cut from one side, then go to the opposite side and work to "reach" the cut where he had previously penetrated from the other side. This back and forth cutting action continued for some few minutes and then Dad started to look up into the crown of that tree. When it began to totter backward, he stopped cutting and, using the flat back side of the pole ax, drove wedges into the kerf of the back cut. The wedges caused the crown of the tree to begin moving away from the up-slope. Dad then inserted the saw back into the widening kerf on the back cut and tenderly cut a little more wood from the "hinge" between the under cut and the back cut. This cycle of inserting wedges and then cutting more wood from the hinge went on for some time, until wedges were pretty well spread out over the back cut. In one or two places, wedges were on top of wedges. Dad worked hard to bring the crown of that tree past the point where it no longer leaned uphill, but sort of downhill. When that point was finally reached, Dad began to cut in earnest. Dad was soaked with sweat by this time. With just a few more movements of the bar in the back cut, that tree twisted on the uncut wood in the hinge, and fell with a *whoooosh*, trailing needles and small limbs on the way down. With a thump it lands, slides a little on the steep hillside. Wow! The top is pointing straight down the hill!

Once the tree began its fall, Dad jerked the saw from the butt of the tree, hit the kill switch, and in one smooth motion, he was standing beside me. He glanced at me, smiled, pulled the Bull Durham from his shirt pocket, and rolled a smoke. He knew his stuff all right, and at that moment I thought he was the greatest, most awesome dad alive!

After we ate lunch, which included barbecue sandwiches flavored with pitch smoke (got to be some nutrients in that smoke), Dad picked up the saw and headed for another tree (stepping in a yellow jacket's nest along the way). He fell a few more trees, and then he took me back to the landing to introduce me to "Sunshine." Sunshine must've got his name from his round, red face. He was the "cat-skinner," and Dad thought it would be a good experience for me to ride with him on the "cat" and see how the logs were yarded from the hillside into the landing.

The "cat" was about the size of a D-4 Caterpillar, probably an International TD-6 crawler. It was a proud moment for me, riding back into the woods sitting beside Sunshine; that is, until he reached the point of the ridge, put the crawler into reverse, and started backing down the steep hillside to a couple of logs. I thought not only would the thing flip over backward, but there was no way that crawler could pull anything but its own weight back up the hill. I was mostly right. After the choker-setter connected the chokers to the winch line, Sunshine simply played out the cable behind the crawler until he was once again had the crawler on fairly level ground. He then put the drum winch in gear to yard the logs up behind the crawler. With the turn of logs trailing behind we then descended the skid road into the landing.

Dad seemed to be working fairly steady following the time of Linda's birth and my entering the second grade in September, 1951. If there were times of drunkenness and violence toward Mom during this time, I cannot recall.

As I stated, Dad had an entrepreneurial spirit, and in early 1952, he obtained a contract to log second growth from the Blackard place a few miles north of town off Dole Road on the north side of Timber Butte. He started the operation in the spring of my second year in school and by the time summer vacation rolled around, Dad had Mom in the woods setting chokers for him. Not that she would work every day, but only on those days when Dad had felled sufficient logs, and had them delimbed and bucked; then he would take Mom with him to set the chokers, so he could yard the logs into a landing. On the days Mom was working, we kids were left at home to fend for ourselves until they returned in the late afternoon. No such thing as "day care." Pat and I (eleven and eight, respectively) were the caregivers for the three younger siblings. We got ourselves out of bed, built a fire in the Monarch range, made breakfast, washed the dishes, made lunch, and then waited for Dad and Mom to come home. Linda was only eighteen months old, and so I'm certain we changed dirty diapers also.

This operation wasn't too efficient, so Dad made plans to move the family into the woods for the summer. He bought an octagonal army tent that was to be our home for the next three months. By this time, I was sufficiently old to know Dad had a drinking problem. I'm sure there were occasions prior to this time where he had beaten my mother, but I cannot remember them clearly. I do remember the ones that followed though. I also remembered that in spite of how hard Dad worked to make something of himself, the alcohol had too tight a grip on him, and it led to his losing all that he had worked so hard to build that summer of '52. Alcohol and logging don't mix.

Dad was one for making do; and what he made "do" for a logging cat was an old Fordson steel-wheeled farm tractor. A tractor with no brakes! I have no idea where he got "The Thing." Somebody obviously disliked him and wanted to see him dead because The Thing almost killed him more than once. Now you have to picture this. Even in the early '50s, The Thing was nothing but a rusty-colored bucket of bolts that provoked some of the most livid streams of profanity to ever come out of the mouth of a human being. First, as I already mentioned, it had no brakes, so you always had to make sure it was in gear before you started down hill. You never left it parked on an incline, unless you left it parked in gear with the engine off, which was rare because once started, Dad didn't want to shut the engine off. It didn't have a starter motor, just the crank handle that stuck out like a loose tooth from the underside of the radiator. Third, it would sometimes stick in reverse; so if Dad was backing up to hitch onto a choker, the choker-setter (me) better be watching to be sure that the clutch would disengage. The thought of what one of those diagonal steel traction plates on one of those rear wheels would do to a body wasn't pretty, especially if the wheel was spinning.

There was the time he literally backed the left wheel into a standing Douglas Fir, and The Thing decided to lock up its clutch. It started crawling up the trunk of the tree. As the tractor backed up the trunk, Dad was cussing a blue streak. He stabbed at the clutch with the left foot, as he worked to balance himself with the right foot to keep from falling off the seat. Just before the tractor tipped, the clutch disengaged, and it slid off the trunk—no worse for wear, which wasn't the case for the driver. Another time, Dad had parked The Thing after backing up to a choker, kicking the transmission into neutral leaving the engine running.

Oops. Hey, Dad, The Thing's on a slope.

He had stepped off The Thing to hook up the chokers to the draw bar when just before he made the hook-up, The Thing, being very independent-minded, decided to coast off on its own—free-wheeling down the skid road toward the landing with Dad trailing in hot pursuit, throwing whatever he could find at it, yelling, "Stop, you blinkety-blank-blank-blank, stop, before I blinkety-blank, blank you, you blinkety-blank-blank-blank." And off into another stream of expletives-deleted. The Thing buried its nose in a slash pile with that tired old four-cylinder engine continuing to percolate. Dad climbed back onto the seat and with a grin on his face, backed it back up the skid road, hitched onto the log and pulled it into the landing. I didn't know what to think about all this, but was learning that this was logging done the Tiny Oliver way—logging done on a shoestring budget and on a wing and a prayer.

The landing consisted of a rollway above a cut in a bank at the end of the skid road. The log truck would back in and park with its log bunk 90 degrees to the rollway. Now a rollway was nothing more than a couple of logs parallel to one another about twelve feet apart. Dad would build one of these wherever he had a proper place to move the logs in preparation to loading onto the log truck. Logs would be pulled from the woods, disconnected from the chokers at the head of the rollway, and then, using muscle power and the leverage provided by a peavy, would be "rolled" onto the rollway. Individual logs would then be "rolled" onto the log bunk on the back of the log truck from the side.

At this particular landing, Dad had built an "A-frame" whose lower ends straddled the left and right edges of the rollway. Rigged with cable, block and tackle, and a pair of cant-hooks, Dad would hook into the middle of a log, and with the old Fordson as pull muscle, the log would be lifted to complete "topping off" the load.

You should have seen the log-truck. Not like the modern beasts in use twenty years later. The gypo outfits hired any hauler who said he had a "truck." For such small outfits, the truck might be an old 2-ton farm truck with its bed converted to log bunks; or in Dad's case, an old World War II Dodge six-pack. These things had dual rear axels and a powered front axel, and generally were used for the short logs. Thus they were called "short loggers." Though powered with a puny flat-head six motor, those rigs were geared for pulling. Shoot, those six-packs would go anywhere, road or not.

To this day, I do not know how he built the rollway and the A-frame. I just know he did. He never hired anybody. He did it all himself, with nothing more than the tools he had around him at the time. He was good with a pole ax. He could notch, slice, hack, and cut until he had the shape he wanted, and he passed that skill with an ax on to me.

There we were, living in a tent in the woods that summer of '52, helping Dad whenever we could. Mom continued helping Dad, working as his designated choker-setter and de-limber. She was a trooper. She could sure work, and she never complained. She'd start the day by cooking us breakfast on an old wood range Dad located somewhere and placed outside the tent under some trees for shade.

We had been in the woods only a couple weeks, when Mom contracted yellow jaundice. She was quite sick for a couple of weeks, and that was one of the few times she was under a doctor's care. She still worked to do what she could in cooking and caring for us kids, but she did not have the strength for going out with Dad to help in the woods. That chore now fell to me, and for the rest of the summer, I became Dad's choker-setter and de-limber, and all around go-fer.

I thought it was great, however, with one problem. It seemed that most of the time, those logs were lying flat on the ground, and I'd have to use the sharp end of a broken limb to dig a hole under the butt end of the log sufficient to poke the end of the choker through, then climb over the log, pull enough of the choker from under the log to circle the log, insert the stinger into the choker, pull it tight, and then wait for Dad to back The Thing close enough so I could hook the loop on the other end onto the hitch on the draw bar.

Was it hard work? Sure. Being the kind of operation it was, something was always breaking, or Dad needed gasoline, or the saw wouldn't start, or he needed beer. I didn't mind a little bit of work mixed in with all the "break time." I thoroughly enjoyed that summer. I can still smell the odor of pitch from sawdust and crushed fir needles, especially when the hot afternoon sun would start to cook them a little bit.

For the most part, I did a man's work; setting chockers, delimbing, and so on. And I still have all my fingers and toes.

One afternoon, when taking a break from peeling poles, Dad asked me if I'd like to "go for a ride." I had no idea what he meant until he took a good sized piece of peeled bark, placed it on the uphill end of the log that he'd just peeled, and then proceeded to demonstrate how to slide down a peeled pole.

Shoot, looks easy, I thought, *even for one my age.*

I gave it a try. Of course, my balance wasn't just right, and I immediately slid off the log. In my attempt to stop my slide off the log, I grabbed at its slick surface as I went over the side. I cut my hand in several places from the sharp nubs that are at the surface of the peeled log. That was the last of the thrill rides for me.

There wasn't a large quantity of poles to cut, probably no more than a couple of truck loads. For the life of me, I can't remember how in the world a logging truck with the long pole-carrying trailer traversed its way up that steep winding road, turned around, loaded, and then hauled those poles off that mountain. It had to have been an army six-pack converted especially for such operations.

The area where Dad was logging was prime rattlesnake country. In addition to peeling logs, Dad was constantly warning us to look before we stepped, and to keep our eyes peeled for rattlers. It was a habit we developed. Late one hot evening, Mom and Dad chased a snake out of camp, attempting to club it to death as it crawled away. The snake took refuge in a clump of poison oak. Blackard grazed some sheep on the northwest side of Timber Butte. Now poison oak doesn't seem to bother a sheep too much, and they would eat the young stuff, leaving clumps of poison oak stalks that would be two or three feet in diameter at the bottom and five to seven foot tall. Well, that snake must have thought that one of those clumps of poison oak looked like a place to seek refuge from the beating it was receiving from the broken limb Mom was attempting to apply to its backside, so it crawled into the stalks at the base of the bush. That didn't stop Dad. He had an old hunting knife in a sheath he kept on his belt. He pulled the knife from its sheath and proceeded to hack into that clump of poison oak until he located the snake. When they got back to camp, he showed us kids the rattles. The poison oak had no effect on Dad. All of us were pretty much immune to the stuff. Maybe we just had a natural immunity against it.

It wasn't all work. We had days off now and then, especially if Dad had been drinking heavily the night before. When the humidity dropped below a designated percentage, all logging operations ceased. This is why many of the larger logging operations would go on a "hoot-owl" shift. Starting early in the morning when the humidity was higher, working by lights, even before the sun came up, to get in as much time as possible before the hot dry afternoons forced a shutdown in operations.

Dad didn't like staying in the woods if there was no reason, and so when the humidity dipped into the fire danger zone, he would load us all into the old '36 Chevy "crummy," and we'd slide off that mountainside down those steep old ranch roads covered with slick serpentine rock. He'd take us to a shady spot along the South Umpqua for swimming, hot dogs, and Pepsi. Dad and Mom would usually get drunk.

On those afternoons when it was too hot or dry to work, we were on a sandbar under some trees beside the river. We were often left on our own when Dad and Mom would make a run into Myrtle Creek for the fixings and drinks (beer for them and some Pepsi for us kids). I know there were times that Mom and Dad left us kids alone at the river when they made their run into town. Whether Linda, the eighteen-month-old was under our care at this particular time, I can't remember, but I do know that the four older kids were alone, and Dad and Mom were nowhere in sight.

At this particular spot, the creek that flowed from the Blackard property on Timber Butte emptied into the South Umpqua right where Dole Road crossed the railroad tracks. There was a deep swimming hole there. At the time, a sand bar extended into the swimming hole, sloping steeply into still, deep-green water. Pat and I were daring one another, seeing who could stand in the deepest water. She went under first, and I followed.

Unknown to both of us, the sand under our feet lay over the top of a rock ledge. We backed off the ledge into deep water. Neither of us can completely explain what happened next. While neither of us could swim, we both found ourselves face down on the sand bar, choking, spitting up snot and water. I have a vague memory of being propelled from the hole, as if pushed by an unseen hand! It happened so quickly the two younger sisters never realized we were in danger. It was several years before we told Dad and Mom they almost lost their two oldest kids that day.

Sometimes we'd hang out at the river until well after dark. Dad would kindle a small fire on a sandbar, and we'd roast wieners and marshmallows. By that time, both Mom and Dad would be pretty soused. Sometimes there wasn't any abuse or any hateful outbursts. There was always the drinking.

While Dad's logging "cat" (The Thing) was ugly, at least it was out of public sight on the slopes of Timber Butte. Not so with Dad's "crummy." Dad was a pragmatic sort of an individual when it came to designing a utility vehicle for use in his logging operation. This was another way of saying he made do. He needed something to haul all his "logging" gear to and from the woods, so he had to have a vehicle in which loggers throw chain saws, tool bags, gasoline cans, oilcans, chokers, boots, aluminum hard hats, rain gear, and themselves. Most of the high-end logging operators used small bus-type vehicles to haul their workers to and from the logging site. Regardless of the type of vehicle used, all of them suffered a high degree of abuse; especially from the rough logging roads that abused and tore them to pieces. In no time at all, they became "crummy-looking." That's how they came to be called "crummies."

Dad decided to make his own crummy. He removed the doors (all four of them), and the trunk lid from the family car (the '36 Chevy). He enlarged the trunk lid opening by chiseling out the back window, and then proceeded to remove the back seat. Of course, these modifications totally destroyed any resale value, but he now had a "crummy," a real open-air special. Problem was, even to the embarrassment of an eight-year-old, the crummy served double-duty as the family car. Imagine the scene to those on Main Street to see this piece of junk pull into Myrtle Creek from off Dole Road with the entire inside of that car open to the world. Dad drove, Mom rode shotgun holding the baby, and four kids were huddled in the center of the rear floor pan where the back seat used to be, hanging on to whatever to keep from accidentally becoming road kill. That's what I was doing (hanging on) when we were skidding down that serpentine slope, heading for the fireworks display in Myrtle Creek, late afternoon Fourth of July, 1952.

One of the roads we could take out of the woods on the Blackard place was a steep trail that had been bulldozed off a cliff face we called a hillside. The traverse down the trail was particularly precipitous, especially in places where a layer of serpentine boulders lay just on the surface of the hardpan. It was too steep and slick to drive up, but if you were careful you could slide, I mean, drive down. Because it provided a decent shortcut to Dole Road, Dad decided to use it.

This road was not smooth. The crummy bounced and jarred as it scooted its way in and out of holes and over football sized rocks as Dad tenuously navigated down the slope. Of course, all of us kids were hanging on to whatever we could find as the crummy made its way down the hill in a controlled skid. For some reason, I was looking through a hole, probably one of the holes through which the back seat had been bolted, to the surface of the "road" directly below, when I was hit in the eyes with a blinding spray of hot brake fluid. The brake line had broken! I screamed, "I can't see! I can't see!" Mom was trying to figure out what in the world happened while Dad was working to control a crummy with no brakes. He quickly applied the emergency brake, locking up the back wheels. We slid to a stop at the bottom of the hill.

In the meantime, I continued to moan and whimper. I was literally blind for several minutes. Dad figured out what happened (can't mistake the smell of brake fluid), pulled his snot rag from his right rear pocket, and then proceeded to wipe brake fluid from my eyes and face.

Thanks, Dad, I thought. *You're snot is not therapeutic.*

In a few minutes, though, things take shape, and I realized I was not blind after all. But now, I have supernatural powers. No. Just kidding. Other than my eyes being red for a few days (probably more from the force of the fluid hitting my eyes than from the fluid itself), I was fine.

We enjoyed ourselves the rest of the evening, watching the fireworks sitting on that rocky bluff off Dole Road, just to the north of town—right at the point where the trace of the Applegate Trail vanishes. Dad never did fix the brakes on that old crummy; he used the emergency brake instead.

The word must have gotten around to Dad's brothers and sisters that Dad had something good going on. About midsummer, several of them showed up at our camp at the same time. Somehow they had found where Dad was logging and had "stopped by for a visit." I met one or two of my aunts for the first and only time. There was Blanche, Nora, Daisy, Betty, and their husbands; and then Dad's brothers, Archie, Bill, and Frank. They didn't stay long, just said, "Hello," and "Good-bye." I guess they came to satisfy their curiosity that Tiny, just maybe, was going to amount to something.

Even though Dad was back to drinking heavily in the evenings that summer, he held on pretty good. It was probably the fresh outdoors and the knowing that he was actually doing something for himself that made him feel good. I don't rightly know. That summer in the woods was very special for me for quite a few weeks; that is, until Bonnie showed up. Bonnie was a few months older than I. She had been brought down from Seattle by my Aunt Peggy and Uncle Dave Summers, a couple of weeks prior to the visit by Dad's other brothers and sisters. We had made a trip back to the house for a short stay, and when at the shack, Aunt Peggy and Uncle Dave visited briefly with Bonnie in tow, and then returned to Seattle; however, Bonnie stayed. She was now under Dad and Mom's care, and we headed back out to the woods for the rest of the summer.

Bonnie was a nice kid. I guess her parents were having some problems, although I don't know the details that brought her to live with us or her relationship to Aunt Peggy and Uncle Dave.

Dad and Mom agreed to care for her as long as needed. Bonnie joined us in the tent on the north side of Timber Butte, as Dad continued to log. As the summer progressed, Dad and Mom began thinking about adopting Bonnie.

Blanche and her husband, Elmer Landers, lived between Winston and Roseburg on a nice little ranch at the end of Landers Lane. They had three kids, two boys, who were a couple of years older than I, and a girl, Judy. (Sometime in the early sixties, both of Blanche's boys were killed in Alaska, when the small plane they were flying crashed into the side of a mountain.)

Later in the summer, following the big family visit, Blanche came out to the camp site for a visit and made arrangements with Dad and Mom that each of us kids would spend a few days with them and the cousins, which we all thought was a good idea. They lived in a real house. I think I was the last in the line of the biological kids to visit, and I remember that I had a pretty good time, and that it ended all too soon. Of course by this time, Bonnie was living with us, and she had to have her turn.

While Bonnie was visiting with Blanche and our cousins, Dad and Mom closed camp, moving us back to the shack. It was time to prepare for the start of school. It was to be my third year. By this time, Dad was drinking heavily and getting meaner as the days went by. Now that I look back, I believe that what precipitated this drinking bout was the fact that Blanche had not brought Bonnie back within the agreed allotted time. Something was going on between Dad and Blanche regarding Bonnie that to this day I know nothing about.

Blanche may have known something about Bonnie's background and thought that Bonnie would be better off living with her than with us. Dad may have suspected what Blanche was up to. When Blanche finally showed up, Bonnie was not with her.

She demanded that Dad and Mom give her Bonnie's clothes. One thing about Dad when he was drinking, you did not *demand* he do anything. He would often say when drunk and steamed, "Don't cross me."

Dad obviously felt as if Blanche had crossed him. In no uncertain terms, laced with appropriate curse words, he told her to get the blinkety-blank out of his sight, or he would kill her! It appeared he was going to make good on his word. He went into the house and came out with the Marlin .22. He chambered in a .22 hollow point and shot a round over the roof of her car as she tore down the pea-gravel driveway…backward. I suppose she was wondering when a .22 slug was going to bury itself in the back of her skull as she, looking through the rear window, exited the property down the driveway.

Dad was mad. He was cussing, ranting, and raving, and I'm sure he would have followed Blanche off that hillside in the old "crummy" if Mom hadn't been hanging onto him crying, "No, no, Tiny, don't do it!"

Somehow, he listened to reason and regained a semblance of self-control. We kids had long since hightailed it out of sight and were watching this all take place from behind the woodpile, an old oak stump, the brush—anywhere other than where all the action was taking place.

It didn't seem like any time at all had passed when we heard a car coming up the driveway again. Dad and Mom were still outside, and Dad recognized Blanche's car. He still had the .22, and he suddenly aimed at the driver's windshield.

I don't know if he would have pulled the trigger or not because it was right then that we all heard, "Tiny, this is the Myrtle Creek Police. Put the gun down, and put your hands up!"

Ol' Blanche had gone and sic'd the cops on Dad.

Dad was no fool. He dropped the gun down and put his hands in the air. It seemed like all the Myrtle Creek cops knew Tiny. Not that they were like old friends. There was no rough stuff, just matter-of-fact, business-like arrest talk. They meant business. Dad staggered around, trying to keep his balance as they worked to get him handcuffed. They stuffed him into the back seat of a patrol car and drove him off to jail.

I cannot clearly describe what I felt when I witnessed such a thing—Dad shooting at Aunt Blanche, the police, the handcuffs, and riding down the driveway in the back of a police car. It was over that quick.

I've often wondered what Dad's state of mind was when he woke sober in the county house. Was he mad? Was he embarrassed? What did he feel? What were his thoughts? More importantly, what was our state of mind? I think that by this time, Mom, Patsy, and I had probably been so numbed by Dad's drinking and physical abuse of Mom that we were beyond rational feelings. I can't speak for the three younger sisters and often wonder what their memories are of these events.

Blanche pressed charges against Dad—attempted murder. I guess there was sufficient reason for the charge, since Dad had fired a .22 round in her direction: enough evidence to get him six month's free room and board in the Douglas County Jail. Dad proved one thing, Blanche was right. That hillside and shack were not the right environment for Bonnie. We never saw Bonnie again.

Survival 101

The "Blanche Incident" was my first memory of Dad being arrested. It was fairly soon after Dad's arrest that we moved. Mom had no source of income, and with five kids, well, she had to do something. I do not remember her visiting Dad during his incarceration, although she may have. They may have agreed that it was best to make the move. Whether they had an agreement or not, the logging operation ceased. All Dad's equipment (what there was of it) was left where last used in the woods. I have no idea what happened to it. Later, after Dad had been released from jail and he took up drinking again, he blamed Mom for not making the effort to go back into the woods and retrieve it. He used this as an excuse to not only verbally abuse her, but also as sufficient reason to once again begin the cycle of physical abuse. How could she have retrieved his equipment? She didn't drive. She would have had to ask Uncle Glen, or somebody else to take the time and make the effort. There wasn't much equipment, anyway—just the old Fordson tractor, his chainsaw, some axes, wedges, chokers, some pieces of block, and tackle, a fifty-gallon barrel of gasoline.

Within days following Dad's arrest, Mom moved us into an apartment on the east end of town, not too far from the Simpson sawmill on North Myrtle Creek. The apartment wasn't much. At one time, it had been a chicken house the owners had converted into a couple of "apartments." But it had electricity, running water, and an indoor bathroom. To me, it was paradise. We didn't have to haul wood off the hillside or water from the well. This is where we lived for most of my third year in school.

While Dad was in jail, Mom was able to obtain welfare to pay the rent, utilities, and to buy groceries. That was the good part. We were somewhat stable, attended the Myrtle Creek Assembly of God, and most important to me, I could have friends over. Then what usually happened in the cycle of abuse, the abuser returned, apologized, pleaded to be taken back again, and promised never to do it again. Sometime in the early spring of 1953, Mom took Dad back.

And so the "breadwinner" has returned, and welfare is no more. Problem is, it was still cold and wet, winter was lingering, and it was a difficult time to find work. We were still living in the rental. Dad tried to find work. Whether it was due to simply no jobs available or the fact that it was probably pretty well known he'd just gotten out of the county house, no work equals no money; no money equals no food.

Aunt Helen and Uncle Glen lived up the street, about a half-mile. Every once in a while, Uncle Glen would drop off groceries, but eventually we were down to a few sour potatoes. Even with a few bags of groceries from those who knew our plight, it was not enough. We were hungry.

I don't know if any on Mom's side of the family, other than Aunt Helen and Uncle Glen, knew how desperate we were. If they did, I can only think that they would have helped. I have to keep in mind that just the summer prior, Grandpa and Grandma had lost their home in the Hubbard Creek Fire, as had Aunt Edna and Uncle Stanley Sjorgren, parents of cousins Dick and Denny. So most of Mom's side of the family were pretty well occupied with their own set of problems, having to rebuild and furnish two homes, and so on. It was a tough time for all the Backlund family, not just the Olivers.'

The facts were that the Olivers were down to eating dandelion greens cooked in a little hog fat and mixed with the remaining sour potatoes. It was during this time of desperation and poverty that Dad snuck into the landlord's chicken house and helped himself to a few pounds of "chicken scratch." Chicken scratch is nothing but dried field corn that has been passed through a roller press to break into smaller pieces. Mom and Dad ran that dried field corn through one of those hand-cranked meat grinders over and over until it was of sufficient fine grain to make something that tasted like corn bread.

In addition to the dandelion greens, we would harvest watercress from the small winter stream that flowed from the steep hillside and past the apartments before dumping into North Myrtle Creek. Interesting, in the years that followed our stays on the Rice property, in season we would harvest and eat hazelnuts, lamb's quarter, camas root, and roots from the lady's slipper orchid. Not that these were staples in any definition of the word, but simply were eaten out of curiosity rather then necessity.

By this time, I was becoming aware of how I dressed and knew that I didn't measure up to the average kid in school when it came to clothing, and even in what I brought to eat in my lunch sack. Often it was just a couple of baking powder biscuits. Sometimes they would have jam on them, sometimes not. On occasion there might be a homemade cookie or two. Not that the cookies were bad because Mom could make some pretty good ones. It's just that as I began to realize that I didn't quite stack up to those around me, it began to work on my psyche, and I began to pull inward. I tried to fit in as much as possible, but there was that underlying feeling that I just wasn't good enough for most of those kids. It was probably all in my imagination now that I think about it; but nevertheless, perception is reality, and so I perceived myself as less than most.

This was the winter and spring of my third year in school. In spite of my feelings of inferiority that were beginning to develop, I was doing well in school—maybe because of my third grade teacher, Mrs. Yokum. She was a smaller, older woman. She treated me with kindness. She always seemed to have a word of encouragement at the right time. I don't know if she knew any of the circumstances going on in my life. I certainly didn't share them with anybody. Whether I realized it or not at the time, she played an important part in validating me through special projects she assigned; but more so, by the gentle kindness and respect she extended. She was just what I needed at the time.

It was in my later years in grade school and into my freshman and sophomore years in high school that I seemed to get in at least one fist fight a year. Not that I was any good at boxing; the good news was, neither were the other boys. It's just that the bullies would single out the one who was different, and they'd keep picking on him until the fists started flying. I could take a lot of garbage, but I usually had a breaking point. I think I surprised several of those bullies when they realized the skinny-looking kid wasn't soft. I got a reputation, and the bullying tapered off.

Somehow we survived that year in the rented apartment—a chicken coop converted into a rentable unit—and toward the end of the school year, Dad convinced Mom we needed to move back to the shack; possibly because he couldn't raise the rent money for the apartment. In the shack on the hillside, there was neither rent nor utilities to be paid, and thus he reasoned any money he made could be put to buying food. So, in a short time, we were back where we started. After a few months or so, the cycle of violence started again. Probably for obvious reasons, Dad couldn't get steady work. His reputation as a drinker, wife-abuser, ex-felon, and so on, were all good reasons for a potential employer not to hire him.

As to being a criminal, Dad was not a thief, as long as you didn't consider him not paying bills he thought too exorbitant. He was neither a cheat nor a con artist. His problems seemed to be all associated with the flesh's craving for alcohol, and thus his lower nature was fed by the alcohol demon, and, consequently the collision with self-control and self-destruction were inevitable.

At this period of his life, Dad was unemployable, and so the lot fell on him to make money any way possible. In the winter months, from my third to my eighth grades, there was always a stipend from the county welfare, but never enough to provide our complete needs; and so Dad, to his credit, did what he could, and what he was capable of to earn some spending money. A significant part of his income came from peeling and selling cascara bark. Because of the role this activity played in our lives, I'll describe this work in a later chapter.

Another way Dad put food on the table was to raise chickens. We raised them for fryers (eating) and for layers. Each spring, around Easter time, Mom would anticipate when the local feed store would make hatchlings available. The feed store was located caddy corner from the Golden Rule, one block off Main Street. The feed store also sold logging paraphernalia and was where Dad had bought his new, blue Homelite a couple of years earlier, now obviously "owned" by someone else following its abandonment on the hillside.

Some years, we'd get the hatchlings free. If not free, we never had to pay more than a few cents a piece. We'd get seventy-five to one hundred of those fluffy little peepers and raise them in the shack until their feathers started showing. We'd house them in strong cardboard boxes placed near the wood stoves for warmth. We'd put some water dishes in each box and feed them "mash," that soft compressed feed that chicks need for their early growing stage. Man, could those birds poop. It didn't smell that bad, but we still had to change the newspaper at the bottom of those cardboard boxes every day.

Once their feathers started growing, we placed them outside in an enclosure made from prune dryer trays that we also used for drying cascara bark. The prune dryer trays were about two feet by three feet, and were made of about one-inch by half-inch wood slats with a half-inch or so gap between the slats for air circulation. When wired together, they made a fairly decent "fenced" enclosure that kept the chicks in and the small predators out. Because we always had a dog running loose, we didn't have problems with skunks, raccoons, or possums near the house; so the chicks were safe outside once they reached their "feathering" stage.

The pen was about eight by twelve feet, and we'd simply set it up under some of the trees that grew around the house; and those birds would go to scratching, eating any slug or insect they could scratch up, along with the grass. When the ground became bare, we'd make it a family affair to move the pen to a new spot. We'd each grab a part of the pen, lift, and in a few steps, have it and the chicks moved. The chicks were able to eat from nature's bounty—supplemented with a daily feeding of chicken scratch, cracked corn, and whatever table scraps were available.

We would try and hold the chicks in the pen as long as possible for their protection until they could fly sufficiently on their own to roost in the trees at night. We'd clip their wings, but in time even that wasn't enough, as they soon became strong enough to jump and flutter over the sides of the pen. After that, they were pretty much on their own. They provided the dog a good chase now and then, until even the dog got tired of the game and pretty much left them alone. In about twelve weeks, the chickens started disappearing from the yard, making their way into the frying pan.

I don't know how Mom could tell a hen from a rooster at such an early age, but she could. She'd save out a couple of roosters and about a dozen hens for laying, but the rest we'd eat, spreading their demise over the spring and summer months. They pretty much stayed around the house as a flock, and we never had any trouble with bugs and slugs within a couple hundred feet of "home." I can still hear the hen's soft "pawk-pawk-pawk" early in the morning as I lay in bed. The chickens would come down from their roost at daybreak, scratching and feeding around the house. The only disadvantage was their poop. My sisters preferred to go barefoot once the ground warmed up in late spring, and they never seemed to mind a little chicken poop on their feet now and then. I never did build calluses on the soles of my feet. I always wore shoes and never had the problem of squishy stuff between my toes.

Except for the piles of chicken poop in the yard, the chickens were a nice addition to the hillside "farm." The job usually fell to the girls to find the laying nests and get whatever eggs they could find. I think they actually enjoyed the job; it was kind of like a daily Easter egg hunt. Only problem was, once in awhile, they'd find an old nest. There is no mistaking the smell of a rotten egg when broken into a hot frying pan.

After we moved back into the shack following Dad's release from prison, Dad bought the old '36 Ford from Uncle Glen. It was pretty well worn out, but Dad made it work. Most of the time, Dad could not start the Ford using the electric starter, as it simply wouldn't turn the motor over fast enough. That old engine did not have sufficient compression to pull the air/fuel mixture into the cylinders using the electric starter. This was especially a problem after it had run for a while. The warmer the engine became, the lower the compression. So before Dad shut the ignition off, he made sure the car was parked on an incline. It always started on a rolling start. This is where Dad switched on the ignition, put the transmission in second gear, and with the clutch pedal depressed, got the car rolling down a grade. As soon as the car had a little speed, Dad "popped" the clutch to turn the engine over. With a puff of white smoke from the exhaust pipe, that tired old flat head V8 would start every time.

He got real creative the summer of '54. The '36 Ford was too small to carry a family of six around. This time, he chopped off the back end with a chisel, pretty much cutting the body off from behind the front seat. Remember, he had honed his car customizing skills when he "built" his crummy a year or so earlier. Disconnecting the rear part of the body, he tipped it off the frame. Then he covered the opening into the "cab" with some heavy plywood, in which he inserted a small window for "rear viewing" purposes, and then constructed a flat bed with side racks. Now we had a flatbed pickup "truck." He even painted it with black enamel using a paintbrush, and from fifty feet away, it looked pretty good. If we kids had to be transported anywhere, we would sit or stand up in the bed.

This modified '36 Ford became the Oliver family's mode of transportation. Except for its "starter" problem, it was reliable and served us well. We were mak'n do again.

During harvest season, when working the bean fields around Myrtle Creek, we'd rise sufficiently early to be in the field before the sun came up, and most mornings, those bean vines were cold and heavy with dew. So there I was, eight or nine years old, picking beans. Even then Dad let me keep some of my money. I quickly learned the value of a hard-earned dollar.

I remember the first summer I picked. I had my own bucket and sack, and I'd place that bag "up the row" in front of me. I'd pick a bucket full of beans, lug the bucket to the sack, dump the beans into the sack, and go back to the place in the row I left off picking; I'd do this over-and-over until the sack was full. I filled my first sack so full I couldn't carry it. As a matter of fact, I couldn't even drag it. Being a fairly astute young man, I knew I could get Dad to carry it to the weigh station. Wrong! He just laughed. He said if I couldn't carry what I picked, he wasn't going to do if for me.

Shoot, I thought, *Now what am I going to do with a seventy-pound bag of green beans?*

I sat on my bucket and studied the problem, went and got another sack, put half the beans in the second sack, and then drug the sacks, one at a time, to the weigh station. What Dad was doing was teaching me to be independent. I learned the lesson. I also learned that I had wasted time. I probably could have picked another sack of beans in the time it took me to solve the problem.

The education I received picking beans, prunes, walnuts, and filberts, continued in the temperate summer climate of the South Umpqua Valley. This education amounted to a doctorate in what-not-to-do-when-old-enough-to-decide-what-to-do.

Dad never took responsibility for the debilitating effects his drinking had on the family, nor did he ever admit he had a problem. That was just the way it was. When sober, there was never a more honorable man, who, in those times of sobriety worked to instill in me character traits I still hold precious: honesty, trustworthiness, being a man of your word, proper etiquette, and so on. He seemed an enigma in this regard. I can remember sitting around the dinner table and Dad telling my sis's and me how to hold a fork, how not to put elbows on the table, and how to hold one hand in your lap when eating. He taught me manners when visiting my friends' homes, which was basically always saying "thank you" to the host and hostess and to offer to help with the dishes after the meal was served. In retrospect, this kind of training seemed incongruous and out of sorts with his drunken character. I thank God that He used a sometimes-sober father to instill etiquette and other social graces that I found useful and proper as a young child and adult.

I do not remember Mom drinking when Dad was not around. I could be wrong, but I remember her drinking only in Dad's presence. I can only think of two reasons for this. One, she drank to dull the pain of an eventual beating; and two, she felt compelled to drink when Dad drank, and in this way, she diverted some of the shame he would have borne drinking alone.

It is interesting for me to reflect on the relationship between drinking "buddies," especially those caught up in alcoholism. Dad had his drinking "buddies"; at times it might be his brother Arch, or some other acquaintance who would stop by. One who stopped by on a regular basis was Ray McFarland.

Dad and Ray hooked up shortly after the end of the Korean War. Ray was recently discharged, married, and began having kids. One day, Dad invited Ray up to the house, and they continued their beer drinking that they had started in the tavern on Main Street. Ray left late that night and returned the next weekend with his wife, Ida, and two kids—a toddler and a new baby in a blanket. The McFarlands then became regular visitors at the Oliver shack.

Ray was well into alcoholism himself, but he was what I'd term a functional alcoholic. He held jobs in the local mills, and as far as I know, was not abusive. As I may have mentioned, as long as we had company, even if the company were other alcoholics and were drinking heavily, Dad was thus preoccupied and relatively congenial toward all. We did not mind company at all, and even welcomed it. Even though there was heavy drinking, things were relatively pleasant. Interesting, too, was that when company was present, Mom's drinking would taper off significantly.

We had some good times with the McFarlands. When the weather was warm, they would often spend the night, both being too tanked up to make the drive home. Their visits were accompanied with lots of food for everybody and treats for us kids. Chicken would be fried, a potato salad made, corn on the cob (Ray's dad grew a lot of produce), and we'd all chow down. Treats might be a watermelon in season, Pepsi Cola, or ice cream.

One morning, Mom made breakfast for everybody and ol' Ray was sitting at the kitchen table sort of hung over real good. He was nursing a beer while Mom fried pancakes and eggs for everybody. We all sat down and passed the eggs, pancakes, margarine, and syrup. Ray loaded his plate up and reached for the syrup, mistaking a bottle of brown apple vinegar for the syrup jar. All of us kids smiled as we watched him pour the vinegar over his pancakes, take a bite, and then make this strange sound. We all chuckling quietly, until somebody tells him that he poured vinegar on his pancakes. He sat up real straight, and said, "Well, we can't waste good pancakes, can we?" He reached for the syrup bottle this time and poured a liberal amount on his vinegar-soaked stack, then proceeded to eat it all, washing the whole mess down with the last of his beer.

Ray never shared his Korean War experiences with any of us that I know of. One thing he shared was his ability to stick needles in his flesh. As I stated, Ray worked the green chains in the mills and thus was in pretty good shape—no fat, good muscle tone, and a good set of biceps. One warm day, he took his shirt off. He was lit up pretty good, and flexed his muscles for everybody. He asked Mom to get him a large sewing needle. She brought him one, and he proceeded to flex his left bicep. We were stunned when he positioned the needle directly above the muscle and pushed it in to the bone. He did this a couple of times, showing no discomfort at all. I suppose it was no more painful than having one's blood drawn, or getting a vaccination. Even so, I still recoil thinking about it.

On another occasion, the McFarlands visited for Thanksgiving dinner. They were to provide the turkey, again a gift from his dad's farm. It was time to put an end to this gray monster, and Dad told me to do it.

"You want me to do what?" I said.

"Chop its head off, Dan. He ain't going to get cooked standing there." The turkey was tied to a tree.

Now I was able to do this with chickens now and then, but this bird was no chicken. It had to weigh at least twenty or pounds, and it was healthy. I struggled to get its wings pulled back so I could clamp them with one hand together with the feet, lift the turkey, and then while holding the turkey on the block, swing the ax. This obviously wasn't a dumb turkey. Each time the ax descended, it'd jerk its head off to the side, and I missed. I finally gave up. Dad finished the job, and we had our Thanksgiving turkey.

Survival 201

During the later part of my third year and into my fourth year in school, Dad would cycle into drunken binges with their predicable results; then would come the sober times when he would work at whatever he could to make a few dollars to put food on the table. There was plenty of logging going on at that time; and while Dad's gainfully employed days in the industry were probably at an end, we at least could scavenge from the efforts of others. During the winter months, the streams and river would flood and carry off the logging debris that always seemed to find its way into the rising waters. Wherever there was a gravel bar, an eddy, or other obstruction in the heavy flow of the river, a driftwood pile would form. When the river receded, there were sound salvageable logs (fir, maple, alder, ash) for firewood and/or cedar logs for fence posts. It was hard work cutting that wood with the crosscut, but we did it, and then hand-carried it over the gravel bars to the utility trailer attached to the car; a trailer Dad had made using an old car's front axel and wheels he'd salvaged somewhere.

Dad usually had no problem selling the firewood. He didn't make a whole lot. Ten to fifteen dollars a chord, or whatever people would pay. He could sell the posts for a dollar apiece to farmers and ranchers and could make some decent money. Although I'm sure he never made wages, we didn't need much to survive on that hillside. The only expense he had was food and incidentals, gasoline for the car, and kerosene for the lamps.

If there was any fruit or vegetables in season that needed to be picked, then the whole family would be out "pick'n" whatever happened to be within a reasonable commute distance from home. For the first few years, we worked the crops in our local area. Blue Lake pole beans, prunes (Italian and Petite), walnuts, and filberts were what we typically picked. Later, beginning the summer between my fifth and sixth grades, we worked in the strawberry fields in Estacada, and a year or so later, the bean fields in Stayton.

In those early years, Dad and Mom kept most of the money, although as I got older, Dad allowed me to keep the larger share; and basically from that time on, I worked to earn my own money for school clothes and other personal things I might need or want. Mostly, it went for clothes. Blackberries grew everywhere along Dole Road and on the banks of the South Umpqua. Mom and Dad would send us kids out to pick as soon as their fruit ripened. There would be great, wide clumps of bushes. First, we'd pick around the edges; but it seemed most of the large, thick, ripe berries would be hanging under vines too far to reach standing on the ground at the edges of the "patch." We solved this problem by going to the closest driftwood pile to locate wide, one-inch thick boards, at least ten feet long. We'd lay them onto the vines and "walk up" the boards, picking as we'd go, laying trenches through those clumps of vines.

We would pick in this manner for hours in the hot sun until we reached some pre-defined quota, which usually was pick until we filled all the kettles and buckets we were given.

Our "buckets" consisted of two or three pound coffee cans. Either Dad or I would use a small nail to punch a couple of holes on opposite sides of the rim. Through the holes, we'd thread a piece of bailing wire, and we'd have our picking "bucket."

Mom, with help from the girls, would can the berries. Nothing we harvested went to waste. She'd make fresh blackberry pies and can the rest, making jellies and jams, and squeezing and canning juice. In season, the canning never stopped—applesauce, peaches, pears, prunes, tomatoes, green beans and corn, with jam and jellies from blackberries, blackcaps, and wild strawberries. Hundreds and hundreds of small jelly jars, pints, quarts and half-gallon canning jars, all stored in a special "fruit house" that Dad constructed in a grove of madrone trees between the house and the well.

I learned that I could make a few dollars a day by picking and selling two-pound cans of blackberries in town. So when Mom had reached her limit (as if I hadn't got my fill of picking), I'd take four of these "buckets," and starting in the morning at a patch close to town, I'd fill them, then walk into town and sell them door-to-door. I'd sell the berries for fifty to seventy-five cents a can, and by early afternoon at the latest, I'd have a few dollars jingling in my pockets. I guess I cut my entrepreneur's wings this way, discovering early that one could get rewarded quite well for their labor if one put out the effort, and had a product that people wanted.

I disliked picking prunes, mostly because they ripened late in the summer and early fall when the yellow jackets were most active. I'd get stung at least once. The yellow jackets would be eating the meat out of those prunes as they lay on the ground, and if you weren't careful, you would grab a prune with a bee on the underside. Ouch!

Bee venom had a bad effect on me. If it was only one sting, I generally would be *okay*, although I remember to this day how painful those stings were. I could instantly feel pain at the point where the venom penetrated, and then chills would spread quickly throughout my body and just as quickly dissipate. Then there was the steady ache of the poison as it began to spread around the point of penetration. If I was stung anywhere on the hand, it would swell up like an inflated rubber glove. Within twenty-four hours, my finger and hand would be two times the normal size with the swelling advancing well past my wrist. The swelling would remain a couple of days and then recede, with the arm and hand eventually returning to normal appearance. But because the skin had stretched, it would itch during the healing process. All in all, it took a week for the hand to return to normal.

Mom and Dad couldn't afford doctors, and so I had no choice but to endure any pain or sickness I might suffer and let the body heal itself. Occasionally, there might be a home remedy, and in the case of bee stings, it was either mud or moist packing of baking soda. I don't think they did any good at all. No matter the remedy, it still took about a week to heal.

Speaking of bee stings, it was within a year or so of our moving into the shack that I came close to dying from an attack by a swarm of hornets. My sisters and I were playing in a small open area in the woods between the house and Dole Road. We were a couple hundred feet down the driveway from the house. This clearing had once been a place where people dumped trash. These were the days before the sophisticated landfills. In those small towns, people would find a place in the country and just throw their trash over the bank alongside the road, or find some hidden field, or sand bar on the river. They were still doing this in the early fifties where the driveway from the old shack met Dole Road, and along Dole Road about a half-mile down river from the shack.

Anyway, the area in which we were playing had been an old "community" dump. It had long since had dirt bulldozed over the trash and the clearing leveled out. Grass grew in the clearing, making it a nice area in which to play. But under that thin layer of dirt, there remained cavities where yellow jackets built nests…in a buried can…whatever. My oldest sister, Pat (such a considerate child at the time), noticed yellow jackets flying in and out of a hole in the ground. I did not notice the yellow jackets. I had a shovel with me. She pointed and dared me to dig. "Yeah, Sis, if you say so." I promptly sunk the shovel into the dirt where she pointed. Imagine my surprise when the entire head of the shovel disappeared into the ground and a swarm of yellow jackets took great offense in having their living space invaded.

I remember pain. I screamed as venom-loaded stinger after venom-loaded stinger found my flesh an available and tender target! All I could do was run and scream! My screams must have been horrible and blood curdling; I flew up the driveway toward the shack in an attempt to outrun the bees. My young legs were no match for a swarm of angry yellow jackets protecting their nest, and so running toward home, I took a swarm of bees with me, getting stung repeatedly during the trip.

I remember making it into the house, but I remember nothing else until the next day. I passed out. Mom told me that I had so many stings that she ran out of baking soda and could only think to wrap me in wet towels and put me to bed. I don't recall if there was any consideration given to the fact that I might have been dying from anaphylactic shock and was in serious need of some anti-venom! But, that's the way my folks were, somewhat ignorant. Shoot, who ever heard of anybody back then going to a doctor for a bee sting? Considering my intense adverse reaction to bee stings, it's a wonder I'm alive today.

Dad occasionally would make a trip up Cow Creek to do some prospecting. Most of the time, the whole family would go. This was more recreation than work. Dad probably had latent dreams of striking it rich, but the Cow Creek channel and its tributaries had long given up their treasures to the shovels and picks of the early prospectors. Even so, while Dad chased his dreams, we kids could play in the water, leaving Dad to dig and scrape gravel from crevices in bedrock in the hope of finding a nugget. Fat chance. All the placer diggings had been gone over numerous times through the years since the time gold was discovered in the area in the late nineteenth century, but it was fun to dream and fun work to do. Cow Creek was where Dad taught me how to pan for gold. In my teen years, I would often take a pan, pick, and shovel and head for the river bed just upstream from the Highway 99 bridge. I could always find some color from the gravel over the bedrock in that area, and actually panned a couple match-head sized "nuggets" from one pocket of gravel.

Dad would also collect chromium ore from the gravel beds of the South Umpqua. During World War II, the ore was valuable.

When walking the gravel beds, Dad had a habit of reaching down to pick up a dark-brown rock. He'd take out his pocketknife and make a scratch on the rock. If it left a light brown scratch, it was chromium, and Dad would carry the "rocks" to the car and add them to his pile of ore behind his workshop at home. He never did anything with the stuff. Just collected it. A point of interest is that about this time, some miner began a small open pit chromium mining operation on a ridge off Timber Butte about a half-mile north of the old shack. It never amounted to much, probably because there wasn't much ore there.

So it wasn't just picking fruit in season. We worked at whatever we could to earn money. Dad obviously couldn't hold a steady job. As far as I know, he never had anything that he could remotely classify as a steady job. At times he would do odd jobs, work in the woods when someone offered him work when he was "healthy" enough to work. He even tried his hand at horse logging. Not that they logged horses, mind you, but Dad and another fellow (who owned the horses and harness), yarded young second-growth timber from small timber plots within a few miles of town using a team of horses.

One of the logging operations Dad was involved in ended in the middle of my fourth or fifth winter in school. Dad had taken a hit alongside the face with a cant hook that his partner had dropped back to him when Dad wasn't looking. It seems that his partner was taking the hooks from a log the horses had just hoisted onto the bunk of the logging truck, and he had let the hook swing from the A-frame back to Dad, who was controlling the hook and line with the horses. He hollered for Dad to duck. Good thing. Dad had time to look up to see what was coming, but not in sufficient time to get completely out of the way. A portion of the hook caught Dad on the side of his face, broke his nose, and almost knocked him out. He staggered around for some time working to staunch the flow of blood from both nostrils but could not completely stop the bleeding, so he plugged his nostrils with some strips from his snot rag. He kept working the afternoon with blood dripping from his broken nose! He didn't see a doctor that night, and he was back to work the next day.

As if a broken nose was not enough, this day he sliced the outside of his right thumb to the bone, from the thumbnail to the middle of his palm. He was sharpening the chain on the saw, and when pushing the chain backwards on the bar to expose more teeth to file, the chain stuck, but his hand didn't. He sliced it open on one of the teeth he'd just sharpened. Again, he bled a lot, but he fixed the cut by wrapping the thumb and palm of his hand with black electrician's tape, and continued to work. Feeling weak in the knees he arrived home early, but because the wound was deep and long he then drove back to town to get the wound sewed up. The doctor noticed his still swollen nose and concluded that Dad probably lost a lot of blood, and instructed him to go home and get some rest, which he did. The next morning, he "recovered" sufficiently to return to work.

The fact that Dad could work like that, with a broken nose, and weakened by loss of blood told me something. I think he really wanted to work, but he was not only the victim of his own weakness for alcohol, but also the victim of a ruined physical body. He had incredible strength, even though he was suffering horribly from a double hernia and ulcers. The ulcers eventually hemorrhaged so severely that he almost bled to death in the winter of 1955.

When I got home from school that winter afternoon of 1955, Mom pulled us kids together and told us that Dad was taken by ambulance to the Veteran's Hospital in Roseburg. His condition was so bad he had to be transferred to the Veteran's Hospital in Portland, where they operated to remove the damaged parts of his stomach. He eventually recovered sufficiently for them to send him home by Greyhound bus.

Man, he looked awful when he stepped off the bus that night. It was after dark, but even so Mom, with kids in tow, had walked from the shack to the bus depot located several blocks south of the Dairy Queen. Lights and shadows from streetlights gave Dad an almost ghostly appearance. He was obviously not fully recovered. The weather had turned cold and a fairly significant snowfall had occurred just a few days prior to Dad's return. Snow had been pushed into piles on each street corner, and I remember the difficulty we had in helping Dad over those slick mounds of snow. As a family, we trudged back to the shack, assisting Dad as needed.

Dad was sick for another reason. The hospital had decided to pull what few teeth he had left and immediately fit him with a set of dentures. So not only was he suffering from his surgeries, but he was also suffering from the teeth extraction. I'll say one thing, Dad was tough. I don't remember him complaining. Mom nursed him back to health, and for some time he was off the hooch.

....

When I think about these events in Dad's life and the toll they had on him physically, I cannot understand the source of his incredible strength. Small as he was, and weakened by the booze and lack of consistent physical exercise, I could never beat the man in arm wrestling or hand gripping. A few weeks prior to his dying of a massive stroke in April 1974, I tried for the last time, but failed miserably at both efforts. He still could bring me to my knees with his handgrip. What made the defeat worse was that he smiled during the process. I wasn't exactly a weakling at thirty-one, in the prime of health, but, no cigar. One must really appreciate Dad's uncommon strength when considering that after several operations by the VA hospital to repair the damage done from years of neglect and abuse to his stomach, he was able to retain his physical abilities with only one-fifth of his stomach. Each time he went in for surgery, the doctors would take out a little bit more until they finally had removed all the bad parts. From about 1960 on, he had to eat several times a day to receive needed nourishment.

About that Marlin .22. Dad purchased the rifle new shortly after he and Mom were married, and, with it, Dad taught me how to shoot. I was seven years old. One of the jobs I had, although I certainly didn't consider it a job, was to put some fresh meat on the table.

The "hillside" we lived on consisted of hundreds of acres of steep, rocky cliffs, with Douglas Fir clinging to benches, mingled with white oak, black oak, myrtle, madrone, maple, cascara, alder, sugar pine, wild filberts, wild cherry, greasewood, poison oak, and azaleas. Oh, the scent of wild azalea blossoms in the spring, how absolutely sweet the smell. In the strength of their bloom, you could smell them a half mile away with no wind blowing. They would grow in the drainage of the seeps and springs that leaked from Timber Butte's south slope, just opposite the bench on which our "shack" was located. The "hillside" was an environment just made for me, and it was in this environment when, if there was nothing else to do, I would take the .22 and go rabbit and squirrel hunting.

Jackrabbits seemed to be everywhere on that south slope of Timber Butte, from the bottom to the top. The best time for bagging rabbits was in the evening, generally a couple of hours or so before the sun set. The sun would be behind the shoulder of Timber Butte, and the south slope would be in shadow. I'd get myself up on the slope, and walking slowly, I would simply scan from the corners of my eye for movement. I could never seem to see them if I tried to locate one by focusing my eyes on an area. It seemed that it was the peripheral vision that caught the movement, which made me stop, and then turn to where the movement originated.

I rarely missed. Not because I was that good a shot, but simply because I never shot at a running target, or from too great a distance. Dad always kept the gun sighted in. I was a good enough shooter to hit what I aimed at. If it was game, it was dead.

We used .22 hollow point bullets for "big game." At the time, "big game" for me was jackrabbits or squirrels. Now if you look at any .22 bullet, it looks so puny compared to a 30.30 or 30.06 slug. You'd think it wouldn't, and couldn't, kill anything. Don't be fooled. Those hollow points would mushroom when they hit, and they'd stop a big old jackrabbit dead—a white tail doe, too. Neither creature is a match for a well-placed .22 hollow-point projectile!

Some of those jackrabbits were big. I'd have the .22 in my left hand and a rabbit or two by the legs in my right hand. Those rabbits were so big their heads would be dragging the ground. Some of them had to weigh ten or more pounds.

We had to watch for boils and other disease in the rabbits and squirrels, especially in the late summer and early fall. They would get huge boils on their sides and on their haunches. If I spotted a boil, I would leave the carcass. Sometimes, you'd not find it until during the skinning process. There was a knack to skinning that kind of game without getting the meat all covered with fine hair and fur. I learned to do it quite well.

The squirrel hunts were the most fun. The watercourses that fed into the South Umpqua in that country were full of myrtle trees. The myrtle tree grows naturally in southern Oregon and northern California, and in certain parts of the Middle East. In the Myrtle Creek area, they grew to quite good size. They produced a nut about the size of a large filbert or a macadamia. I guess they were edible if one could get past the bitter taste. The gray squirrels seemed to love them because they would get fat and sassy when the myrtle nuts ripened in the fall. They'd sit up there on a limb with a nut between their forepaws, scolding you with their *kuck-kuh, huck-kuh* chirp. Some were intelligent enough to recognize danger and would scramble for safety, while some would just sit on the limb and chirp and scold away. Others would poke their head out from behind the trunk of the tree—first from one side and then from the other side, daring me to shoot. I didn't argue. I shot.

We ate a lot of rabbit and gray squirrel during our time on that hillside. I didn't eat much of it, especially squirrel. Too tough and gamey tasting for me, no matter how Mom cooked it.

Like I said, I was a decent shot and I didn't waste ammunition. Dad taught me well, teaching me never to shoot unless I know what I'm shooting at and to never shoot at a running target.

"That's for show-offs and people who like to waste their money."

"Usually," he said. "They make a lucky shot, and suddenly they think they're Annie Oakley." Dad taught me well in a number of areas; how to respect and use a rifle was just one of them.

I killed my first deer when I was nine years old. At the time, I didn't think it was a very big deal, but now that I look back, it indeed was a big deal. Think about it for a moment. This was the early fifties, probably '52 or '53. Here I was, this skinny kid out hunting for meat for the table. It was part of the work that I did. Why, today, if the authorities caught wind of a family living in the circumstances we lived, they'd haul the kids off under protective custody and put the dad and mom in jail and throw away the key. They'd call it "child endangerment" or something like that. Why, who would even think about such a thing as to give a nine-year-old a .22 rifle and then let him go hunting? Yes, actually hunting to kill something. Not only would there be child endangerment charges, but, animal abuse charges, hunting out of season, reckless endangerment to the environment, ad-infinitum.

For the Olivers, hunting was always "in season." When we needed venison, we simply went hunting for it. There was no license to buy—just ammunition.

I well remember the day of my first deer kill. It was about an hour from sunset. It was a warm, early fall evening.

I walked north from the shack toward the base of Timber Butte.

Once onto the faint trace of a trail, I followed it until it sloped down toward the small streambed in which, higher up the canyon, was built the small covered collection tank that at the time still provided potable water for Myrtle Creek. At this lower spot on the mountain, and at that late time of the year, the stream was dried up, although springs higher up continued to provide a source of water for Myrtle Creek's water collection system.

I had seen deer many times and at different places all over the steep slopes of the mountain that circled the basin in which the old shack was built. I had learned how to be sufficiently quiet when in the woods to increase my chances of spotting a jackrabbit or squirrel. This time, it was a deer.

There were dry oak and maple leaves on the trail; but even so, I was doing a good job of being quiet because I spotted the doe in a clearing on the opposite side of the dry creek bed before she spotted me.

Now I know of grown men who have been struck both dumb and blind by "buck fever," but I don't remember any of that. I remember propping the rifle alongside a small oak and taking aim just behind her right shoulder. Before I could pull the trigger, I must have moved, or made a noise that spooked her, and she darted toward the far side of the clearing.

My response was almost instantaneous. I whistled. You know, the kind of whistle where you curl your tongue under your upper front teeth and make that shrill, loud whistle to get somebody's attention. Dad had taught me this trick when hunting rabbits, and when I used it, they would usually stop to try and figure out what made that noise, which allowed me time to sight and get off a killing shot. It worked for that doe, too. She stopped in her tracks and turned back to face the source of the sound. This gave me time to get off a single round aimed directly into the chest between the forelegs. *A clean heart shot,* I thought.

She immediately bolted to my left, running parallel to the dry streambed, disappearing behind a clump of broad leaf maples growing from the side of the steam. There was silence, except for what sounded like rustling leaves, as if someone was kicking leaves into a pile. I followed as quickly as possible, thinking that I had missed her completely, all the time hoping that she had stopped just out of sight and would allow me another shot, but nothing. No movement. No noise. I followed her tracks to the edge of the dry streambed, looked upstream, downstream, across the streambed. Nothing.

I was dog-gone disappointed and discouraged walking back to the house.

Dad was outside. He'd heard me shoot, as I wasn't that far from the house. As I walked past, he asked what I had shot. *Probably thought I was shooting rabbits.* I told him I had shot at a doe and that I had her dead in my sights, but I obviously missed and she got away. He asked me where it all happened, and I explained.

"Well come on then, let's go see if we can find her," he said, with a touch of excitement.

Like I said, it wasn't that far from the house, probably less than 300 yards; and so it didn't take us long to get back. I showed Dad where I made the shot, where the doe stood and where I thought she had gone. Dad found blood.

With a knowing look he said, "You were too close to have missed. She's probably nearby somewhere. If you hit the heart, they can run some distance before they die."

He tracked her to the brink of the streambed where I had stood earlier. He looked down into a pile of leaves in the bottom of a dry hole, pointed, then said, "There she is. No wonder you couldn't see her. She's half covered with leaves."

We both dropped into the hole and pulled her from under the leaves. Now this was probably no more than fifteen minutes from the time I had made the shot, so even in the hot weather, she was still in good shape.

Dad then asked me for the hunting knife so he could bleed and field dress it. I said, "Knife? What knife?"

It was then that I got the shortest, most intense lesson on the subject of never going hunting without a hunting knife. "How in the blinkety-blank are you going to dress the blinkety-blank thing?" he chided. "Get the blinkety-blank back home, find the blinkety-blank knife, and be back before I finish my blinkety-blank cigarette."

Shoot, I had such an adrenaline rush by this time that I was back before he took his first blinkety-blank puff.

Dad showed me how to bleed and field dress an animal that early fall evening. No nonsense, just plain facts on what to do, when to do it, and how to do it. He concluded by saying, "*Okay*, that's the way I expect you to do it from now on. And by the way, if you kill it, you pack it home." *Gee,* I thought, *I must be back in the bean fields.*

Dad and I packed the meat home. We then hung the carcass from a limb of one of the oaks close to the house and finished skinning and quartering. We cut the back strap (tenderloin) from each side of the backbone and quartered the rest, putting each quarter into clean pillowcases, and then hung the sacks down in the well, the coolest place we had.

That was it. No fuss. No fanfare. No, "Boy, isn't Dan quite the hunter." I'm sure there must have been a pat on the back somewhere, or some compliment, but I don't remember one. I do remember the meat tasted good.

Mom knew how to cook venison. From the front and rear quarters, she would slice the meat into small filets. What was too small would be ground up into "deer burger." The small steaks were placed inside a paper bag in which was a cup or so of flour seasoned with pepper and salt. The bag was shaken to get the meat coated with the mix, then the meat taken out and put in a hot skillet with some Crisco shortening for frying. After the meat was cooked, Mom would make gravy for the potatoes. Into the same hot skillet, Mom would put the rest of the flour from the sack, stirring the flour mix until it became brown. Then she'd mix in some canned milk mixed with water, salt and pepper, a thickening agent; and stirring occasionally, it would begin to thicken into a nice-tasting brown gravy. The gravy would be put on boiled or mashed potatoes, and with some corn on the cob or other vegetables in season (if not in season, then canned veggies) supper was on. Mmmmm, good.

The "Chittim" Years

It tastes awful, gaggingly awful. Take my word; it is nasty-tasting stuff. The scientific name is "cascara" for Rhamnus purshiana (Latin). The colloquial name for cascara is "chittim"; even more colloquial, "shittim."

On the slopes of Timber Butte, the cascara tree grows mainly in the draws, gullies, and benches where seeps or springs occur. The trees are nothing to look at—relatively small when compared to the oaks, madrones, and alders. The bark, with a grey-white mottled look, is relatively thin. Usually, the trees would be no more than fifteen or twenty feet tall, and maybe eight to ten inches in diameter. If you weren't paying attention, you could mistake an alder tree for a cascara tree. The bark was not only similar in color and thickness, but the leaf also had a similar look and size. When in doubt, though, all one had to do was peel a thin strip and taste the inner side of the bark. The decision was never in doubt when measured by cascara's bitter taste.

"Extract of cascara sagrada" from cascara tree bark has been recognized as a tonic laxative and prescribed by doctors since about 1877. When brewed as a home remedy, it makes the most awful tasting "tea." When someone in the family became constipated, Mom or Dad would locate a cascara tree and peel a small quantity of bark. Mom would steep the bark in boiling water, making a most foul-tasting liquid. No matter whether honey, sugar and/or lemon were mixed with it, there was nothing that could make it palatable.

"Quit squirming," Mom or Dad would say. "Drink it. It'll make you poop." I drank a dose of that foul, bitter tasting liquid once, and it cured my constipation all right. It cured me for good. I never had another case of constipation. I didn't care how plugged up I was, I was never going to admit it, and I never drank that foul brew again.

The tree is native to the Pacific Northwest, and when there was no other source of income, Dad would have all of us out somewhere on those draws and watercourses off Timber Butte looking for, and peeling, cascara.

Being one of nature's laxatives, cascara was harvested for commercial use and used in various kinds of over-the-counter laxative products. You can talk to any northwest country boy or girl that grew up in my period of time, and they can probably remember peeling and selling the bark, or knew somebody who did.

You really couldn't make a living at it because, number one, it was hard work, and number two, the buyers (usually a feed store) could never pay enough for anyone to even make wages. Besides, the price changed constantly, depending on supply and demand.

In addition to supply and demand, what was paid depended on whether or not the bark was green or dry. If it was dried, the buyers paid more. It was a heck of a lot of work to dry the bark. Then you had to smash it up into small pieces in order to get sufficient quantity into a gunny sack to make it weigh out. Because we had time on our hands, we'd earn extra by drying the bark.

....

Peeling cascara bark is a heck of a hard way to earn a living. Then again, we didn't need a whole lot of money to live.

The bark had to be peeled when the sap was running. You couldn't peel in the late fall, winter, or early spring because the bark seizes tight to the cambium wood of the tree. You had to wait until late spring and summer to peel. It was usually hot and dry at that time of the year too, so it made for some uncomfortable times on those hillsides.

Peeling the bark itself was relatively simple. The trees were small enough that I would climb into the tree and peel the small branches while Mom or Dad would peel the trunks down to ground level. Sometimes Dad made it easy on everybody and would simply cut the tree down with an ax or a bow saw.

Like I said, Dad was creative, and using what was available and with tools at hand, he designed and formed some useful peeling tools from flat files. Peeling was a family thing. Usually it was Dad, Mom, and I that did the peeling. The girls, as they were able, would scrape off moss and then stuff the gunnysacks with the wet, green bark.

It was hard enough walking up those steep slopes of Timber Butte with the empty sacks, tools, water, and lunch, to get to the cascara trees. It was even more difficult hauling the sacks down the hill and back to the house. I hated that part of the job. It was doubly demanding in that we often had to make several trips to haul our day's peeling back to the house and prepare it for drying.

The work wasn't done when we got the bark off the hillside. We still had to lay it out on old prune dryer slats. (They had been stacked out of the way ever since the last batch of chicks outgrew their use for the prune dryer fence.) The dryer slats would be set up on blocks of wood off the ground about 6 to 8 inches to allow air to move up, under, and around the bark. In that hot, southern Oregon sun it only took a couple of days for that thin bark to dry to the "busting" stage.

After the bark was dry, one of us (the girls usually) would hold the sack open and throw in some of the dried, curled up bark. Then, Mom, Dad, or I would use a baseball-bat sized mallet that Dad had made from a madrone limb to tamp the bark, breaking it into small bits in the bag. More bark would be added, tamped, and the process repeated until the sack was full. We'd pack a lot of bark into those bags. We could get sixty to eighty pounds into a sack, depending on the size of the sack, of course. We'd stack the sacks up into a pile until we were done.

When sufficient quantity of bark was collected and processed, we'd load up the green, '39 slug (Dad had retired the old '36 Ford), and Dad and Mom would be off to the buyer with a load of bark. We kids would wait at home for them to return with groceries. Usually there would be ice cream and pop for us kids, and of course, beer or wine for Dad and Mom.

"Chittim" peeling was often interrupted with Dad's spells of drunkenness and abuse. It's difficult to remember the exact instances and times of the violence that Mom endured from the drunken hands of Dad when we lived in that shack off Dole Road. It was almost routine during the drinking periods. We kids learned to recognize the point where Dad's progression into drunkenness turned on the mean streak. It was like a switch thrown by some demon that occupied a hidden closet in his mind. Things would be fine until a certain alcohol threshold was reached in the bloodstream. Then, kaplooie! It was time for us kids to head for the tall timber and start praying somewhere on the slopes of Timber Butte.

The preamble to a beating was name-calling (that was the cue to get out of the house), and then it deteriorated into physical abuse that would only stop at the point in time where Dad drank himself into unconsciousness, or where Mom simply left the house to hide with us kids.

Don't misunderstand. The beatings were not constant, but continued on and off during a binge; some cursing or other form of verbal abuse, a slap, a grabbing and twisting of arm, and hair pulling, all intermixed with drinking. Sometimes, there'd be no physical abuse, just the verbal. In all these times and regardless of the cycle, we kids learned to stay out of his way, and if close, not look Dad straight in the eye; for if you did, you would usually be on the receiving end of his threats.

Though Dad often threatened us kids, I cannot remember him ever actually hitting any of my sisters or me during his bouts of drunkenness. Patsy tells the story of one time when Dad was drunk and took his anger out on her, spanking her with a piece of kitchen wood. She states that she was terribly bruised. There was always the fear of what he would do, or was doing, to Mom, the tell-tale signs the next morning—the bruises, the swollen and cut lips, the black eyes, and the overall soreness throughout the body. She was always the first one up in the morning fixing breakfast, bringing "Daddy" his coffee—doing all in spite of her aches, pains, and obvious discomfort. How she was able to endure that abuse time-and-time again without throwing in the towel and just leaving, I will never know. I'm sure it was because of us kids that she endured.

I cannot adequately describe the fear we kids would experience during the times of drunkenness and abuse. It was thick, heavy, and hung like a shadow all around us. The absolute ugliness of Dad's drunken, angry countenance was terrifying to witness. We simply learned to stay out of his way after he became incoherent; crazy is a better term. We would do everything in our power to agree, assuage, conciliate, and acquiesce to his moods to prevent an episode of abuse. When a certain point of alcohol in the bloodstream was reached, the result was inevitable. We fled his presence. Alas, Mom could not, or would not, and we often feared for her life, cringing and crying somewhere outside the house as we heard his curses and her cries of pain.

Dad would drink only when he had a "certain amount" of money. To his credit, if there was any money, food was the first commodity to be bought. When "payday" occurred from selling a load of "chittim" bark, Dad and Mom would continue on into Roseburg and shop at one of the wholesale grocery outlets, completely filling that green slug's trunk and back seat area with groceries—cases of Sego milk, boxes of dried milk, canned corn and peas, sacks of beans, flour, sugar, and necessary toiletries. It was mostly staples, but also cans of corned or roast beef, and other foods that were preserved and would not spoil without refrigeration.

At that time, you could buy oleo-margarine in plastic sacks that contained a package of yellow dye that you would "pop," and then by kneading the bag, work the vegetable dye through the white vegetable oil and have something that looked like butter. There would be MJB coffee by the three-pound can, a sack or two of white flour, twenty-five pounds of sugar, fresh vegetables for salads, and a couple hundred pounds of potatoes, and usually treats for us kids. Not a whole lot of candy, but usually soda pop and some mellorine (vegetable fat) ice cream. We didn't care one way or the other if it was made from vegetable fat or the finest dairy cream, it tasted good. The best part was it all had to be eaten immediately because we didn't have a freezer.

We peeled "chittim" bark, on and off for at least three years through the summers of my fourth, fifth, and sixth grades. It wasn't like it was steady work, but when Dad needed money and there was nothing else to do, we peeled.

The last serious peel was indeed quite memorable. Dad learned of some bark located on BLM (Bureau of Land Management) land southwest of Dillard, fifteen miles out in the middle of nowhere. Actually, if one is familiar with that country, the location could easily be located today. The South Umpqua River flows north from Myrtle Creek through the Dillard and Winston areas. Dillard was plotted about halfway between Myrtle Creek and Roseburg. Dad had previously scouted the area. The first thing we kids were aware of was that we were packing the Dodge with cooking gear, bedding, food, axes, peeling tools, some extra clothes, and off we went. Dad stopped in Dillard for cold beer.

But this was fun. We were going camping; no driving back and forth. For some reason, I never considered the summer we spent in the woods on the Blackard property during Dad's gypo logging days as "camping." Then, we just moved our living quarters. For some reason, this camp had a different "feel" to it—a real, honest-to-goodness camping experience.

This was before the days of all the readily available, and affordable, modern camping paraphernalia. What a sight that old green Dodge slug must have made, going down the road with a mattress or two rolled up and tied to a fender, the trunk stuffed with what, to most people, would be classified as garbage, and five kids, squirming and fidgeting in the back seat, wondering where we were going and when we were going to get there, but loving the trip anyway. Who cared about the trip? We were going camping, and Dad knew how to camp.

We crossed the green steel bridge that spans the South Umpqua at Dillard and turned south on a gravel road that ran parallel to Highway 99 on the west side of the river. After a couple of miles, and directly across the river from the Ford sawmill complex, we made a right turn onto Rice Creek Road and drove for several miles until Dad pulled the green slug onto an old dirt road that began to climb up and away from the creek bottom. I'm certain, now that I look back, that this road and creek were probably named after the early Rice family whose property we lived on. For some time the road climbed until we came out on top of a fairly open and somewhat flat piece of land that sloped off to the Southwest. By now, we were about as far from civilization as I had ever been.

Like I said, Dad had previously been up in the area scouting out the lay of things. When the road broke out on top, we came to a barely noticeable fork in the road. Dad took the road on the less traveled side of the fork, and within a short distance, the road dead-ended. He said he wanted to show us an old homestead. We stepped out of the car and walked among the remains of old rusted springs, downed field fencing, and rotting lumber, kicking old cans, and bottles in our path. The house had been abandoned for years and in time, the foundation rotted and the house caved in on itself.

"Watch out for rattlesnakes," Dad warned, as we made our way among the debris. This was sufficient warning for all of us to beat a hasty retreat to the old Dodge. Yes, indeed, Douglas County was, and still is, prime Timber Rattlesnake country, as we would soon find out.

There really wasn't much to see at this abandoned homestead, and so with all of us back in the green slug, Dad drove away from the skeletal remains. He turned onto the opposite fork in the road and continued to drive further from civilization on what now was no more than a bulldozed road that traversed down the hillside, eventually dropping into a creek bottom. Some logging had been done in the area years earlier. The road, though void of gravel and rock, at least in the dry season, provided a reasonable surface for the green slug.

Dad had permission from Bill Blackard, who leased the BLM acreage (the same rancher whose timber he had cut on the north side of Timber Butte some four years earlier), to peel any and all cascara we could find in the area. What a beautiful area it was. The camping site was open and flat and immediately adjacent to Tompson Creek. It wasn't what some would call a stream. No, it was a creek. There's a big difference between a stream and a creek, at least in my mind there's a difference. A stream has sufficient flow of water that you can't jump across it, while a creek you can, at least in selected places. Most importantly, a creek, like a stream, has fish in it. This creek not only had some good-sized trout in it, but it had crawdads too! Shoot, I knew Dad was going to expect me to peel some bark first, which we did, but I wanted to fish that creek. *What a camping site*, I thought!

The old logging road that guided us into our camp continued across the creek and then crossed a small clearing. I asked Dad where it went, and he told me that it climbed the south wall of the canyon until finally breaking out on top and dropping down the other side into the Cow Creek water shed. The road dropped down alongside Doe Creek, then paralleled the creek until it met the main stem of Cow Creek at a point about ten miles west of Dillard.

At various times, Dad would enchant us kids with his stories about Cow Creek Canyon and prospecting and panning for gold, when the only way in and out of the canyon was by rail.

He related one story that I can only assume was true. It seems he was way back in the drainage somewhere between Dillard and Glendale and was traversing up, over, and down a mountain to reach a creek on the other side. He had reached the top and was descending the other side. While still a thousand feet or so above the creek, which he could hear below, he took a breather. In looking around, he noticed gravel under his feet, and being curious, dug a ways down and put a couple shovels of gravel into a gunny sack. He then continued on down the mountainside to the creek to satisfy his curiosity.

He said the gravel was rich with gold. At one time, the gravel from which he extracted the gold had been part of an old riverbed. It must have been ancient.

Now this, I said to myself, *is a real camp*. Bedding, and what cotton "tick" mattresses we brought along were simply rolled out on the ground with blankets for covers. We didn't have tents, sleeping bags, coolers, or any of the modern camping gear that makes camping so comfortable today. All camp paraphernalia was existing household simply put to camping use. What the hey, it worked.

Dad built a fire pit, which he lined on three sides with rocks from the creek, building a U-shaped wall about two-foot square and a foot high, then placed a sturdy piece of tin on top for a cooking surface. Firewood, from dried limbs, and whatever we could find just lying around, was cut into smaller lengths and fed under the tin through the open end. That was our "stove."

Our cooler was a covered galvanized tub, in which we placed rocks until it rested on the creek bottom in sufficient depth of water to receive some convection cooling effect from the water around it. Not too efficient, but better than leaving the mayonnaise, meats, and other vegetables out to spoil. It must have worked, as none of us ever contracted food poisoning. The other foodstuffs we just kept in the car, to keep it away from the critters. We used water right from the creek, boiling it and using it for drinking water. For washing and other uses, we used the water directly from the creek, heating as we needed it.

That first night was an experience. It was around midsummer. Now typically during that time of year in that part of Oregon, it *does not* rain. If there were clouds, they were clouds that "promised" rain, but would only cast a few lightning bolts, followed with the rumble of thunder. That's what we thought this storm was going to be. Sometime in the night, it started to rain. Here we were out in the open, no tent, no cover of any kind, except for some low-limbed cedar trees about a hundred feet from camp that grew around the base of a large broken outcropping of rock. Dad was quick to move us all under the trees with the bedding, and we spent the rest of the night in complete dryness, as those thick-boughed cedars shed water as long as it wasn't a prolonged down pour…which this wasn't. It quit raining in a few hours, and we woke to a bright sunny morning. After a few hours of sun, the ground was dry, and we reclaimed the flat spot with our bedding, spending the rest of our camp sleeping under the stars.

We worked in the early morning to avoid the heat of the day and relaxed in camp during the hot afternoon. Mom and Dad would sit in the shade and drink beer, while we kids played in the water. I'd go fishing toward sunset and usually catch sufficient number for all to have a fish or two for breakfast the next morning.

The peeling went pretty well, as there was a good growth of cascara in the area, and it was relatively easy to access and peel. We quickly ran out of gunny sacks in which to place the bark, so Dad was making trips home with the bark to place it on the drying racks, then driving back to camp late in the evening with whatever replenishments of supplies we needed, and beer.

After ten days or so, we had to break camp and head back home to finish drying what we had peeled, break it up, and take it to market. Within a week, we were back in camp. After setting up our second camp, Dad made a return trip home to bring a load of dryer racks out to camp. Now we had a fully operational cascara peeling, drying, and bagging station right alongside Rattlesnake Rock, as we would soon discover was the name of the place we made camp!

This second camp lasted around two weeks, peeling during the mornings, packing the bark back to camp, spreading it out on the prune dryer staves, then relaxing during the heat of the day.

As I said, the creek carried a sufficient flow of water to maintain a supply of native cutthroat trout and lots of crawdads. I cut myself a straight slender stick to which I attached a large fork (Mom never missed it) that I had fashioned into a sort of pronged "gig." I'd gig a mess of crawdads every now and then, cut off the pinchers, pinch off the tails, place them in a pot filled with salt water (a two-pound coffee can with a wire bail on it), and boil them until done. They tasted pretty darn good. I guess with all the fish and crawdads, I was the major supplier of fresh meat for the camp. I'd supplement the water-fare with a fresh-killed bush or jackrabbit from a late evening hunt. Life was good.

The creek had a major drawback; it didn't have a hole deep enough in which to swim. You could cool off by sitting in the water, and it might come up to your waist if you pulled some rocks out of the way to make a depression in which to sit your butt. It was on one of those occasions that I got the idea to build a dam. My building skills were honed several years earlier building rabbit hutches for Dad's failed rabbit fryer venture. I had also built a tree house or two, and as I thought about a dam, a plan began to take shape in my mind.

The creek bed was about three feet lower than the flat clearing on which we were camped, and the elevation was the same on the opposite bank. The bank on both sides was almost vertical, with the creek bed flat, tiled with smoothed stones, and about fifteen feet across. Two large cedars grew almost at bank edge, one on each side of the creek. My plan was to place a large pole across the creek with each end butting up against the upstream side of the two cedars. I would then lean boards (if I could find them) against the pole, with the lower end slanted upstream and poked into the creek bed. My thinking was that the water would back up against the boards, with the pressure of the rising water holding the slanted boards against the pole and forcing the lower end into the creek bed. The weight of the water should hold the pole against the trees. If my thinking was correct, and I could keep it from leaking too much, it just might work.

I first had to find a pole long enough and of sufficient diameter and strength to hold against the weight of the water. I have no idea where I located it and how I was able to drag it to the creek and lay it across the creek from bank-to-bank, about three feet above the water. I must have had my sister's help. Soon it was in place, up against the upstream side of those two cedars on opposite sides, lying across the creek just as I had pictured it in my mind. I also have no idea where I found sufficient quantity of one-inch boards, but I obviously did. It took a couple of afternoons. It might have been too hot to peel chittim, but it was not too hot to build a dam. All the time this was going on, Dad and

Mom were just watching. As I began to layer the last few boards to close the gap on the creek, the water was already rising.

In my spare time over the next couple of days, I worked to fix the leaks. On about the third day, we had ourselves a nice little swimming hole that was being furnished by an abundant supply of clear cold water. It probably averaged three feet in depth, fifteen feet across and about fifty feet long.

Not a bad engineering feat, I thought, as I surveyed my handiwork.

I needed a boat now, and so when we weren't using the galvanized washing tub as a cooler, I would scoot down in it with my knees around my chin, have my sisters push me out, and paddle with my hands around the "pool." A flat-bottom washtub leaves much to be desired when it comes to balance. A canoe is child's play by comparison. Maintaining any sort of upright position required much attention to how one moved. Any sudden shift caused it to abruptly flip. I learned quite a bit about the different types of rocks in the creek bed, what with my face planted on the bottom time and again. I finally wrangled the washtub into obedience. Persistence and determination paid off, and I eventually learned how to "paddle my own tub."

All the time I was building my dam, I cannot remember Dad helping one bit. I wonder what he was thinking. I also wonder what he was thinking the night of the "marshmallow incident."

Dad had worked himself into a pretty good mood with a few bottles of Olympia beer that afternoon. He and Mom had driven over the ridge into town for a beer and food run (I think that was the priority), bringing back some hot dogs, Pepsi, and marshmallows for us kids. After dark, we were sitting around the campfire. Dad removed the piece of thick iron that formed the cooking surface over the fire pit, and we were roasting those large, fluffy, powder sugarcoated Campfire-brand marshmallows. They were packaged in thin cardboard boxes two layers deep. They were the best-tasting marshmallows I have ever eaten. Why'd they stop marketing marshmallows like that? Probably when they decided it was cheaper to mush them all up in a plastic bag.

You know how it is roasting marshmallows. You cut yourself a stick about three or four feet long, scrap the bark off the thin end, whittle a point on it; stuff one, two, three, or more marshmallows on; and then see how fast you can burn them. At least it seemed that's what my sisters did. Even at my young age, I could never figure out how anybody could hose up a task as simple as roasting a marshmallow. Dad showed us a new way.

Dad probably decided my sisters were having way too much fun trying to set the grass on fire. Their roasting attempts usually resulted in a pleasing, albeit primitive, display of fireworks as they wildly waved burning brands of marshmallows in the air in attempts to put the flames out. Dad suddenly interrupted the fireworks display, asking us to find and bring him the wire-mesh popcorn popper (you know, the type you can use over a bed of coals). He dropped about a dozen marshmallows into the basket, sliding the lid over the top. He had this smug, ain't I smart, look on his face.

Ha, now I'm going to show you how to really roast marshmallows, he must've thought.

He placed the "popper" over the coals and proceeded to shake it. It didn't take long for even us kids to decide that this wasn't the way to roast marshmallows. As soon as the wire-mesh warmed, the marshmallows began to stick to the wire, and the more they stuck, the harder Dad tried to shake them loose.

It became quite comical. I think this was the only time I laughed at Dad so hard I cried, for in his early state of drinking, his mind was not as sharp as usual. It took a few seconds for him to realize what was going on, though his efforts prior to that dawning were quite funny. The harder he shook the popper, the madder he got, not at his audience that was having the greatest time laughing at his expense, but at those stupid marshmallows that wouldn't cooperate in that wire mesh popcorn popper. Finally, the whole thing caught fire, and he was waving this flaming torch up and around, and over his head flinging flaming brands of marshmallows around the camp, shouting, "stupid son of a blinkety-blank," and other terms familiar to our ears; until in disgust he drowned the flaming thing in the swimming hole. We never mentioned the "Marshmallow Incident" in his presence after that, and for some reason Dad never bought another one of those wire mesh popcorn poppers. *Wonder why*?

So we worked and played away the days—peeling, drying, and sacking, until one evening about two weeks into camp and well into August. The days were hot and dry, and on this particular day, we had quit work earlier than usual. I had gone fishing upstream from camp about a quarter mile or so. There was a nice hole from which I had previously caught trout, and I wanted to try again.

Sheep had made their little trails all over the hillsides and down into the creek bottom, where they'd stop for a drink. The trails would usually continue across the creek. A few hundred yards from camp, one of these trails pitched down the road berm that had been created by a bulldozer as it had pushed dirt from the hillside into the creek bottom. Sheep had made a small trail that traversed from the right side of the road, down the berm, and into the creek bottom. This trail pointed in the direction of the fishing hole I had in mind.

In the creek bottom I went off the trail, moving upstream to a point where I could toss a hook with a worm on it into the large, deep pool. I was well shielded by some low bushes, so I knew I was not casting any shadow of movement into the pool. I quickly pulled out a couple of nice fish with two consecutive casts, when on my third cast a real lunker took my hook and bait. My heart was pounding as I quickly tied on another hook, rebaited and made another cast. No luck. On my earlier cast, I had the fish on my line and had pulled it out of the water, but his coming loose and falling back in had sufficiently ended fishing that hole for the day. Time to move to another hole.

The road was probably twelve to fifteen feet above the streambed and well shielded from view. I charged up the trail traversing the side of the berm under a full head of steam, eager to get to the next hole. I had sufficient momentum and was moving pretty good when I broke over the top onto the road—and just about stepped on a rattler! Talk about adrenaline. I remember being in mid-air over the snake, and somehow I broke all the laws of physics by being able to change direction while remaining suspended two feet above the snake. I ended up six feet to the right of my original direction of travel. I can't remember how I did all that in mid-air. I'm sure I alarmed the snake, too, because before I could get my wits about me and find something larger than my fishing pole to beat the thing (I wasn't about to use my fishing pole), it had slithered off the road, over the bank, and down into the streambed. I followed the snake but eventually lost it in some of the leaves and bushes in the creek bottom.

This incident ended any enthusiasm I had for fishing. I hoofed it back to camp. While cleaning the few fish I had caught, I recounted the story to Dad and Mom. About the time I finished the story, Mom takes off with the .22. A few minutes later, we hear a "bang," and she comes back to camp with a set of rattlers. She had found the snake (at least, she found *a* snake) killed it, and was back in camp.

Mom hated rattlers.

I was still bored. After it cooled down that afternoon, I decided to go rabbit hunting. This time, I headed the opposite direction from camp, which was back up the rutted dirt-logging road that brought us into the area. It was getting close to the sun sinking behind the hills. It wasn't quite sunset, but was that kind of early dusk that's formed by a mountain shadow in early evening when at the bottom of a canyon. It's also the time the rabbits come out to pose for target practice.

I hadn't gone too far when I rounded a turn in the road and noticed some movement about ten feet in front of me. *Small snakes,* I thought to myself, as I stood over them. They were no more than seven or eight inches long, and probably just hatched. It seemed to take a moment for the fact to sink in that I was looking at freshly hatched baby rattlers! I stomped on them, left their dead carcasses in the road, and continued on, killing a nice fat bush rabbit, leaving it alongside the road. I would pick it up on my way back to camp. I had gone only about a hundred yards from where I had killed the baby rattlers when I noticed movement under the greasewood up on the right side of the road. *Hmm, king snake*, I thought as I saw black and white rings that identify the kind. I was taught not to shoot a king snake because they often feed on other snakes, which included rattlers. I wanted to be sure. Then I saw the rattles!

Now the interesting thing about the Timber Rattler and the Western Diamondback is that the last quarter or so of their body length is comprised of alternating black and white rings. If that's all you see, you think you're looking at a king snake. However, when the tail came into view from behind some brush, that "king snake" had the longest set of rattles I had ever seen! I followed the movement of the snake until I could locate its body. It was huge! It was probably no more than ten feet away and was crawling slowly under the brush parallel to the road. I finally located its head and summarily proceeded to execute it by emptying a magazine of thirteen .22 loads into the body. Finding a large, forked stick, I scooted, pushed, and pried its body onto the road. It literally stretched from one rut of the road to the other. It had to be somewhere between five and six feet long, with its body the width of a man's forearm!

I didn't know it at the time, but I may have been looking at a world record Timber Rattler. I don't think it was a Western Diamondback, but it could have been. Anyway, I cut off its rattles (fourteen and a button), tossed the carcass over the road bank, and headed back to camp, picking up my rabbit on the way back. Of course, when I got back to camp, I told Dad and everybody else about the snakes as I waved my new trophy set of rattles in front of them. After sufficiently impressing everybody about my snake-killing skills, I went to work to dress the rabbit. By the time I had finished the job, Dad made the decision to break camp and make like a sheepherder, getting the flock out of there. For some reason, the snakes were moving, and he figured we must have been camping pretty close to their dens. Little did we know then. We broke camp quickly and headed back home, coming back the next day to pick up the bark and whatever else we failed to locate in the dark the night before.

Dad described to Bill Blackard some time later about all the snakes suddenly coming out and where we had been camped. Bill told him that the pile of rocks where we laid our bedding that first camp night when it rained was known for its rattlesnake dens and was appropriately named Rattlesnake Rock! We had made two different camps only about a hundred feet from the base of that broken pile of rock, and it wasn't until that final day of the second camp that we saw any rattlers at all. I think about the fact that on the first or second night of our first camp, when I was crawling under my blankets, a small garden snake crawled out from under my blankets. Maybe Dad was thinking about that when he made the hasty but good decision to break camp that evening. Dad may have had a drinking problem, but he wasn't a fool.

The following summer, we peeled cascara again, but not like the operation we had the previous year. The summer between my seventh and eighth grades was the last of our chittim peeling. We had pretty well depleted the cascara from the slopes of Timber Butte, and Dad began to range farther from home in order to find peelable trees. The last cascara we peeled was in the Ten Mile area along the banks of Ten Mile Creek. Dad had located some trees and had obtained permission from the landowner to peel. This was the summer I learned to drive. I was thirteen.

Dad still had the green Dodge slug. He surprised me one morning after we pulled off Highway 58. We had barely started across the flat field toward the creek about a quarter mile away when Dad stopped the car. I was sitting between Dad and Mom in the front seat. He put the car in neutral, and he told me to change places with him.

"Huh?" I said.

"You heard me," he said, with a kind of twinkle in his eye. "Get behind the wheel."

It still didn't register until he began to "show me the gears."

This was before automatic transmissions were in vogue. Most cars had a three-speed manual transmission with the gearshift lever mounted on the steering column between the steering wheel and the dash. Later, after I had my first car, I learned that such shifting mechanisms were called "three on the tree."

Well, predictably, it took a few tries. First I had to get the "H" pattern planted in my mind, push the clutch down, put the transmission in "low," give it some gas, then let out on the clutch. This was known as "killing the engine," and was a necessary ritual of the learning to drive experience. It was all about learning how to apply the throttle while letting out the clutch.

"*Okay*," Dad said. "Start the engine and try again."

He was patient, and on my second or third try, I got the ol' Slug going.

"Good," he said. "Now, put'r in second, boy. Use the clutch! Use the clutch!" He shouted at me to be heard over the grinding gears.

"Oh, yeah, sure."

After a few clunks and jerks, I had her in second gear, and we were cruising across that field.

"Turn. Turn!" Dad shouted in my ear, as he grabbed the steering wheel to turn the Dodge slug away from the maple tree I had sighted in on from the far side of the field. He jammed his left foot on the brake, quickly bringing the car and its screaming load of kids to a halt.

Dad had a project on his hands, and he wasn't about to quit. With everybody still in the car, he backed it up, got it lined up on the far side of the field, and we started at it again. In a couple of passes across the field, I got the sequence of starting the engine, shifting, turning, and braking sufficient to satisfy Dad.

That was the extent of my early driving lessons, and the last of our chittim peeling.

We Called It Fun

Reading was an activity I thoroughly enjoyed, especially adventure stories in which I could vicariously project myself into better worlds and times. After all, my world, while reality, really wasn't where I wanted to be. Reading transported me into more bearable circumstances.

We all had library cards, even Dad; and we'd spend an evening every now and then at the city library checking out books that suited our interests. Dad would only do the library visits between binges. Those times were especially enjoyable, as we would then appear a normal family. It was an inexpensive form of entertainment, but in looking back, I learned much about history and how others lived, survived, and accomplished. I read many of the classics. If we had extra time at the library, I would often get lost in a volume of Encyclopedia Britannica or Americana. The Myrtle Creek Library filled an important role in my education as a pre-teen.

Another thing I loved was music. Nothing formal. No music theory, no singing lessons, no guitar or harmonica lessons. Just learning by listening and doing. I sang, and then learned to play the harmonica, then the guitar. It's what we call "playing by ear." I had an ear for music, and I sang and played whenever I had the opportunity. I probably started singing before I could walk, listening to Mom and Dad. Later, as I watched and listened to Dad or Mom playing the harmonica, I thought I would give the instrument a try. I took right to it, even learning to "tongue" the reeds, which is how the individual notes are played.

So there I was in the second grade, playing for some class function. I brought the house down, too. The cameras were flashing, and the talent scouts were fighting amongst themselves in attempts to sign me to a long-term, high-paying contract. Reluctantly, I had to say, "No. I need to go home and cut wood."

Dream on, country star.

Some time after turning nine, Dad taught me a few chords on the guitar he bought from Great Aunt Lilly. Before long, we had a little family band going. Of course, the instrumentation was a little limited, but we had the voices, and all could sing. I loved those times outside under the stars on a warm southern Oregon evening, playing and singing. Sometimes I'd play the guitar and Dad the harmonica, or we'd switch instruments; or Mom would play the harmonica, with pretty much everybody but the harmonica player singing whether they knew the words or not. Of course, I did not realize it at the time, but the music was feeding my soul. It left me comfortable with myself and provided an outlet for self-expression.

While I never learned to read music, I learned chords, rhythm, timing, inflection, fills, and, in time, learned to play guitar instrumentals.

I wasn't a great singer, but I could carry a tune, and I felt the message in the song. I developed my own style, and in my own way I appreciated music. I appreciated it for how it made me feel and how it made others feel who listened. While I didn't love it sufficiently enough to learn the theory, I loved it for what it provided me: both a sense of well-being and accomplishment. Considering the situations and circumstances of my life, I probably developed my musical abilities as far as I could.

When asked to play and sing, I did. It didn't make any difference if they were personal friends, immediate family, cousins, uncles, aunts, whomever. I'd sing the songs I learned from Dad, the songs learned in school, the songs I learned listening to Mr. Stone's '78s, and the songs I learned listening to the *Grand Ole Opry* when we had a working battery in the radio. Back then, most of the early years in school required a certain amount of class time in music. Music appreciation was what they called it. We'd learn and sing songs, such as, "Oh, Suzanna," "Home on the Range," "My Old Kentucky Home," and so on. The songs Dad taught me were the songs he learned as a young man growing up in the early days of country music, "Cowboy Jack," "The Wreck of the Old 97," "The Wreck of Old Number 9," "Waiting for a Train," "The Letter Edged in Black," "Wreck of the Titanic," and others. Of course, there was the usual list of gospel songs.

I loved the country music that was popular then. Occasionally, we could pick up the *Grand Ole Opry* on the battery-powered radio we had in our early years on the hill. We didn't have a record player, but Mr. Stone did. Often when visiting with him, we'd sit and listen together to '78s of Bob Wills, Eddy Arnold, Cowboy Copas, George Morgan, Little Jimmy Dickens, and Hank Williams. Too often, on my way home from school or on weekends, I'd lose track of time listening to those '78s of his. *Gosh*, I'd say to myself, *if only I could sing like that*. I'd daydream of singing as good as those of whom I listened. To listen is to learn, and so I learned "San Antonio Rose," "Your Cheating Heart," "Almost," "Take an Old Cold 'Tater and Wait," "Get Your Cold Feet on the Other Side," and "I'm Walking the Floor Over You," just to name a few. In learning, some of the singing and instrumental styles of those early country artists were impressed on me, and I unknowingly blended their styles, creating my own.

In those early years, I sang for the joy of singing, and for the joy it brought others. My early guitar playing consisted of the major and 7th chords, with a minor chord thrown in once and a while. I learned early to put in runs between chord changes, and I'd pick up a new "lick" now and then, eventually progressing into forms of the boogie-woogie and blues. Instrumentally, I learned to play the "Steal Guitar Rag," "Under the Double Eagle," "Wild Wood Flower," "Aura Lee," "Red River Valley," and others; and while I knew each mistake I made, most listening never seemed to notice or care.

I enjoyed the accolades adults would give when I'd play the guitar and sing those old songs, and maybe with a tear in their eye, they would pat me on the back and tell me how much they enjoyed my playing and singing. I don't think I let their approbation go to my head. There was a certain humility I had that was fed by an inferiority caused by the situations and circumstances in which I lived. Even so, the compliments I received provided much needed nourishment for my soul. The music sustained me in those times when it would have been easy to slip into an attitude of self-pity and hate due to the cards life dealt me. There's something about respect shown by adults to a kid. It does something for them.

We didn't have money for toys, other than those we received as Christmas gifts, and because they were not expensive, they would soon break or wear out. Thanksgiving and Christmas were times we kids looked forward to, not only for what the holidays represented, but because they were times for visits to Grandma and Grandpa Backlund and the opportunity to see all the cousins. The two main holidays were the times the Assembly of God Church, Myrtle Creek Fire Department, or Chamber of Commerce remembered us, sending somebody to the home a day or two before the holiday with food boxes. Memories of those holidays are replete with stomachs stuffed with foods we otherwise could not afford. The Christmas boxes usually contained a small gift for each member of the family.

Apart from the occasional gifts we might receive at Christmas, our toys were limited to what we made ourselves, or what Dad made for us. Decorations for the tree were all handmade. We'd make white strings from popcorn, red strings from madrone berries, and green and red strings from pasted loops of colored construction paper.

Dad wasn't unaware of his kids' need for entertainment. We were not without our swings made from ropes tied to a limb on one of the large oaks that grew in abundance around the house.

Sometimes, the swing would be a single strand of hemp rope with a tire attached to it; at other times, the typical two strands with a board notched at each end for a seat. And because the limbs from which the rope was hung were at least fifteen to twenty feet off the ground, we could get some altitude before our common sense would take over. Maybe alongside the main "seat" swing, there'd be a single rope with a handle tied in the end about head height. You'd reach up, grab the handle, and then push off with your feet. The trick was to be able to turn 180 degrees after your feet left the ground, so you could catch the ground with your feet on the back swing, and then push off again for more height.

On one occasion, I was getting some air using the handle swing when the rope broke. I ended up in a pile with my legs in a strange angle behind me; I seemed to be all twisted up and unable to breathe. I thought, *I've broken my back! I've broken my back!* I started screaming and crying uncontrollably, crying and shouting at the same time, "My back's broken! My back's broken!" My sisters were scared to death and went running off to the house for help. Everybody came pouring out of the house to see what in the blinkety-blank all the racket's about, and by the time they came running up the trail to the swing, I am up and walking under my own power. I met them coming up the path to the swing. I was embarrassed, of course, but hey, what the heck, that was the first time I'd ever had my back broken. I just healed quickly.

Dad built teeter-totters and merry-go-rounds. Even though these were simple contraptions, they did the job when it came to fun. No need to explain how a teeter-totter is made, but some explanation is required to describe how Dad made two different types of merry-go-rounds.

For the first, simple type, he began by digging a hole and "planting" a twelve-inch diameter "post." Using a handsaw, he'd cut the top square to the post about two feet off the ground. Then either he or us kids would go down to the nearest driftwood pile to locate the biggest board we could find; that is, if he didn't already have the board he needed, which he usually didn't. We'd be looking for something like a two-by-ten at least twelve feet or longer, the longer the better. Dad would then drill a hole in the center and thread a large bolt through the hole down into an appropriately sized hole in the top of the post. Then he'd make a couple of seats with handles at each end of the board, and after greasing the surface between the top of the post and the under side of the board, *whoop-de-do*, a two-seat merry-go-round to play on. Put an equally weighted kid on each end, tell them to hold on to the handle, and with a third one pushing from the center, the board would soon be spinning.

We all had a little mean streak, and there was nothing more enjoyable than to get the board spinning so fast that the centrifugal force would slide a rider or two off the end of the board. Of course, the down side of those attempts would be that the person doing the pushing would sometimes lose their footing, and the board would run them over. You'd have to quickly duck to keep from getting your back scraped or the back of your head conked.

The second type of merry-go-round was an attempt of Dad's to model the style used in the school playground. For this one, he planted a fourteen-foot long pole sufficiently deep, and then with about ten feet or so showing, he leveled the post on top and placed a cross made from two four-foot lengths of two-by-six bolted at a ninety degree angle on the top of the standing pole. Like with the simpler merry-go-round, he fastened it to the top of the post with a bolt through the center of the "X" down into the top of the post. He drilled a hole out at the tips of each end, from which he fastened ropes with handles we could reach standing on the ground. Again, the idea to get two or four kids of equal weight to balance the sides, and then by hanging onto the rope handles and running in a circle, you could get the centrifugal force working, and you'd start swinging out with your feet leaving the ground every 180 degrees or so.

This latter style of merry-go-round was sufficiently well-built that even one person could get it going pretty good, and I particularly liked it until the time I was in one of my elevated flying positions and the rope broke. I landed face down with my sternum impacting the corner of an old wooden box that someone had left just outside the circle that our feet made contacting the ground. Unfortunately for me, it wasn't far enough removed to prevent an injury like I suffered when I hit the corner of that box. It took me weeks to recover from the bruised chest. It was black and blue for days and was so painful I had a difficult time breathing. I may have broken a rib or two, or even cracked my sternum; but because I was still breathing, going to a doctor for diagnosis and treatment was not a consideration. Suffer through, and be the tougher for it. I'm not certain I even complained to Mom or Dad. Wouldn't do any good anyway; we couldn't afford a doctor.

We made toys from such simple things. For example, many of the larger white oaks had large, low, and limber branches that reached out from the trunk for some twenty feet or so parallel to the ground. We would stand under the outer reach of these "toys," jump to grab hold, then pull the limb down. Then while one or two of us kids would hold it down, a third one would crawl up and anchor their butt in an outer fork. Then we'd release our hold on the limb, which would swing the rider up and down; or we'd pull the limb to one side as far as we could, and then release it. In this case, the rider would go swinging parallel to the ground. Wahoo! Ride'm cowboy! Then it would be the next rider's turn.

Tree houses were something that I learned to build by trial and error. I was probably in the fifth or sixth grade when I took an interest in this form of house building. I located a likely tree, just at the lower edge of "yellow jacket" clearing. It had a pyramid fork of three branches about fifteen feet off the ground that made an ideal location from which to anchor the sub frame of the "house" I was planning in my mind. So after a thorough study of the construction details and how to put it all together (about five minutes) I headed off to the local builder's supply (the drift wood piles of the South Umpqua) to locate my construction materials.

It took several weeks of free time to scavenge sufficient boards and nails to even begin the job. I'd pull the nails from the boards, straighten them, then carefully place my hard-won hardware in a one-pound coffee can for safekeeping, with the lumber stashed close to the trunk of the tree. I then cut to length and nailed the necessary two-by-sixes (using whatever spikes I had) to each fork of the tree, creating a somewhat level set of braces for my sub frame; then added a square sub frame made from two-by-fours, to which I nailed one-by-fours, and one-by-sixes for flooring. I created an opening in the floor to enter the house from below using "steps" made from short pieces of two-by-fours nailed to the trunk directly under the opening, I then proceeded to build the sides (with openings for windows) and a roof. Size-wise, it was probably no more than six feet square and four feet high, but to me it was my castle. Such an accomplishment deserved a celebration. I would have a "smoke."

My buddy Gordon Simmons and I had learned to make pipes from old dried corncobs, and so, after a reasonable amount of care (about ten minutes) I had one constructed of the proper length, hollowed out, with a small hole at the bottom for a pipe stem. The pipe stem consisted of another piece provided by the local flora and fauna, a hollow vine of correct size and length. There it was, a pipe fit to inaugurate the "completion and open for use" of Dan's first, full-fledged tree house, fort, refuge, and all around personal space.

Now all I needed was tobacco.

For the life of me, I'll never know why I just didn't use some of Dad's. He smoked a pipe on occasion and had *Prince Albert* or *Half-n-Half* lying around somewhere in the house. I could have easily borrowed a couple of tablespoons that he would never miss. But no, I got it in my craw to make my own tobacco, like the Indians, from crushed, dried oak leaves. How in the world did I get the idea that Indians used dried oak leaves? Bad idea. Crushed, dried oak leaves burn very quickly. *And hot!*

Hey, I thought. *The first puff wasn't all that bad. A little rustic, has a rather bitter after taste, though. Hmm, let's draw a little longer, and this time let's inhale.* Wrong! That second puff was probably the puff that cured me from smoking. I took a deep drag, and along with the effects of the hot acrid smoke, the dry cob caught fire, startling the dickens out of me. I dropped the flaming mess into a nest of dry leaves under the tree. I had to drop through the opening in the floor, down my two-by-four steps, and stomp out the beginnings of a small forest fire; so much for grand openings.

But overall, the tree house was indeed a grand and permanent sort of structure.

Ten years or so later, on leave from the Air Force, I visited the old home site. Remnants of the old tree fort were still attached to that White Oak.

As I've alluded more than once, the shack was built on the most "level" spot on a sloping hillside, up slope from Dole Road. No matter where one stood on that hillside, it was either up or down. There were two driveways from Dole Road to the house. One was straight up from the road, and in dry weather was generally the "driveway" used, as it was the most direct route. In wet weather, the direct route was too slick, and we used the longer, more circuitous route. Although equally slick, it was not nearly so steep, and a two-wheel drive vehicle could usually make it to the house. There were times, though, when even this route was too wet and slick to make it all the way to the house. Then Dad left the car where it stopped, and we walked the rest of the way.

The "driveways" converged at the house, which provided a slopping parking area between the house and Dad's work shed. I mention all this because the "road" continued up past the house into the woods. While the old road had been long abandoned and overgrown, it was still sufficiently wide that a vehicle (in dry weather) could drive to the end, a point where it intersected with the pipe trench in which lay the city's six-inch water main. In the beginning, the road had probably been used to provide service access as close as possible to the cistern built into the bottom further up the canyon. What was nice about this "road" (more like a wide dirt trail through the woods) was that it had a steep pitch to it. It was just right for my favorite sport. Extreme coasting using homemade "go-carts."

Dad showed me how to make my first go-cart. Go-carts were four-wheeled contraptions made from whatever wheels, axles, bolts, boards, and nails we could scavenge. Again, we went to our local builder's supply for source materials, the ever-productive, ubiquitous driftwood piles of the South Umpqua. What I needed was lumber and nails. I also needed axles and wheels; their source of supply was the local dump, located at the point where our driveway intersected Dole Road. Wheels and axles from old wagons, baby buggies, two-wheeled scooters, you name it, all were fair game for use on our contraptions. Wheel size didn't matter, as long as they were round and had a hole in the middle for the axle.

The first cart build began the day Dad took me into the woods. I provide sufficient detail on how go-carts are constructed so that any ten- or twelve-year old can do it with the few tools mentioned. Dad has his pole ax with him, and after roaming around looking up into the branches of the madrone trees, he selected a tree, felling it with a few swings of the ax. He then cut a perfectly formed "Y" from the tree. The "Y" was formed with about a three-inch thick piece of trunk, forming the stem of the "Y" and two smaller branches, the arms. We trudged back through the woods to the workshop where Dad proceeded to use a handsaw to square up the ends of the "Y." He had two half-inch diameter rods (the axles) about two feet in length, and using a hand drill, he drilled a hole the size of a six-penny nail an eighth of an inch in from each end of the axle.

He assembled the wheels and axle in the following manner. First, he placed a large washer on the inboard side of the wheel, then came the wheel, then another large washer on the outside of the wheel, followed by a nail of appropriate size inserted into the hole at the end of the axle. He may have used a cotter pin instead of a nail, I can't remember exactly. I just know that a nail with the correct bend in it is an adequate substitute for a cotter pin. He then pushed the wheels outboard as far as possible, making contact with the washer/axle pin, measured the distance between the wheels and then cut a two-by-four to the measured length. Next, he centered the axle on the length of two-by-four and fastened it in place by alternating nails on opposite sides of the axle and bending them over the axle, using sufficient quantity of nails to ensure the axle was securely fastened to the board. This constituted the rear axle/wheel assembly that he then nailed to the underside end of each arm of the "Y."

The front axle was built the same way, but this time Dad offset the axle slightly on the two-by-four, which allowed space for him to drill a hole through the center of the two-by-four, and the end of the "Y" stem. He then bolted the front axle to the stem of the "Y." Now the "cart" could be steered.

The last thing to be built was a seat, which consisted of nailing a couple of one-by-sixes to provide a place on which to sit. By sitting on the "seat" and placing one's feet on the front axle assembly, you could push with either the right or left foot and thus have steering. Pushing forward with the left foot put you into a right hand turn; pushing forward with the right foot, put you into a left-hand turn.

With two or three of these so-called "go-carts," my sisters (cousins, friends, whomever) were greatly entertained racing one another down the old road that met the driveway at the shack. We would stage races, pitting equally matched karts and kids, racing one another down the trail from the uphill side of the house. Side-by-side, down the course, skidding into and out of the turns and often into one another.

We'd come rumbling and clattering out from under the canopy of trees, squealing, "You cheated!" "You cut me off!" "I'm gonna beat you next time." With dust and gravel flying, we'd throw ourselves into a sideways skid in the pea-gravel-coated parking area between the house and the workshop.

Generally, these carts would last only a few weeks, as most of the wheels were not made for the stress we put on them, especially baby buggy wheels. Buggy wheels looked good but tended to buckle under the centrifugal forces we applied in the corners. Once in a while we'd get lucky and locate wheels that had ball-bearing hubs. Boy, could carts built with such wheels go. For the fast carts, I designed a "hand brake." The hand brake consisted of a stick nailed to the side of the frame. If the speed got too fast, you simply grabbed the stick, pulled back on it, and the opposite end dug into the roadbed. It provided a brake of sorts. Most of the time, if your speed was too great, you simply steered with a rope and used your feet for braking. Ha! That's where the term "brake shoe" came from.

Like the merry-go-rounds, these carts were the cause of occasional pinches, bruises, slivers, and cuts. But even so, the carts were great fun and most friends and cousins who visited thought so, too.

There was a "brake" on another toy I recall. This toy was an old two-wheeled scooter we salvaged from the dump. What a find it was. It was complete! It was all there, the wheels, the handle; you know, the kind with eight-inch solid rubber wheels and a metal frame between the wheels. We kids couldn't understand why anyone would throw away such a fine treasure. It had a "U"-shaped kickstand that you'd kick under the rear wheel to allow it to remain "free-standing" when not used, and a handle bar about waist high that you used to steer the front wheel. And we could coast it down the driveway. We took turns. It was my turn when I discovered the reason it ended up in the dump. It had an intermittent "brake" on the front wheel!

It was tricky, lulling its rider into a false sense of safety, until suddenly the front wheel locked up. On my third or fourth run, I had a good head of steam down the driveway, and the next thing I remember, I was flying over the handle. I couldn't explain it. I must have hit a rock, or a hole, or something. I hit the ground with my nose and proceeded to bleed all over my shirt.

All those who witnessed this event thought it was quite funny. You know, comments like, "Gee, Danny. You looked so funny. You just sailed right out there over the handle bar."

Well I wasn't going to get any sympathy from this bunch of pikers, and so I gave the scooter to Ellen (the next youngest and closest to me in age), and I went to get a wet washcloth to stop the bleeding. I came back just in time to see Ellen walking up the driveway, dragging the scooter behind her, crying and bleeding all over her dress. The scooter had thrown her, too, in exactly the same way and in about the same spot. Come to find out, the front wheel had an evil tendency to go cock-eyed on its axle and lock up. That was the last time Ellen or I ever rode that thing. We never trusted it after that. We salvaged the wheels and used them on another go-cart.

So, for the most part, toys were what we made. Dad showed me how to make bows and arrows, whistles and "airplanes." For a bow, he showed me the value and strength in a good piece of Pacific Yew wood. Again, in a driftwood pile he had located an uprooted Yew tree. From a dry branch, he created what he said was a "bow." *Looks like a worthless piece of wood to me*, I thought. *Sure, it's nice and smooth, and the wood is pretty, but it doesn't look like a bow, because there's no "bow" to it.*

He had formed and shaped a four-foot length that had no curve, and I couldn't help but thinking that it didn't look much like a bow. It looked more like a nice walking stick.

He couldn't find a string that was sufficiently strong for the bow, until he decided that a thin piece of flexible braided wire would work well. He got the curve he needed, attached the wire, and then proceeded to make a couple of arrows from straight cedar. He whittled the arrows into long shafts, keeping a "larger" head on the front end of the arrow for balance purposes. He said this way, he didn't need any fletching on the end. He then proceeded to show how accurate his little bow and its simple arrows were. I don't know how he was able to draw that bow. I couldn't begin to do it, but he did. He demonstrated by punching holes in a cardboard box at about seventy-five feet distance, on which he painted a target. He then demonstrated the strength of a short, compact Yew bow by launching one of the arrows straight up, *out of sight!* Panic ensued. For some reason, on my part only! I couldn't see the arrow, and thus had no idea where it was going to land. And so I ran to a point where I thought the arrow wasn't going to land. It landed directly in front of me, bouncing off the hard dirt of the path I was on. "Oops," Dad said.

Over the years that we lived on the hillside, I used Dad's method to sculpt several bows and sets of arrows, some better than others, but none as good as Dad's.

Somewhere at sometime, I had obtained a commercially manufactured bow with a draw strength that did not exceed my abilities. While it was much better than any I could build, its drawback was that when I let the arrow fly, the string would smack me good on my right wrist. I couldn't afford a wrist guard, so I used a Cracker Jack box. I punched both ends out, pulled the box over my hand, and positioned it around my wrist. It worked fine.

Dad taught me how to make small wing-shaped toys that were tethered at the end of a string. You swung these flying contraptions in an ever-expanding circle over your head, playing string out with each rotation. As the "wing" turned in the air at the end of its tether, it made a whirling, fluttering sound that would change volume and pitch depending on the speed in which you could "twirl" it. We had no swivel on the end, and the string would knot up after a few circles, so you had to "re-wire" the thing with an unused piece of string.

Another toy was the thin carved airplane. It also "flew" as you circled it around your head with it tethered at the end of a string. One string was attached at the end of the wing, and the other string at the end of the tail fin. They were attached to a control stick in your hand, and as you turned in a circle, the plane "flew" (more by centrifugal force than actual flight). You could make it climb or dive by twisting your wrist to change the angle of the "control stick" in your hand. It worked. It really worked—until you got dizzy!

Then there were balsa wood, propeller-driven airplanes. If I had some loose change, I'd buy these at the Five and Dime Store on Main Street. Ah, what great fun, to wind its rubber band power plant to maximum number of knots, and with a launch from your extended arm, it would fly up and away, down the driveway; usually ending its flight in the top of a madrone tree past the clearing on the down side of the house. I became quite good at climbing into the thin tops of these scrub madrones to shake the plane loose. And then I'd do it all over again. I even made a launch ramp. Those planes had a set of wheels that rolled quite well; and with a smooth inclined surface on which to roll, those balsa wood contraptions would gain sufficient speed to launch themselves toward the nearest tree. I kept wondering what part of the wood gave the plane sufficient intelligence to know where a tree was located. Those planes would fly against the wind if it meant they could land in the top of one of those madrones.

As much fun as the balsa wood planes were, there was yet my favorite flying toy, the coffee can lid. When I think about this "toy," I think about what might have been. Oh yeah, I could've been rich.

In the fifties, they marketed coffee in one, two, and three-pound cans. These cans had a lid that was removed by inserting the prong of a small metal "key" into a metal tab under the outside lid of the can. By turning the "key," a metal strip was removed from around the lid, after which you could put your fingertips under the knurl of the lid and pull to remove your fingernail…I mean the lid. The lid had a "lip" around its outside. When the lid was placed back on the can, it provided a fairly tight seal. Once the coffee was used, can and lid were tossed into the trash. Many of these cans and lids ended up in the community "dump" that was conveniently located where our driveway met Dole Road. I'd rummage through the trash, and whenever I came across a coffee can lid, I'd add it to my collection. When I collected a few dozen of 'em, it was time for some fun.

I don't remember who showed me that these coffee can lids could sail quite a ways through the air when you tossed them, very much like one tosses a Frisbee. As a matter of fact, these coffee can lids made a whole lot better Frisbee than a pie tin. Maybe it was fairly common knowledge that these lids could fly, but then, I discovered how to "really" make them fly.

The underside of the lid had about a quarter-inch "lip" on it. It also had a raised bulge in the center. I learned later that this curvature was like an airplane wing; it's what gives a wing lift. These coffee can lids had the basic characteristics of a round wing. However, they had one drawback. The lip of the lid caused the lids to gradually begin tipping to the left or right (depending on which hand one used to throw them), and when they did, they basically plummeted straight down to the ground. I discovered that by using a hammer and bending the lip back into the center of the lid (toward the bulge) and flat against the underside of the lid, that they flew straighter and further, when thrown "bulge up."

Now, of course some of you may be asking why I had to collect so many of these things; after all, wouldn't just a couple of them be enough to play catch with? Hey! The only thing these metal-flying disks had in common with a Frisbee was the fact they could fly. I didn't mean to imply that I played catch with them (you could get cut by a piece of exposed metal). It was a lot more interesting and fun to throw them from the bluff overlooking the Highway 99 bridge. My objective was to get one to fly far enough to land in the South Umpqua River!

On the bluff, at the highest point where Dole Road crests, I'd walk out, and find a flat spot that gave me some footing. The railroad tracks and the river were pretty much below me, and I'd begin flinging those lids, one at a time into space, a couple hundred feet above the river. If it was windy, forget it. The air had to be pretty calm; and when it was, those modified coffee can lids would sail. Most would make it over the railroad tracks, and a good 50 percent would end up in the river. Occasionally, one might make it to the far side of the river. But then there was that one, that special one, that perfect one. All the dynamics of physics were working in its favor—the perfect lid, perfect air currents, perfect toss, perfect spin, and perfect angle of attack. It was a sight to see as it sailed, and sailed, and sailed. A puff of wind lifted it at just the right time. It was high, stabilized, still flying, and high over the tracks, now over the river, now across the river, across the gravel bar on the far side. It was still sailing—straight into oncoming traffic that was slowing down to make the left turn onto the bridge. *Blam!* It hit the hood of a car. I can only imagine what the occupants thought, *What the blinkety-blank was that?*

I could never duplicate that flight. No matter how many lids I tossed from that cliff afterwards, I never broke that distance and time record. Without a doubt, it was the longest coffee-can lid toss in history, obviously a world record, and nobody to witness.

Of course, the Frisbee wasn't invented yet, and so, maybe if a "light" had come on that day in some crease of my cerebral cortex, I might really have something to write about. Think about it. The signs when entering Myrtle Creek today might read, "Welcome to Myrtle Creek, Home of Dan Oliver, inventor of the Lid."

A grass whistle; who ever heard of such a thing? I did. Talk about a simple toy. The first time I heard the sick squawking call from a blade of leaf grass, how I wanted to be able to do the same thing. It was early in our stay in the shack that I woke one morning to this horrible sickly squawking of a chicken or some other animal in some sort of death struggle. But it was Dad playing music on a blade of grass.

You take a blade of grass, and place it tightly between the base of your thumbs. Then by placing the other end between the first joints of your two thumbs, you can bring tension on the grass. This forms a "reed" between your thumbs that you can blow over and create the most horrible-sounding screeching noises. It will wake the chickens at midnight when done right, and will be sure to incur the wrath of all moms, aunts, and grandmas while bringing chuckles from all dads, uncles, and granddads; and the respect of every child who wants to learn how to do the same thing.

Summer months at home were generally great fun. Of course, I am not considering the negative side that resulted from Dad's drinking, but from a purely pragmatic viewpoint, I have to consider my summers as being fun. We lived outdoors as much as possible. As soon as the weather turned warm, it was too hot for sleeping inside. We did the obvious thing; we moved outside. We kids would claim the underside of our favorite tree for shade purposes, and that became our space until weather would force us indoors. Of course, the best shade trees were the fir trees, which had this sadistic characteristic of shedding small droplets of pitch onto your blanket and pillow during the day, and your hair and exposed body parts at night. No matter, the summers were hot and dry, and thus no rain for most of the summer. The only downside was the mosquitoes and other night-flying bugs and insects. Even so, it was more comfortable outside than inside.

Many times, our evening meals would be prepared over a second wood range Dad had procured and located outside, or we'd simply build a "campfire." In either case, when too hot to cook inside, Dad and Mom would make a trip to town for some hot dogs, watermelon, potato chips, and Pepsi, and we'd have us a little camp-out in our back yard.

The problem with our "free-range" chickens is that they tended to make pests of themselves during the preparation and eating phase of our outdoor living experience; thinking any food left unattended, or even when we were eating, was "free," thus the term "free range." In an effort to discourage such free-range foraging, Dad presents me with this homemade slingshot; one he made from the "Y" of a tree branch and some leftover inner tube. I remember the time well. It was about mid-morning. It was going to be another hot day, and we'd be eating outside.

"Here, Dan," Dad said. "When the chickens come around before we eat tonight, just plunk a bit of pea-gravel at them with this thing as a form of discouragement." He told me afterward he didn't realize the mistake he was making. Shoot, as far as I was concerned, chicken season was now open, and I had instructions to fire at will.

She was the first and only chicken I killed with a slingshot. She approached the picnic table under the shade tree so innocently, scratching and clucking, trying not to be too obvious, not knowing that everything was lining up against her. Her time was up, and she was heading for the frying pan; wasn't even close to dinnertime. I had been practicing on tin cans at ten feet and never in my wildest dreams thought I'd hit a chicken at fifty feet. Wrong! It had to have been the same forces working that day that brought about the "perfect coffee can lid toss" across the South Umpqua River. No thinking was required. You just do it. I loaded a smooth, round piece of pea-gravel into the leather pouch, pulled back on the rubber, and let'r fly. *Cute little thing*, I thought as I watched the pebble hit her smack dead center on the side of her head. It broke her neck and with her head now on backwards, she began staggering in circles. I was more surprised than scared. I'd actually hit something with a slingshot at the impossible distance of fifty feet! Of course, the "something" happened to be one of Mom's laying hens. The sis's were witness to my willful and malicious act of chicken-slaughter and had Mom and Dad outside before the rock bounced of the chicken's head to hit the ground. Dad's reactions to such events could be so unpredictable. He chuckled, picked up the still kicking chicken, and put the poor thing out of her misery.

"Here's supper," he said, as he handed the chicken to Mom, also telling me, "No more chicken-shooting, son." He let me keep the slingshot.

I thought it was interesting how I felt at the time I committed this "fowl" deed. I had killed rabbits and squirrels many times prior to this and never felt any remorse. I did when I killed that chicken. Probably because it was not planned; it was accidental, and it was unnecessary.

In the fall, flocks of robins would descend into the madrones to eat the ripe berries. Dad at one time had killed a dozen or so that we cleaned and cooked, finding that each bird provided sufficient "white meat" for several bites. It was something that we only did that one time.

The robins were thick this particular fall, and I was scattering pea-gravel via the slingshot, all over the hillside in attempts to kill one. (This is why I told you I was so surprised when I killed the chicken at fifty feet.) I could get within ten feet and still not hit anything. Frustrated, I climbed into one of the madrones next to the house and waited. A robin landed not more than three feet from me. Couldn't miss, and I didn't. Again, I felt so bad about what I had done, that I decided I'd never kill another bird just for the fun of it.

I never again used the slingshot to kill. Cans and bottles were open season though.

In the dog days of summer, we'd be down along the river late into the evening, sometimes well into the dark, roasting wieners and marshmallows after a day of swimming. I guess this was a benefit in Dad not having a steady job. He was always available to take us to the river.

Except for the drinking and the usual drunken rages that Dad would go into in his deeper binges, these were days made for a kid. We'd arrive at our favorite space alongside the river late in the morning before the heat of the day would strike. We had many favorite spots. Cow Creek was one of them, but when selected swimming holes started getting too crowded, Dad located spots on the South Umpqua closer to home, generally with no other people around.

We kids would play in the water from getting in, to getting out, and we became as brown as the oak leaves in fall. I might burn some in the early days of late spring or early summer, but usually only once, because I hardly ever wore a shirt, except to sleep or when walking through stands of poison oak and blackberries.

At one spot we found, about two miles from town, Dad would park the car on the shoulder of Dole Road. We'd carry our food, drinks, watermelon, and blankets from the car, cross the railroad tracks, and hike into the maple and alder trees that grew between the tracks and the river. A blanket would be spread on the sand in the shade of the trees. We kids would unload our arms of grub and goodies onto a blanket and head for the water.

This particular spot was where Dad tried to teach me to swim. I was probably between fourth and fifth grades, and I desperately wanted to learn, but soon exhausted Dad's patience. He left me to learn on my own. I did.

Discouraged with my attempts to swim on top of the water, I had purchased a set of swim fins and a full-face mask using my blackberry picking money. I guess I thought it would be easier to swim under water. And it was. I discovered how easy it was. Another benefit of being able to see clearly underwater was that it overcame my latent fear of those deep, dark holes where you couldn't see the bottom; you know, where the man-eating pollywogs lived. And so with the fins and goggles, I could really scoot around under the surface. Soon I was diving to the bottom of the deep holes, keeping company with the suckers and crawdads.

Hmm, no man-eating pollywogs, I thought.

In no time at all, and on the first day I used the facemask and fins I was dog paddling, then swimming. I was so proud of what I could do I swam completely across the river before I told anybody I could swim. My daring feat came as a great surprise to all. Dad thought I had used a board or some piece of driftwood to get to the other side.

This was also the place of the great raft incident.

Some time before we started using this swimming hole, the railroad had replaced a good number of the telephone poles that paralleled the tracks. Basically, the wood planted in the ground had rotted, but the wood above ground was sound. The telephone crews had simply discarded these "worthless" poles at the place they were cut from the ground. The poles still had the cross ties and the metal straps and bolts used to secure the cross ties to the upper portions of the poles. Dad, being one to recognize value in somebody else's discards, decided he could make a raft from these poles, cross ties, and miscellaneous hardware. All he needed was the crosscut saw, a pole ax, brace and bit, and an adjustable wrench to secure the square nuts to the bolts.

Work consisted of locating five or six poles, bucking them into appropriate length, fastening them together with a cross tie bolted at each end into each pole, and launching the thing.

Being cedar, the poles were relatively light, and thus were easy for Dad and me to carry, after we had cut them into the desired length. We had finished our bucking and had moved the seven or eight "logs" down to the water's edge for bolting together. Dad sent me back to get the tools we had left under the trees. I reached under the cross cut saw with the flat side of my right hand to pick it up and lifted it about waist high. But before I could get a grip with the other hand, it slipped from my right hand and fell with teeth pointed down. Three of the pointed teeth penetrated my leg just below the right knee, gouging three nice holes that fairly spurted blood. I was sort of in shock, stumbled down the bank to where Dad was, and showed him my leg and tennis shoe full of blood. He didn't say much, he just told me to get in the water until it stopped bleeding. I did. That was the extent of Dad's doctoring.

Sheese, I thought, *Wonder what medical school he attended?*

I've often thought of why I did not contract tetanus, typhus, or polio from exposure to that foul South Umpqua River water at that time of year. Here I was, just a kid, swimming in water that, even without puncture wounds, a healthy person would still be susceptible to such diseases. All that day I was in the water, as well as many days afterwards during the healing process, and with no ill effects.

I don't think Dad really knew how bad the wounds were. I limped for a couple of weeks as they healed. On one occasion, he got on my case, thinking I was putting on an act for sympathy, which I wasn't. I was hurt, and neither Dad nor Mom seemed to care. At least, that was what I was thinking at the time.

In a few days, in spite of my limp, we had the raft ready to go. For some reason, Dad had it in his mind to put a sail on it. Justice for his lack of care and concern for my wounds was about to be served.

He took a bed sheet and with a few poles and some rope for bracing and steering, he made a sail in the center of the raft. He decided to try it himself first, with no passengers, good thing.

He launched into the slack water of the swimming hole, and then with the wind blowing upstream, he sailed the "craft" pretty as you please out into the center of the river. He was soon out of sight on the other side of a house-sized boulder that blocked our view as he sailed upstream.

He was gone for quite a while, and we were beginning to wonder if he just hadn't taken the thing upriver all the way to Myrtle Creek, when he eventually came from around the far side of the boulder. The mast was broken, the sheet and rope were a snarled soaked mass in the center of the raft, and Dad's in the water, holding onto the raft to provide steerage as he kicks with his feet for power. He was in a good mood though, probably because he had time to think about how funny it was. He told us how he was making good time up river and congratulating himself on being a real sailor when he comes to the point where some riffles enter the slack water. He was going too fast and he buried the nose of the raft into the riffles. The weight of the water on the front of the raft and the force of the wind in the "sail" flipped the raft upside down. Dad was thrown clear. It took him some time to place all the pieces of his broken sail onto the raft, and collect what pride he had left before making his way back downstream.

"Oh, by the way, Dan," he said. "Go check the driftwood piles for some one-by-six boards. I need to make some paddles."

I learned the raft building trade well, too. Later, in one of my high school summers, I built a similar raft and used it in the slack water just downstream from the Highway 99 bridge. I, too, built it under some maple and alder trees. However, I was well over a hundred feet from the water's edge, and I needed help in moving it. I recruited my good buddy Gordon Simmons for this purpose.

It was a solid raft. I had bolted the cross ties in place, and there was no way it was going to fall apart. We used a couple of small roller logs under it to help move it to the water. I had crafted a couple of paddles from some 1 x 6s with a pole ax, and after getting the raft into the water, told Gordon to shove off and step on. He shoved off but didn't step on. I found myself alone on a rather unwieldy sort of water vehicle, floating down the South Umpqua in a late spring runoff. At first it was a little spooky, but I got the hang of the paddle and had no problem getting it back to shore where I tied it up to some brush overhanging the water. And there, I left it for later use. After the water had receded somewhat, Gordon finally found the courage to get on board. And so we had our times on the river; that is, until one day the raft wasn't where we left it. I knew it was just a matter of time before some low-life located it and either stole it or simply turned it loose to drift downriver.

I loved to fish. Now most fishermen would call what I did anything but fishing. My fishing consisted of pulling as many trout as I could from the Blackard stream that flowed from springs on the north side of Timber Butte.

I remember the first time I saw the stream "fished." It was during the winter or spring of '51 or '52, and Dad took me fishing with him. It was after a rain, and the creek was flowing pretty well. The water was muddy, but Dad seemed to know what he was doing, and in a matter of just a few minutes pulled a sufficient number of fish from the stream to fill a large kettle. He simply fished with a line tied to the end of a flexible willow pole. No fuss, no bother, just all business. And so, that's how I fished the Blackard stream (as I came to call it) when I became old enough to ride my bike the several miles down and back.

I'd find an old Prince Albert tobacco can, dig some worms, put the worms in the can, take fifteen or twenty feet of fishing line, several No. 6 or No. 8 single-barbed hooks, and head for the Blackard property. In a half-hour or so, I'd be at the stream. I'd hide my bike in some blackberry bushes alongside Dole Road, then locate just the right willow branch, which grew in ample supply along the river and creek banks. It had to be about six feet long, not too thick and not too thin. Using my pocketknife, I'd cut it to length, trim off the leaves, and proceed to "rig up." A few twists of line around the end of the pole, tie on a hook (no weight, mind you), and thread a worm onto it. It was that simple. I was ready to fish. (One important benefit fishing in this fashion provided was that I never had to carry a fishing pole. It was especially important not to advertise the fact you were going trout fishing when trout season was not open.)

"Don't let them see you," Dad said. "A shadow over the water, a stone clicking against another stone, any such thing like that will spook those fish, and they will not bite."

Through Dad's verbal lessons, and by trial and error, I learned how to fish small streams. I'd sneak up on a likely looking fishing hole using a rock, a bush, or a tree as cover. Once properly in position, I'd release the end of the line I was holding, and guiding the hook with the tip of my pole, drop the worm-covered hook in the water at the place I desired. If all was working according to Hoyle, *blam*! Fish on! Most were around six- or seven-inches. Some reached eight-inches. "Lunkers" (any fish over eight-inches) were few and far between.

I began fishing at the point the creek emptied out of the culvert that ran under Dole Road and the railroad tracks.

The water dumped into a nice-sized hole on the downside of the culvert, from which I could catch two or three fish. I'd then enter the culvert, exit it, and walk upstream, fishing each hole as I went up to the falls. The "falls" were as far as the fish could go, probably no more than a third of a mile from the road, and then I'd turn around and fish the creek downstream. I usually could catch a few more.

The creek always seemed to have fish in it. I would fish it only a couple of times a year, giving it time to rebuild its population. Usually though, I would take twelve or fifteen fish each time. Seasons and quantity mattered not to me. I fished when I felt the urge. And that's the way it was. I don't know if "fun" is the word to use. Maybe a more fitting word is "therapy." I needed an outlet such as this, and so I used it whenever I felt a need to visit my "therapist."

Friends on the Hill

He was my friend. I addressed him as "Mr. Stone." Mom and Dad used his first name, "Clark." He lived "up" the hill from us in a small tarpaper shack no more than fifteen feet from the dust, dirt, and gravel of Dole Road. What I mean by "up the road" is that he lived just short of the crest of the hill between our shack and town. If you were going to or coming from town, you passed Mr. Stone's place.

Unlike the Olivers, Mr. Stone really was a squatter. The accurate definition of "squatter" is one who takes up residency on property without permission or other legal authority. The Olivers had permission to live on the Rice's 40 hillside acres in return for functioning in the role of property caretakers. It is my understanding that, at least initially, Mr. Stone was a true squatter.

In my visits with him over the years, I learned he built his small shack at its chosen location, asking permission of no one. Of course, after his shack was built, it was too late for permission, so he squatted. Sometime afterward, he had obtained permission to stay. Shortly after building, he obtained a connection to a city water line and electric power via an empty home located a couple of hundred feet closer to the crest of the hill, at the place where Dole road began its serpentine descent into town.

Dad and Mom knew the Stones prior to our moving onto the Rice property. Mr. Stone's wife died shortly after they moved into their shack, before I had a chance to know her. Funny how, at the time, I never questioned certain things, but looking back, I ponder about the circumstances that led to the Stones' need to squat on others' property. They indeed must have become "homeless." I never knew the reasons. Interesting how we are sometimes curious about some things, but not about others. I suppose we were all just too busy to wonder the why and way of situations and circumstances of the Stones. It wasn't our business anyway. We had our own problems.

As time went by, and as a result of stops to visit Mr. Stone to and from town and school, he would tell me a little bit about himself. As a young man, around the turn of the twentieth century, he moved himself and his family from Missouri in a covered wagon, homesteading at the confluence of Gold Creek and the South Umpqua, several miles downstream from Tiller, Oregon. This was about 40 miles upstream from Myrtle Creek. For some reason, in his "senior years," he moved from his home to squat alongside Dole Road.

Shoot, at that time in the early '50s, Mr. Stone was somewhere in his mid-sixties. Times back then were a little rougher on the flesh than the past half-century, and so at sixty-five or so, Mr. Stone was an old man. He was short, about Dad's height, but on the heavy side. He had a full head of white hair, no teeth, and seemed to always have one of those Sherlock Holmes-type pipes or a cheap stogie clamped tightly between his gums. Oftentimes, the pipe wasn't lit. It would just hang there, with the bowl resting on his jutting chin.

Down slope from his tarpaper shack (about fifty feet or so) Mr. Stone built a covered storage area. He sided the shed with old boards, pieces of plywood, and other materials, and so the contents of the structure were somewhat protected from the elements.

I was curious about the contents of that shed, but my sense of propriety would not permit me to snoop, other than cursive glances through the ventilation openings in the siding. I'm still wondering what treasures he may have stored in the shed. One thing I know he had in storage was a disassembled covered wagon. He had kept the parts in good condition under the protection of the shed's roof. I'm sure he had other memorabilia therein, but I never entered to snoop, even though it would have been easy to get inside. I still wonder if any of the wheels of that old wagon touched a bit of the Applegate Trail.

Mr. Stone was always dressed in bib overalls. Of course he wore shirt, socks, and shoes, and an old Fedora-type hat when he made his biweekly trek into town for groceries and incidentals. That was his uniform, always clean and neat, everything about him was an exact fit for the role he played.

He received a Social Security stipend, and on something like sixty dollars a month he survived; and because he had no other expenses, he survived quite well, at least by Oliver standards.

Like the Olivers, Mr. Stone had an outhouse. But unlike the Olivers, he had water at the house and electrical power. He was "uptown." Why, he even had a couple of electrical outlets in the main living area and a bare bulb hanging from the ceiling in the middle of the main room. The main living area wasn't more than ten-foot-by-ten-foot, with the bedroom off the main living area that was barely big enough to hold the bed and some storage shelves on which he stored his nonperishables such as canned food, beans, candy, and the like. He had another bulb hanging from the ceiling in the bedroom. Both bulbs were switched on and off at the socket. He had tied a string to the short chain that dangled from the socket, and then tied the other end of the string to a nail on the doorjamb. When you entered the room in the dark, you could easily locate the "switch" by flailing an arm around until you hit the string, usually breaking the string in the process.

The living area had a cushioned wooden rocker. It was what I eventually termed the "Stone Throne." Immediately to the left of his throne was a wooden kitchen chair. This was the company chair and was where I'd sit as we talked; I'd lose myself as he regaled me with his stories of times gone by, with my left elbow resting on a checkered red and white oil cloth laid on the table.

He had a portable phonograph player and several dozen '78s of country songs from the '40s and early '50s. I couldn't get enough of Little Jimmy Dickens, George Morgan, Hank Williams, Lester Flatt and Earl Scruggs, Tommy Collins, Roy Acuff, and a few other early artists whose names I cannot recall.

Like the Olivers, Mr. Stone heated his home and cooked on a wood burning range. You entered the house through a small door off the porch, the porch being covered by a shallow, sloping roof. His water source was a faucet connected to a sink on the front porch. It was on that porch his old mongrel red dog, Rover (part Irish Setter), made his bed on a hairy, flea-infested blanket. That dog was old when I first knew Mr. Stone, obviously a relic of his days on the upper South Umpqua and Gold Creek. The dog hung on for a couple of years. He loved that dog. He cried when he buried him in a shallow grave on the bluff overlooking the South Umpqua. Old Rover was one of Stone's last links to Gold Creek.

Mr. Stone played a critical role in my early development. He was a friend, howbeit, an older friend. You know, the kind of friend who is just there, and whom you subconsciously know will always be there. It was my habit early in our relationship to stop and visit whenever I was on my way home from school or town. He always had some treats, not only for me, but for my sisters, too. Sometimes it might be a banana; other times a Hershey bar, or hard candy.

As I sat in that old high-backed kitchen chair, he'd talk. He'd talk about the early days homesteading on the South Umpqua, about gold panning on Gold Creek, and how to fish for "cats."

I was wondering what he was frying up one afternoon, and he said it was "cat" that he'd caught in the river. Man, I thought that was awful that he would rescue a drowning cat from the river, kill it, and then eat it—until it became clear that he was talking about catfish. He shared some cooked cat with me. It was good, solid meat chunks rolled in flour, and fried in Crisco oil. From that time on, I used any excuse I could contrive to go fishing for "cats." Many times, the entire family was down at the river in the late spring and through the summer fishing for them. They weren't that big, probably no more than twelve or fourteen inches, but once the bony heads were gone, everything else was solid white meat.

The two things I didn't care for about a catfish: first, they are hard to kill, and second, they are hard to skin. Well, maybe there are three things I didn't like because if you have ever had your skin pierced by one of their sharp gill spines, then you know what the third thing is, pain. The trick was to get the fish skinned without getting punctured by those spines. Their skin is exceptionally difficult to get off the meat. You have to cut around the entire base of the skull, then take pliers, grip the skin, and pull back toward the tail, and in that way skin the fish. It was made less difficult by pinning the head of the fish to a board with a nail, to hold the fish firmly in place so you could get enough pull with the pliers to rip the skin off. I'm not funning you. It was that difficult to "skin those cats." And they were difficult to kill. Even with a nail through their head and completely skinned, they would still be working their gills and making swimming motions with their bodies. This sounds kind of morbid, but that's the way it was. We weren't being mean. The fish were nothing more than food, and pretty good food at that when rolled in peppered and salted flour and then fried in some good ol' Crisco oil.

Mr. Stone would have me cut and stack fire wood. Unlike our place, Stone had two covered woodsheds in which he would stack split wood for his cooking range. He'd have a couple loads of mill ends bought from one of the planer mills. While he was capable of splitting and stacking the wood himself, he would pay me twenty-five cents an hour to do it for him. He knew I was a hard worker and knew that I could use some spending money.

For me, Mr. Stone was like having a grandpa next door. He was someone to talk to and someone to just be with, and someone to work for when I needed some cash to take in a movie at the

Rio Theater. Whether he understood the role he was playing in my life or not, he played it well.

Mr. Stone was a good carpenter and handyman. Between his house and the storage building (the building in which he stored his old covered wagon), he constructed a small workshop. In that shop, he had a large trunk-sized, custom case in which he stored his woodworking tools: chisels, handsaws, rasps, planers, and the like.

Some time around the mid-fifties or so, Dad told me that Mr. Stone wanted me to stop in the next time I passed his house.

He said, "Clark's got something he wants to give you."

I followed Mr. Stone, and in that shed he showed me what he had built: a large wooden wagon. It was like one of those metal Radio Flyer wagons, except this one was made from half-inch plywood. The corners were braced with pieces of iron screwed to the wood. It had rear wheels under the wagon and a front axle that pivoted, to which was attached a metal tongue for steering. It was just like the Radio Flyers. And it was red, too and impossibly heavy. It was the Mack truck of coaster wagons. All it needed was an optional Ford flathead V8 to be functional.

While I could see the great care with which Mr. Stone had assembled the wagon, it missed the boat on the ergonomics and human factors side of its design. It was heavy, and thus hard to pull, especially uphill, which was half the distance to town and half the distance from town. And when you wanted to coast, the small utility wheels, even though they had ball bearing hubs, were too small. The gravel on Dole Road acted like a drag brake. In later years, I'd reflect on the effect gravel had on the speed of that wagon and wonder if that's how highway engineers got the idea for making the runaway truck turnouts on the steep downgrades. I came to hate the thing and eventually used it only when hauling groceries for Mom from the store. After all, I didn't want to appear ungrateful for the work and effort Mr. Stone had expended on my account. He enjoyed seeing me pulling the red "Mack truck," I mean wagon. I often thought of having it "accidentally" get away from me and lose itself in that gap in the rock where Dole Road sort of "hangs out in space" over the river.

It was no secret to anybody that Mr. Stone knew Dad was a drunkard and wife-beater, but I do not recall him ever broaching the subject. He knew our living conditions; and yet, to his credit (and wisdom), he never criticized Dad in front of us kids. He was just a good man and a good friend, and I thank God that he was there to provide an element of sanity and security in a world that was shaky, insecure, and at times outright terrifying.

....

Mr. Stone died in '68. He was eighty-three, I think. He was one friend whose funeral I would have attended had I known he had passed away. However, I was stationed at Minot Air Force Base at the time and didn't know that he had died until Mom mentioned it in a letter, some weeks following his death. I just feel compelled to say, "Thank you, Mr. Stone," for just being there, and for being who you were—if you only knew the role you played in rearing me.

....

I mentioned in the first chapter that I had two companions on the hillside. Saddy and Sandy were their names. Both dogs had similar characteristics, and I deeply loved them both. Saddy was first.

After Dad was released from jail following the "Blanche Incident," we had become acquainted with a Mrs. Evers, who lived a couple miles from town up North Myrtle Road, not too far from where we lived in the small apartment just north of the Stimpson Lumber Mill. As I mentioned earlier, Dad could not find steady work following his release from the country jail, but on occasion he would do odd jobs for Mrs. Evers. Mrs. Evers was single at the time and for the sake of propriety, he would take one of us kids with him to her home when working, and we'd play with a medium-sized and friendly Chow-mix dog she kept tied to a post. She must have known we kids loved that dog, and so after we moved back to the shack she visited, asking Dad if he would take the dog. Dad asked us kids if we wanted a dog. *Are you kidding me*, Dad? We named the mutt, "Saddy."

Being part Chow, Saddy's tail curled up and over her back, and she had that sort of furrowed contemplative brow, giving her a perpetual sad look. Maybe that was why we named her "Saddy." She hated gray squirrels and found great pleasure in running the hillside until she treed one. She would keep the squirrel treed all day, barking in the process. The only way to get her to shut up and back home was to go up and shoot the squirrel. Man, there were times at night I wanted to shoot her. Ha!

One weekend Dad's brother, Archie, visited, bringing cousins Kent, Jim, and Benton (age descending order). Kent, around sixteen at the time, asked permission to take the Marlin .22 and go shoot some birds. Obtaining permission, he took Saddy with him. A couple hours later, he walks back into the yard. Saddy was trailing him, head down, laboring to walk. Blood was seeping from a wound behind her right shoulder. A froth of rose-tinged bubbles hung from the corners of her mouth. A lung shot! Kent said he was shooting at a bird and didn't realize where the dog was. I've always wondered how someone could shoot at something and not know what was around and behind the possible trajectory. But accidents happen, and you can't undo what's been done. Kent was obviously upset over what had happened, and we never really thought anything else about it at the time.

As doctors seemed to be out of the question for us kids, vets certainly were for the dog. She was dying anyway. A vet would have simply put her out of her misery. We made her as comfortable as possible on a bed under the eves of Dad's workshop, hoping against hope that a miracle might happen. But, in hindsight, we should have put her out of her misery; she suffered so. All night, she moaned and howled as she lay on her deathbed beside the workshop. We'd go out and check on her throughout the night, but there was nothing we could do. She died sometime in early morning. I skipped school to bury her. Using Dad's soldering iron heated over a blowtorch, I burned her eulogy into the wooden end of an old apple box. The acrid wood smoke mixed with the salt of my tears burned in my nostrils. Somehow I was able to write, "Here lies Saddy the best dog I ever had." I could still locate her grave today. I dug it at the base of one of the electric power poles on the property that supported high-voltage lines feeding Myrtle Creek's electrical power station. The power poles are long gone, but not the memory.

Dad knew I missed that dog. One afternoon a few weeks later he brought home a flea-invested black puppy. That poor old pup had so many fleas that neither Mom nor Dad would let us kids play with it. They treated it for several days with flea powder, but it didn't make a dent in the flea population on the pup. Dad decided to put it out of its misery with a bullet from the .22. He tied a short rope around the pup's neck and took him into the woods, telling us kids that he wouldn't be long. We waited for the report from the .22, but it never came. In something like fifteen minutes or so, Dad comes walking into the yard with the pup still tied to the rope.

"Couldn't do it," he said. "There I was with the rifle barrel pointed at the pup's head and a bunch of 'skeeters landed on his nose. That dog looked at me with such a pathetic look on his face that I just couldn't do it." He returned the pup to its original owner.

A couple weeks later, Dad brought a short-tailed, sandy-haired pup home. We kept her. We named her "Sandy." As she matured, we were all struck by the similar looks and character traits when compared to Saddy. Slightly smaller and thinner, but in all other aspects, she was Saddy reincarnated, but with one exception. Sandy had a bobbed tail. We were inseparable, and she too hated squirrels. She was faster than Saddy, though. She once chased down a jackrabbit going uphill, and caught it! Must've been a sick rabbit. *Probably an early ancestor to the one I frightened to death some fifty years later.*

Her departure was also tinged with sadness. She was less than three years old when we moved off the hill in '59, following Dad's last arrest and incarceration in the Douglas County Jail. We could not keep her in the rental across from the Golden Rule, and so Mom gave her away to a family who lived a few miles up South Myrtle Creek. They said they would give her a good home. Shortly after her "adoption," I walked the four miles to visit her. It broke my heart. She was tied to a short leash. She so wanted to go with me, pulling and tugging on her leash, whimpering and crying as I walked away. Again, I cried.

Gordon Simmons was his name. Because of our long friendship, I considered him my best pal. He and I were classmates and buddies pretty much from first grade until sometime in the mid-sixties, when marriage and family responsibilities took priority.

While Gordon and I were in the same grade, he was about a year younger than I. Back then, as now, there was a cut-off age for entering first grade, depending on one's birthday. For me in 1950, it was November 15, and because my birthday was November 30, I did not start school until I was almost seven years old. Gordon's birthday was a few weeks earlier than mine, and so he was able to squeak into the first grade as a five-year-old. This may have been the reason Gordon allowed me to assume the role of leader; it just happened naturally.

Gordon was raised in town and had a stable family. His dad, Ray, worked in the sawmills, and later, at the Riddle Nickel Mine. Whereas I had four sisters, he had two brothers and a sister. He was the eldest, wore glasses, was as skinny as I, and even in the summers, was white as a sheet. He'd sunburn easily, and unlike me, he hardly ever took his shirt off for that "summer look" that most of the kids had at that time.

My first recollection of our budding friendship occurred in the second grade. He lived a few blocks from school and typically he would walk home for lunch. On occasion, he would invite me to have lunch with him. In the third and fourth grades, as we became older and more responsible, we'd spend time together on the weekends and he'd invite me to spend the night at his home. Yes, he'd visit with me at "the shack," but he never once made any derogatory comments about how I lived, where I lived, or about Dad or Mom. We'd roam the hills around Myrtle Creek and in our pre-teen and teen years spend time on the river, during all times of the year. I often think that it was because of friends like Gordon, a friend who accepted me for who and what I was, that I ended up being somewhat stable and adjusted.

Here was where Dad's training was impressed on me. As a youngster, Dad gave me lots of freedom. If I wanted to go visit Gordon, I would simply ask permission. He'd tell me what time to be back (later I'd tell him what time I'd be back), and if I was going to eat at Gordon's home, I was directed to show proper etiquette. Dad taught me much about etiquette. "Yes sir," "No sir," "Yes ma'am," "No ma'am." He explained how to sit at the table, passing food from left to right, always saying "Thank you," or "No thank you"; and not to put elbows on the table, and always to compliment the cook, regardless whether I liked the food or not, and to offer to help with the dishes. And I did.

Sort of ironic, don't you think? Dad obviously was trained in such decorum, and yet, he couldn't hold a job, couldn't provide (well) for his own family, was a drunkard and a binge drinker, beat his wife, and failed in so many ways to be the kind of man I want to believe he desired to be. Even when Gordon may have been around the house when Dad was drinking, even in his most violent and drunken stage, he somehow would change his conduct. Of course, if I knew that Dad was in one of his drunken binges, I simply would not have friends over to visit.

Early in our friendship, Gordon was the one with the bike. I didn't have one. We'd often be seen riding double around Myrtle Creek. Back then, bikes were in basically two sizes, bikes with twenty-four-inch wheels, and bikes with twenty-six-inch wheels. Gordon got his bike when he was barely able to ride the twenty-four-incher. And as he grew and could have easily ridden a twenty-six-incher, he never owned the larger bike. As long as we palled around, which was until I left Myrtle Creek just before starting my senior year, Gordon still had that bike. Of course, we both got our driver's license as soon as we turned sixteen and that pretty much was the end of our bike riding. In those early years, before I got my first bike, Gordon and I could be seen on any given weekend riding double on his twenty-four-incher. Sometimes Gordon would pedal; sometimes I'd pedal.

It's interesting how, as we age, that we long for some of these old connections, and thus motivated, reach out across time to re-establish old ties or strengthen relationships that have deteriorated into rusted memories. It was in one of those pensive moments in the mid-'90s that I desired to re-establish contact with Gordon. I hadn't seen him nor even called him for at least twenty years. Finally I got off my duff and made a few phone calls in an attempt to locate him.

At the time the melancholy mood descended, I was visiting Mom in Winston (Winston is located about midway between Roseburg and Myrtle Creek on Old Highway 99) when I made the call. There was no listing for Gordon Simmons, but I noted a listing in the phone book for a Randy Simmons, who lived in Riddle. Randy is one of Gordon's younger brothers. I made the call, introduced myself, and told Randy I was attempting to locate Gordon. Imagine my shock when he told me Gordon had died of a heart attack at age fifty-two, just a year or so before I called. Also, their dad and mother (Ray and Vera) had died the same year! So, lesson learned. Don't delay if your heart stirs you to contact an old chum.

About the sixth grade, something good happened again for me by the hand of my third grade teacher, Mrs. Yokum, and her husband. I can't remember the exact year, probably sometime in my sixth grade.

Let me back up a little in time. At the beginning of third grade, Dad was still serving his sentence of six months in the Douglas County Jail for attempted murder. In that critical time I was beginning to pull inward, thinking that I would never measure up to the rest of the students for any number of reasons that you can probably imagine. When things looked bleakest, I was assigned to Mrs. Yokum's third grade class. She was a good person. She was small and thin, wore glasses, and her hair was done up in a bun behind her head. In class, she always had an encouraging word. It was in my heart to please all adults, and I guess she took notice. I got decent grades, worked hard, and liked to draw. She was just what I needed. I began to come out of my shell.

For the Thanksgiving season of third grade, she asked all kids in her class to create a Thanksgiving scene. I threw my heart into the project. I drew a house in a small valley surrounded by fields of corn and pumpkins, split rail fences, and pasture in which I drew horses and cows. It was the total farm scene. I finished it with watercolors. I was proud of my accomplishment, and I knew that Mrs. Yokum was proud of me as well. The scene was selected as the best scene of any student in her class and consequently was put on display in the hallway outside her classroom. Mom kept the picture for several years, but then, in one of our moves, it was either lost or tossed. Mrs. Yokum and her husband had no children. Their home was directly behind the Simmons home. Occasionally, they would notice Gordon and me playing and would make pleasant conversation with us, always precipitated with a "Hello. How are you boys doing?" Or, "What are you boys up to today?" One of them, or both, obviously noticed that I did not have a bike, and so they conspired to do something about it.

One weekend when I was visiting Gordon, Mrs. Yokum interrupted our play. She asked that I follow her to the front of their garage, which was just off the alley between the two homes. There were stairs along the outside of the garage, and at the top of the stairs was a landing, with a door giving entrance into an attic. The door opened, and Mr. Yokum wheeled this bike down the stairs. He told me that they wanted me to have his old bicycle. He'd slapped a fresh coat of paint on the thing. I was speechless. I was absolutely stunned that anybody would give me something like that. I didn't care that it had handle bars as wide as a Texas longhorn; but if I had known how heavy that old bike was, and how difficult it was to pedal it up and around the hills of Myrtle Creek, I might have cussed him at the time. But not really, for now I had a bike! Dad had taught me proper manners, and though at first speechless, I finally was able to render my thanks.

Like I said, it was old and heavy. Probably a product of the thirties the way it was built and looked. I reckon it weighed forty or fifty pounds. Shoot, I didn't care. I was taught to never look a gift horse in the mouth, and while it seemed as big as a horse, I rode it everywhere. In the eighth grade, I made my first paper route deliveries on that tank of a bike, and it could carry a load. I guess you could classify it as a bike-truck, 'cause I think if it had a pickup bed it could have carried as much as a pickup.

As a youngster, this brute of a bike built up my thigh muscles and wind. After several months of riding, I finally developed sufficient leg strength and lung power to pedal the bike up the hill in both directions whether coming from town or going to town. Anybody who knows Dole Road as it takes off from US Highway 99 at the north end of town knows how steep that road is. Conquering that hill with a single-speed, heavy bike was a major accomplishment.

I got the idea one day to coast down the hill (from the top) without using the brake, enter our driveway with a full head of steam, and try pedaling from there without having to bail off the bike and push the remaining distance to the house. The problem was the berm of gravel between the outside edge of Dole Road and the entrance to our driveway—a sure recipe for disaster.

I'd been practicing for weeks on how to hit the gravel berm at a forty-five-degree angle at high speed without having the front wheel jerked cock-eyed by the gravel and throwing me over the handlebars. The technique was simple: concentrate, hold the handlebars for all you were worth, and pray. In my practice runs, the theory worked at speeds lower than maximum velocity; but in such runs, there was never sufficient momentum after exiting the gravel berm to reach the house without bailing off the bike.

Maximum velocity should do it, I mused. *Yeah*, I repeated to myself, *maximum velocity*.

It was a cool day when I decided to test the maximum velocity theory. Not that I had planned for a cool day, but the fact that it was, led to my wearing my heavy Navy wool coat. It cushioned my fall. Everything started right. From the crest of Dole Road I started, just beyond Mr. Stone's tarpaper shack. Pedaling as hard as I could, my speed soon exceeded my ability to keep my feet on the pedals, so I free-fell the rest of the way, holding trajectory down the hill, channeling all my strength from shoulders, arms, and hands to the handlebars to hold the front wheel straight through the gravel berm; so much for theory. Have you ever noticed how different the world looks upside down? I had a good look as I did a one-eighty and began a flat spin over the handlebars. It was kind of slow motion, like I was suspended in time, pin-wheeling over the entrance to the driveway. After several hours in suspended animation, I came to earth, landing on my left shoulder, sliding a few feet, looking up at the blue sky. You know how it is after one of these types of accidents. You don't know whether or not you ought to try to move. So you don't. You just lie there. There's a fear that you broke something, but you're afraid to test any extremity to see if it moves, or even check if they're all there. Not only were there no injuries, there was also not even a tear in the heavy Navy wool jacket I was wearing. I brushed off the dust and gravel, picked up the bike, and pushed it up the driveway. Shoot! So much for my grasp of science and physics. *What a bike, not even a scratch*, I thought, as I pushed my two-wheeled RV up the driveway.

Thank you, Mrs. Yokum, for that bike. You'll always be in one of those special warm corners of my memory.

In the eighth grade, I decided it was time to retire the old bike. Dad was in jail for the last time, and Mom had moved us from the shack into the rental across the street from the Golden Rule. I had returned from a berry and cherry-picking trip with the Gallios family (more about this trip later) and had obtained an *Oregonian* paper route that put money in my pocket. With the money, I bought a three-speed "English racer." These were light bikes (for the time) with thin, high-pressure tires, and a three-speed rear hub. The shifting was done using a single small lever on the handlebars. Brakes were the "caliper" type, one for each wheel.

I bought the bike, on my own contract, from the Western Auto Supply store on Main Street in Myrtle Creek. The manager, for some reason I'll never know, trusted me. He noticed me eyeing the bike in the window one day and came out and began a conversation. In the course of our conversation, I mentioned I had a paper route. With a knowing grin he said, "I don't care if you can pay cash now. But, if you have ten dollars for a down payment, and agree to pay five dollars each month until paid off, you can have the bike now." I had the down payment. I walked out of the store pushing my new bike. I never discussed the deal with Mom. I made the decision and deal by myself. Never signed a paper either! Nothing but my word. I had it paid off in six months and never missed a payment!

My entrepreneurial side was kicking in. Shortly after buying the bike, I bought a new Clinton two-cycle lawnmower from the same store for a budding lawn mowing business. A few of the townsfolk had asked me to cut their grass, and I obliged; however, I had to use their too-often cantankerous old power mowers, and on one occasion, a dull reel push mower. I could do better. Again the store manger (probably the owner) sold it to me for five dollars a month, nothing down. I'm certain that a few people in town knew the "Oliver family." And maybe he did. People talk. I choose to believe that he knew sufficiently about me, and knew I would not betray his trust. Like with the bike, we never signed papers. We had a verbal contract. He simply kept a ledger in which he entered my payments, and after each payment, he told me how much I had left on account.

Acts of kindness and trust of this type do a great deal in forming character in a person. Dad taught me that when I gave my word, never go back on it. I still remember the words. *A man is only as good as his word*, and I never considered faulting on my obligation to make the payments.

Yes, I had friends. Obviously I was befriended by the Western Auto Supply man. At the time, I never considered him a friend, just a man who showed me the good side of adults. Like Mr. Stone, his simple acts of goodness made an impression.

I had a friend who was killed.

Bobby Hulie was the first of any of my classmates, friends, or family whom I personally knew to die. He died before he finished the sixth grade.

I don't remember when I first met Bobby. While Gordon was my main buddy, I had other friends whom I visited with from time to time, and Bobby was one of them. Like us, the Hulies were having a rough go of it, struggling to just make ends meet. But they were a happy family. I can't remember how many kids they had, but they had a few, with a good mix of boys and girls. Some were older than I; some younger.

I believe we become acquainted with the Hulies in the year or so after Dad was released from prison for taking a pot shot at his sister, Blanche. Sometime after his release, he began studying and attending church with the Jehovah Witnesses. That was when I met Bobby. The Hulie family were Jehovah Witnesses. And Dad and Mom became friends with Bobby's folks.

Now, if my description of where we lived gives the impression we lived on the side of a mountain, it could not hold a candle to the mountainside the Hulies lived on. Like the Olivers, they had no electricity and no running water. But by comparison, their home seemed large, warm, and inviting.

The house was located on a bench bulldozed from the side of the mountain directly across the South Umpqua from Myrtle Creek. The "road" (the remains of an old logging road) to their house branched off Weaver Road and began a steep traverse up the slope of the mountain directly above the railroad bridge that crossed the river at that point. There was nothing to stop any vehicle if it left that slippery, bumpy, excuse for a road, until you hit Weaver Road, probably bouncing into the community swimming hole by the railroad bridge. Those thoughts were in my mind every time we drove down that steeply-descending grade to intersect with Weaver Road.

Bill Hulie was one of the many gypos in that country who attempted to scratch a living logging patches of second growth. And because he obviously had a contract to log some second growth on the mountainside, and because there was a house up on the mountainside, that's where they lived; that's where Dad also worked when Bill needed some extra help; and that's where we'd visit when invited.

Bill employed Dad off and on in his logging "operation." Dad had me with him one late spring day. It was one of those days in Oregon we call "dry." (*Dry* meaning it wasn't raining hard.) Dad took off from the muddy landing with pole ax, wedges, chainsaw, gas, and oil, trekking up slope and out of sight to do some falling. I remained in the landing area, skirting hither, thither, and yon keeping out of the way of loggers and equipment. My intent was to be alive to make the trip home with Dad after quitting time.

Now when I use the term "equipment," I'm not referring to skid steers with gigantic tires and chains, nor even small cleat track dozers, or anything so sophisticated or expensive. Mr. Hulie's logging equipment consisted of a World War II Army surplus jeep (chained of course), and a farting horse.

I was standing off to the side of the landing, when here comes this jeep in compound low gear, four-cylinder engine whining, tires spinning, and mud flying as it towed a "turn" of logs into the landing. Talk about a workhorse! Even today, I can hardly believe what I saw. This piece of what passed for yarding equipment had several logs (they weren't giants mind you, but were of sufficient size) rolling and turning behind it in the trough of mud called a skid road. The "equipment" operator (driver) was making good time down-slope towing the logs. But when he pulled into the landing, he had to make a turn to his right to lay the logs against other logs previously yarded and laying in the mud to the left of the jeep. He hit the landing with the engine still screaming and the mud flying, mud soft and deep.

I had the feeling I'd been there, done that, as scenes of my physics-momentum experiment with my old heavy bike became painted over the scene. The Jeep was in a right turn in about a foot of sticky goo, and the logs suddenly dug in, causing the Jeep to flip onto its right side. Stuck? Not really. The driver climbed out the driver's window, as steam poured from the right side where the hot exhaust lay buried under the mud. He calmly walked back up the skid road, as if this event was nothing out of the ordinary. No cussing that I heard. Some time later, he returned with Mr. Hulie and Dad. All three obtained a hand hold on the side of the Jeep in all that mud and tipped it back on its wheels. The driver got back in, pressed the starter button, and lo, the engine burbled back to life (end of the tail pipe's still buried in the watery goo)! I was impressed then, and I'm still impressed today. No wonder our soldiers loved the jeep during the war.

Oh yeah, about the horse. Bill used the horse to yard timber off slopes too steep for the jeep. Occasionally, Dad was the horse wrangler (or whatever they called loggers who used horses for this purpose). One day, I was riding the back of this brute of a gentle work animal as Dad walked it up the skid road to get a log or two. Because of what I experienced that day on the back of that horse, I believe there is some truth to the eco-argument regarding the greenhouse effect made worse by certain, large vegetation-eating animals. If it's not true, then that horse was an exception. As Dad lead it up the skid road to get that turn of logs, that horse let a good one—*ffft, blurt, poot, phoot*—every single step. Yep, the horse may have had a flatulence problem, but it could sure yard out the hard to get logs.

On the times when the Hulies had the family up for some social time, Bobby and I and the rest of the older kids would get the biggest thrill playing on their rope "swing." Now that swing was a "swing." Today, swings have so many safety features they should not be classified swings. A more appropriate name would be sway. The Hulie swing had no safety features. As a matter of fact, it was designed to be dangerous; the more dangerous, the more fun. Ah, a swing in the classic definition.

As I previously described, the Hulie house was built in the middle of an old dozed landing on a very steep hillside. At the edge of the berm, where the dirt had been pushed onto the downside of the slope, was a large madrone. The tree was perfectly placed and equipped with a proper limb at the perfect height, thus providing the initial element of danger. On that limb was a three-quarter inch manila rope with a round stick tied in the middle at the end of the rope. This qualified as the second element of danger. The object was to hang onto the stick with both hands, back up to take all slack from the rope, then run (keeping the rope taut) in an arc until you launched yourself over the lip of the cliff. This latter act constituting the third and final element of danger. If the rope, or handle, didn't break, or you didn't lose your grip to gravity, you'd find yourself swinging in a wide arc twenty or thirty feet above the ground until your momentum swung you around to land back on flat terra firma on the opposite side of the tree. What a thrill the right kind of danger gives! Amazing what parents would allow kids to do back then. The dads would get into the "swing" of it, too. The moms and younger kids were the only ones with any sense; not that the younger ones didn't want to have their turn.

As Dad took me into the woods with him on occasion, so Bill took his son...my friend, Bobby. We all got the news in school one Monday morning. If my memory is correct, the school had been notified and my sixth grade teacher, Mr. Misner, told the class that Bobby had been killed the weekend before.

My reaction was strange. I felt no sorrow or loss, even though it was my introduction to the death of someone I knew, someone I called friend. Even today, I cannot explain why I reacted the way I did. I recall Mom asking if I wanted to go to the funeral. She said it wouldn't be open casket because Bobby had been hit by a log his dad was falling. The story we heard was that Mr. Hulie was falling an old snag, one that was rotten on the inside. Such trees are tricky to fall, and this one did not fall as predicted. Bobby was standing in the wrong place.

"No," I said. "I don't want to go to the funeral."

Interestingly, other classmates attended the funeral. I didn't. I'm still puzzled by my reaction. Ah, Bobby. I did miss you, and yes, eventually, I mourned my loss.

I had other friends. I'll introduce them to you in the chapter titled "Good Influences."

Goodbye Canvas-Sided Shack

Some things we desire to forget, but cannot. They seem to be permanently etched on plates of stainless steel in our memory vaults. Such was my last memory of the old Maytag washing machine the day my sisters and I were huddled around the wash-tubs rinsing blood-soaked towels and rags. It was spring. I was in the eighth grade.

Some months before, Dad began the spiral into another drinking binge. It had deteriorated to the usual point of verbal and physical abuse on the ever-available object of his anger, Mom. By the spring of 1958, Mom had taken up serious drinking herself, making batch-after-batch of home brew, and together she and Dad would begin drinking as soon as it perked alcohol. It was probably what a brewer would term "green beer," meaning that it was not fully aged. They didn't seem to care as long as it had alcohol.

In the months leading up to this time, if beer and wine were not available, Dad would drink anything that had drinkable alcohol. He was drunk more than he was sober. Although the home brew was plentiful, Dad's beverage of choice was store-bought beer or wine. The wine was cheap, "fortified" versions. One could buy a bottle for fifty or sixty cents. At twenty percent alcohol by volume, a single bottle would produce a pretty good drunk. Dad and several of his buddies also drank bay rum. I believe it was the same thing they used in some barbershops for after-shave lotion. I can still recall the smell. When I came into the house and noted its unique, sweet smell it was time to head for the slopes of Timber Butte because the "fit was going to hit the shan" sooner than later. I don't know if Dad was drinking home brew or not on this particular drunk, or whether he was lacing it with wine, bay rum, whiskey, whatever. In any case, his drunks were deeper, and his abuse toward Mom had reached the level of violence when, this time, he almost killed her.

Generally, Dad could control his violence until company was gone, but as soon as the coast was clear, Dad would loosen his self-imposed restraints, and ratchet into violence, beginning with the bad-mouthing, cursing, and general verbal abuse toward Mom, making excuses and fomenting reasons for why his words and actions were justified. He quickly reached the point of physical violence. In these later periods, and especially this last time, it was not simply slapping, hitting, or hair-pulling. It reached the stage of outright physical violence that often left Mom so abused she could not function for several days, literally with the "stuffings" beat out of her. Fat and bloodied lips, black eyes, and bruises everywhere from fists and kicks. Once he had kicked her so hard in the back, she could barely walk. It took weeks for the limp to go away. In those times when Dad knew he had seriously hurt her, he would hold off the abuse (realizing when sober what he had done in his drunkenness), until she recovered, then it would cycle all over again. I could not understand this element of his abuse. He had to know he was hurting her and would stop short of permanent injury, but not this time.

During this particular period (my seventh and eighth grade years), I had reached a point in maturity that I knew Dad had something seriously wrong with him, and that if he didn't stop, he was going to kill Mom. At one time, he had borrowed a .30 caliber carbine from one of his friends, and in one of his drunken rages, fired a shot at Mom. Whether or not Dad intended to kill her didn't matter to any of us. All of us kids knew that Dad had taken a shot at Mom with a high-powered hunting rifle! Maybe he wouldn't miss next time.

And so here we kids were, down in the creek bed at the washing tubs, rinsing bloody towels and rags that Dad would bring to us as he carried clean rags back to the shack. We kids knew something serious had happened, as huge clots of blood were in the rags. He wouldn't let us kids go to the house to see Mom.

We had been sitting in the house some time earlier eating breakfast, when Dad suddenly went crazy. I really think he was drinking bay rum at the time, as it made him more violent and crazy than wine or beer, I don't know. He had been at it all night and was still at it into the morning hours. I just know that when the plates and dishes started flying, we kids bailed out the door. Mom stayed, as usual. This time, a broken piece of dinner plate struck her on the right temple, severing a major artery. Mom told us later that the blood came out in spurts with each heartbeat.

It took Dad a few moments to realize what he had done, then he frantically tried to stop the bleeding, but no matter how much he tried, he couldn't. We kids were old enough to realize that if Dad didn't do something soon, Mom was going to bleed to death. We were all crying. Mom's pleadings eventually got through to Dad as he quickly sobered due to his failed attempts to staunch the flow of blood, and he eventually took her to the doctor. I'm sure both Dad and Mom concocted some kind of story on how it all happened, but I know Dr. Faber knew what was going on.

Mom was back on her feet in a few days after drinking lots of liquids, and though somewhat weak, she seemed to be taken in by Dad's attention and somber contriteness. Certainly, he must have known that he had come close to killing her, and that if she had died, he would have spent several years in jail on a manslaughter charge, leaving five kids to foster care or adoption.

At this time in Dad's life, he was too far into the alcohol binging stage to stop, and after a few weeks, he was back at it again. This time, he hit Mom so hard in her left eye that she thought she was going to lose her sight. It's a wonder he didn't kill her, or at least break the eye socket. I cannot recall ever having seen such a horrible-looking eye. The entire left side of her face was horribly swollen. It was so swollen, it took over a week for the swelling to recede enough for her to see through the swollen slit. From the outside looking in, it was an awful thing to see. It was like looking at a bright red blood clot with a black spot where the iris was.

This time, Mom finally had enough. She was fed up with the verbal and physical abuse. When we kids were at school, and Dad was passed out, she walked into the police station in Myrtle Creek and filed charges; Dad was arrested for domestic violence and abuse. For the second time in our stay on the hill, he was hauled off to the Douglas County Jail at Roseburg. Again, peace reigned. By now, it was late spring of 1958. I was just about to graduate from the eighth grade, and Mom was about to move off the hillside for the last time. This last move occurred when I was away from home picking berries and cherries with the Gallios family in the Sandy and The Dalles, Oregon areas, which I write about in the next chapter.

Soon after Dad's final incarceration, Mom moved us from the shack into a comfortable rental in Myrtle Creek across from the Golden Rule. She had Uncle Glen Thackery move Dad's '48 Ford into a single car garage detached from the rental. Rent, utilities, and a food stipend were provided by welfare. Mom took in ironing to help pay for other incidentals. Shortly after Dad's release from jail, he visited Mom, but she did not want anything to do with him. He took the car and left.

Dad had to live somewhere, and so he worked for Bill Blackard as a ranch hand for a few months, living in an old shack on Bill's ranch off Dole Road (on the same ranch Dad had logged in '52). I think that job lasted only as long as Dad was sober. I believe he lost the job because he couldn't stay away from the bottle. I assume this was the case, as I had little opportunity to see Dad during their separation.

Mom and Dad never divorced. Though not divorced, she dated a time or two, and at one time was seriously contemplating marriage to a fellow who was showing her some attention and affection. She sat us kids down and told us she was thinking about divorcing Dad and marrying this bum, but I could see the handwriting on the wall. He, too, was an alcoholic, and I told her that. A short time later, the guy quit showing up, and as far as I know, Mom never had any more "gentleman" friends.

Now, it seems to me that Mom was no different than many abused women whose abusers exert a mental hold on their victims. I am not an expert in any sense, but certainly by experience and observation have gained a right to an opinion. Abuse can be physical or verbal, but, regardless the type, the abuse extracts a horrendous toll on the psyche of the victim and any kids who witness it. Abusers put the blame on the abused.

Interestingly, in the mind of the abuser, the object of his/her abuse is the one who is to blame for all the problems of the abuser. If the abused were just a better person; if the abused just understood what the abuser was going through; if the abused would just do a little bit more in this area, or that area, then all would be right and the abuse would stop. The one on the receiving end of the violence attempts to placate the abuser in all the named areas. Regardless the effort of the abused to measure up to the standards of the abuser, the abused cannot win, nor can they change the abuser. Love doesn't work. Nothing works.

Like I mentioned earlier, I do not know what goes on inside an abuser's mind that causes them to act as they do. I just know that the abused can never win. No matter what they do to placate, or even tiptoe around certain subjects or decorum, when the abuser reaches a certain point, self-control is lost and they give in to a violent side of their nature.

Abusers come from all levels and backgrounds; some are simpleminded and foolish; others educated, erudite, articulate; from poverty to wealth, religious and secular; they all seem to have the same psychological hold on those they abuse. No matter how often the abused may "step out of the relationship, the abused seemed to be pulled back over and over again. Now, please do not misunderstand me. I know that women and even children can be abusers, but in my case, I focus on the male abuser. Strange, when one thinks about it, and it seems so obvious to those looking in from the outside, but it seems the abuser and the abused can't do without the other. They seem to have a symbiotic relationship; each feeding some innate, inward need in the other that can't be identified, and yet is somehow nourished in the relationship.

During Dad's and Mom's lengthy separation, I bumped into Dad on Dole Road one afternoon. I had walked from town to the old shack to look around. I had not seen Dad since he was released from jail. After stepping onto the road off a shortcut trail I used through the brush, there was the black '48 Ford. It was parked on a wide spot on the right shoulder of Dole Road.

Dad had passed out in the driver's seat. He wasn't too passed out, 'cause my shoes grating on the gravel as I stepped close for a look must have awakened him. I had initially thought he was dead. He was really toasted. Barely able to talk, he told me to get into the passenger seat and why I did I don't know, but I complied. I should have run, but he was Dad, and I was programmed to obey. As soon as I slid into the passenger seat and closed the door, I knew, with no shadow of doubt, I had to get back out of that car. He wasn't rational. He was drunkenly insane. He was dangerous. Reasoning with him was out of the question. Fear began to constrict my throat and paralyze my frame, even though I desperately needed to run.

He cursed at everything in general. He was so drunk, he wobbled and weaved as he sat behind the wheel, his eyes red with alcohol and fury. Spittle spewed onto the dash as he cursed the world and everything in it he could blame for problems real and imagined. Nothing would appease him or make any difference in his attitude. I then realized the fear that Mom must have experienced just before that first blow, and I did not want to be in that car another minute, nor did I want to be riding with him when he got it started. As he attempted to find and press the starter button with a stabbing thumb, I overcame my paralysis, opened the door, and bolted across a grassy area into the thick brush off the side of the road.

"Come back here you little son-of-a-blinkety-blank," I heard Dad slur. "I'll kill you, you little expletive deleted, ad infinitum, deleted." I knew he was drunkenly insane, as Dad never used those terms directed at me. He probably thought I was Mom. Who knows? I didn't care what he was thinking or why he was calling me names, 'cause he'd never catch me on that hillside. In the receding distance, I heard the car start, and with the engine racing and gravel thrown from spinning wheels, Dad raced up the road into town. It was almost a year before I saw Dad again.

I knew little about alcoholism then. One thing I know now is that when that absolute lowest point is reached, a decision for survival must be made. The alcoholic either continues the course of death, or in a sober mood, decides that if they don't change, they will die. Dad must have reached that low point. He made the right decision.

I learned from my cousin, Ben (Arch's boy) that some time after this incident, Dad showed up at their home in Roseburg. Uncle Arch's home was on a hill on the southeast side of Roseburg at the far end of a gravel lane, high on a hilltop. I learned in conversations over the ensuring years with Ben that Arch, too, was an alcoholic and like Dad, in his drunken stupors, Arch was also an abuser. But that's a story Ben will have to tell.

Somehow, Dad got admitted to the Veteran's Hospital in Roseburg following our incident on Dole Road to detox, and for more stomach surgery (ulcers). Ben told me that Dad was in bad shape when he showed up at his home. He was emaciated and looking like death warmed over. To Arch's credit, he took Dad in. He lived with Arch and his family for some weeks, slowly recovering and gaining strength. Dad began seeing Mom again, and she decided to take him back. Some eighteen months had passed in their separation, and though we were all somewhat uncomfortable with one another at first, we settled into living in Myrtle Creek as a family once again, but now in the Cornutt rental right at the intersection where Dole Road meets US Highway 99 at the North End of Myrtle Creek. I think money played a role in Mom and Dad reconciling once again. But then again, I like to think he also missed his kids. Dad, indeed, seemed to have changed. We started studying at home with Jehovah's Witnesses, again, until there was disagreement over doctrinal issues. Dad had them leave. Dad also listened to Herbert W. Armstrong (Radio Church of God) and even sent for the group's magazine, *The Plain Truth*. This magazine and the organization behind it would play a major role in my life beginning in the mid-sixties. But that's a story in itself that needs to be told in another book.

This was the status of the family through my junior year in high school, after which Dad loaded the family into the '57 Studebaker pickup, and we headed for a strawberry pickers' camp in Estacada, Oregon, and later the bean pickers' camp in Stayton, Oregon.

We only returned to Myrtle Creek in the fall of 1961 for our household furnishings as, after the conclusion of the pole bean season, we had rented a home and settled in North Plains, Oregon. I was to finish my senior year at Hillsboro Union High School. But now, what about those strawberry and bean picker camps?

Fruit-Picker

As much as it is distasteful to admit, experience as a fruit-picker helped form commendable habits in me. I say this with a note of negativity because at the time I was engaged in such work, I did not necessarily view it with a great deal of pride. There was always a sort of sour taste on my tongue when using the term "fruit-picker." In retrospect, many wonderful lessons were learned in that form of labor that served me well in my varied careers.

I mentioned in one of the earlier chapters that from about six years of age, the Oliver family would pick produce in the Myrtle Creek area. Blue Lake pole beans in the late summer, and as the season progressed, we'd pick prunes, then English walnuts, and occasionally filberts. While such "pick'ns" could easily be available to anyone who had the need and the will to work in the local area (the Olivers certainly had the need and the will), my "professional" fruit-picking career kicked into high gear in Estacada, Oregon, in the early summer of 1955.

I learned later that Mom and Dad had planned this initial sojourn some weeks in advance. Mom responded, via mail, to an ad in the *Oregon Journal* for strawberry pickers in the Estacada area. One pre-dawn morning, a car struggled up the steep driveway off Dole Road. After brief introductions, Mom and Dad began packing blankets, clothes, cooking gear, and food into the car parked by the front door with the motor running and the lights on. Within a short while, Mom and all five kids were in the car driving north on Highway 99 with a stranger. Shoot, as far as I knew we were heading for Mars. Dad stayed home. He had been hired for the summer to help a man on a small horse logging operation.

The "stranger" was Bill Randle, the owner of several strawberry fields east of Estacada with some small cabins in which the pickers could live during the berry-picking season. Obviously, Mom had written the Randalls to make arrangements for Bill to drive to Myrtle Creek and pick up a family of "berry pickers." Back in the fifties, the north Williamette Valley and its west and east foothills comprised ideal berry-growing environments. Strawberry fields were everywhere, and there usually were not enough pickers to go around. Few were the regulations limiting who could pick and the age of pickers. Growers would buy a worn out school bus and then way before dawn, drive miles into the surrounding cities and towns to pick up a load of school-age kids and some moms, haul them to the berry fields, and then drop them off back at home at the end of the day. Bill must have desperately needed pickers. He had driven over two hundred miles to pick up a woman and five kids, the oldest kid only in the eighth grade, and the youngest not yet in school.

So here we were, six hours later, driving through Molalla, past the tavern on Main Street with its marquee of a rearing stallion attached to the outside wall over the door, then another twenty miles northeast, through Estacada. The Randall farm and its berry camp lay in the rolling south west foothills of Mount Hood, about ten miles east of Estacada and on the south side of Eagle Creek. The land was a patchwork of open pastures, berry fields, logged over areas, and second-growth timber.

The "berry camp" was a hundred yards or so from the Randall home. The camp consisted of a dozen or so single-room cabins encircling a common area that contained a water pipe with a single faucet. At the edge of the "compound" were "his" and "her" outhouses. That was it. This was home for over four weeks.

At least the cabins had a wooden floor. They were the size of a medium-sized bedroom, maybe twelve feet by twelve feet.

Each contained a wood-burning cook stove, a small eating table, a couple of chairs, a single bare light bulb hanging from the ceiling, and a double-bed bunk bed. There were no mattresses, just straw. Some would think this an austere description of a type of prison or concentration camp. To me it looked fine. We unpacked and Mom quickly had the place in tip-top shape. Boy, she could make do.

My seasoned training as woodcutter was quickly applied attacking a huge pile of "pond lilies" off to the side of camp. I soon had several armloads of split wood and kindling placed neatly behind the stove. Mom soon had a fire going in the cook stove to take the dampness out of the place, and we made our beds. She placed a blanket over the straw in the bunk beds, followed by sheets and blankets, and with pillows in place, beds were made for her and the girls. A bed was made for me against one wall of the cabin using a small "tick" mattress we had brought from home. This was our home during our first berry-picking season, which lasted into early July.

The Randalls were extremely kind. They treated their pickers with respect, and as needed, when hauling the berries into Estacada at the end of the workday, they would inquire if any adults needed to go in for groceries or other necessities. When space was available, pickers would hitch a ride on the berry truck when it made its daily delivery to the drop-off station. The driver would drop the pickers off at the grocery store in Estacada and pick them up on the way back with its load of empty berry crates for use in the next day's picking. Some pickers had their own transportation, and when able, would also ferry those who had no transportation back and forth to town.

The mornings were chilly the first couple of weeks, the fields heavy with dew, and the strawberries cold. Oft times, we'd be picking in the gentle rains of the late Oregon spring. We began picking before sun up and picked well into the afternoon on most days, breaking for about an hour in which we would hike from the fields back to the cabin for lunch.

Because I was allowed to keep what I earned, except for a small stipend I paid Mom for "room and board", I continued my education regarding the value of a dollar. The more I concentrated on picking, and the longer I stayed on the job, the more berries I picked. The more berries I picked, the more money I made.

What a simple formula, I thought.

This type of "piece-work" taught me the value of a hard day's work and value of the money it produced. Even as an eleven-year-old, I could pick as well as most adults. I was earning five to eight bucks a day, averaging probably 120 to 150 pounds of berries; on several days, over 200 pounds. I could usually out-pick Mom, and she was one of the better pickers.

Work consisted of grabbing a couple carriers in which you placed six hallicks. A hallick was about 5 inches square and two-inches deep and held about two hundred pounds of berries. No. It just seemed that way toward the end of the day. A hallick held a pound, or a pound and a half of berries. You'd claim the next unpicked row adjacent to the last claimed row, trek to the starting point, and begin picking according to how the "straw boss" (usually the owner, the owner's wife, or an inexperienced picker they hired for this purpose) wanted the berries picked. Of course, they only wanted ripe berries. No rotten or green ones, but what the hey, the occasional rejects were easily covered by berries that met picking specifications. Besides, it took time to pick the bad ones. Why waste the effort? First, we'd fill our stomachs, then fill the hallicks, rounding out the berries on top with fat, ripe, juicy ones; and by the time the carrier was full, you'd have ten or twelve pounds of berries in it. You'd fill one carrier in this manner then a second one. When full, you'd haul the full carriers to the "weigh station." There, another waged employee would weigh the carriers (deducting the weight of the carrier), punch your ticket to indicate the number of pounds, and you'd repeat the process, over and over again.

Some growers had you transfer the berries from the carriers into crates before they were weighed. A crate had space for twelve hallicks, or double what a carrier held, but with two carriers heaped up, you had about a crate and a half of berries. The owners, or other hired help, would stack the full crates onto a flat bed truck. At the end of the day, a driver would haul the berries to a collection dock, and from there, load them onto a larger truck for hauling to the collection point in town, or directly to the cannery. One thing I remember is it was one heck of a lot of backbreaking work.

So this cycle was repeated. Pick the patch, move to another patch, let the picked patch ripen, and then in a few days go back over it again, over and over again for four to five weeks until the plants stopped producing.

In the morning hours, with the vines wet with dew or rain, the lower half of your body was wet and cold. Your hands would ache from the wetness and the chill, and you couldn't wait for the sun to break over the top of the firs (when it wasn't rainy or cloudy) and slowly dry the vines.

Your hands were stained of course. You could always tell who was "in the berry pick'n business," no matter where people were gathered—whether at the grocery store, the movie house, or the swimming hole. Just look at the hands.

As we picked through June and into early July (usually the season was over by the first week in July), we all sported good tans, especially on the back of our neck and hands. Most pickers also sported a sort of "bent at the middle look" from all the stooping during the picking season, but all quickly recovered.

As the season progressed, one got used to the back pain, and the knees toughened up. It seemed to rain in the early days of the season, not only making things miserable for all, but causing the berries to have rotten spots, which you'd have to watch for, and if not too large, punch out with a thumbnail. If they were too rotten, we were supposed to throw them away, but there was more than one large reject that would somehow find its way under good berries. Shoot, like I said earlier, the effort was made, and the berry was picked. Why waste it?

Gosh, were some of those berries large. Delicious, too! There were two types of strawberries widely planted at that time, Northwests and Marshalls. These were the ones I remember. While they were especially good to eat, and grew to incredible size in the lower elevations of the Cascade and Coast Range foothills, they spoiled quickly. Of course, genetic engineering has pretty much solved this problem, but what we gain in preservation, we lose in taste and texture. Man, I miss the taste of those early varieties.

One of the perks we pickers had was that the owners allowed us to take as many berries to camp for shortcake and eating as our hearts desired. I could never get enough of those berries, whether eaten fresh in the field or cut up and sweetened with sugar and spooned from a bowl, over fresh-baked shortcake or hot pancakes.

We worked the Randall farm during four picking seasons stretched over a period of seven years. In the second season we picked, the Randall's put us up in an old farmhouse rather than a picker cabin. I think they thought they were doing us a favor, but the house was drafty and cold. It rained a lot that year. All the pickers had colds and runny noses. About mid-season, I became quite ill. It started as a sore throat that didn't get better. After several days, I had a difficult time swallowing, with the pain so intense in attempts to swallow even hot soup; the liquid would be ejected out my nose as my throat reacted to the pain. I seemed to be carrying a low-grade fever, too. Eventually, I became too sick to work and just stayed in the house the last week or so. Interestingly, Mom didn't seem to think anything was too out of the ordinary and never took me to a doctor to get a diagnosis and treatment—just a sore throat. Little did she know that I had an abscessed tonsil.

Dad set her straight when he arrived at the end of the season to take us back home. I was still too weak to do much talking, as my throat ached to even talk. It was like I had lockjaw. I could barely open my mouth. Dad sensed it might be serious after he learned from Mom that I had been sick for some time. He asked me some questions and without hardly any hesitation said that as soon as we got back home, I was going to the doctor. He told Mom that he suspected I had Quinsy, which was the formal name for an abscessed tonsil.

Dad had several bouts with the problem as a young man prior to marrying Mom. His experience may have saved my life. Generally, when we kids got sick, the folks applied home-remedies and let our young bodies fight it off. My body wasn't fighting this one off. What makes Quinsy so dangerous is the potential for the putrefied pus sac on the tonsil to break inward into the muscles of the neck, and thus pollute the blood stream. In such cases, a person could quickly die from blood poisoning. Treatment could be lancing, and/or antibiotics, such as Penicillin. Doctor Faber prescribed Penicillin, and within a day or two, the swelling was going down, and I was beginning to feel better. With such simple treatment, I quickly was a good as new.

....

My body's proclivity for the illness is probably hereditary. Later, as an adult, I would suffer three additional bouts with the illness. The second time, I was in the Air Force stationed at Minot Air Force Base, North Dakota. Again, by the time the Air Force dispensary doctors had properly diagnosed what I had, I had lost almost fifteen pounds. None of the younger doctors seemed to be at all concerned about the cause behind my inability to eat. They'd prescribe some large horse pill for my "strep throat" and send me home with orders for a day of bed rest, then back to work on the flight line, but usually with no improvement. Finally, on my third trip or so to the dispensary, I received a diagnosis by an older, experienced physician.

He was a gray-haired "Full Bird" Colonel who, upon prying open my mouth and taking a look inside exclaimed, "Oh my god, you've got Quinsy." He began ranting and raving for all to hear asking who it was who had been treating me, and "Don't you idiots know that this airman could have died from this?" *Boy, that sure makes me feel a lot better,* I said to myself. He immediately came at me with a very large "aspirator," a long suction-type syringe with a hollow needle about the size of a pencil (the needle looked that big to me).

Okay, Doc, I thought. *The disease hasn't killed me, so what's with the weapon? Are you going to speed up the dying process?*

He was in a hurry and didn't use any painkiller, and as quick as I can write this, he had penetrated the boil on my tonsil to remove one full syringe of bloody-white pussy goo. He got the remainder in a second syringe.

The pressure was immediately relieved. I was feeling much better. He gave me some oral antibiotics with orders to see him personally in two days. It was a good thing, too, as my throat begun to swell shut again. But this time, he admitted me to the Veteran's hospital in Minot for intense antibiotic treatment and a couple more treatments with the syringe torture. I was released on the fourth day.

....

In the late '50s, we moved our "summer work program" to the Schumacher berry and pole bean farm west of Stayton. There, we could pick strawberries, rest a week or so, and then be paid to "string" the bean fields. Bush beans would be at the picking stage, and we would hire out to pick them, racing the bush bean combines that were just then being marketed and used to replace human pickers. By late July, the Blue Lake pole beans would be ready for picking. So in short, the family had pretty much full-time employment through the summer without having to move from camp to camp.

The Schumacher farm was located in the flat, fertile, sandy loam fields of the North Santiam River, east of Interstate 5, about midway between Stayton and Jefferson. It didn't make any difference who one picked for, the work was the same. It was hard, backbreaking work; but even so, when I worked, I did not waste time. I was extremely serious about earning money because now I was heading for my mid-teens, and cars were on my mind big-time—and girls, but mostly cars.

Summers in the Schumacher "bean camp" were idyllic in many ways. It was the best time of the year to be a teen in Oregon. The rainy season was past, the skies were blue, the clouds fluffy and white, and the weather sometimes comfortably warm, but mostly uncomfortably hot. For the summers, Dad would stave off the alcohol demon. Oh, he'd have a beer on occasion, but never to excess. He seemed to have his drinking under control. Again, we were around people, and Dad knew there was certain behavior that was frowned upon...drunken rages...wife beating, that sort of thing.

Many of the camps in the mid- to late-'50s were probably still much like the fruit camps of the Okies and Arkies in the thirties. Small shacks were thrown up by the farmers around a common water spigot, with men's and women's outhouses on the periphery of the camp, and a woodpile to supply fuel for the wood ranges inside each cabin.

Boy, how those outhouses would stink in the hot August afternoons. I became quite good at holding my breath. I could get the job done in no more than three breaths, hopefully without swallowing a fly during my quick inhalations.

There were no laundry facilities. Some of the women did their laundry on scrub boards, heating wash water on their stoves and washing clothes by hand in camp, just like we did at home. Others would use the laundromat in town.

Neither were there bathing facilities in those early camps. We did our bathing in the river. We must have stunk rather badly at times, but because all smelled the same (bad), who was to notice?

The state eventually stepped in, and in the late fifties began passing legislation that forced the growers to make major improvements to their camps. By the time my "fruit-picking" tenure was ending (the summer of 1961), the growers had provided shower facilities, although they never did get rid of the outhouses.

It wasn't all work. Some afternoons would be too hot for any activity, other than trips to town or swimming. Usually picking would end, and quickly we'd wash off the deep stains, change into clean clothes, and head for town for groceries and incidentals, soda pop, candy, or ice cream, then back to camp for swimming. At Shumacher's, the North Fork of the Santiam was only a short walk past the fields. The water was cool, clear, and refreshing. There were times along the banks when several families would "pool" the hotdogs, marshmallows, watermelon, whatever, and we'd spend the heat of the late afternoon alternating between the shade and the water.

In the summer of 1961, we had taken our latest dog, Penny, with us. She was half Pomeranian and half Cocker Spaniel. Though small, she had a great love for water and would join us as we swam in the cool deep pools along the sandy banks of the Santiam. She also loved to fetch. She especially loved chasing rocks. Now what in the world was this rock fetish she had?

One afternoon, I was lying on the sand, plunking hardball-sized rocks into the water when the dog ran and leaped into the water. She swam to the point where the rock had disappeared and dove! That's right. She ducked her head under water, elevated her back feet, and headed for the bottom! She came up with a rock in her mouth. The water was only three or four feet deep at that point, but her little exhibition drew the attention of all who witnessed her feat. She would dive three or four times, grow tired, rest, then want to go at it again. Animals can be so entertaining.

And there were movies. Stayton had a community movie theater (this was before the days of the megaplex theaters), and a number of families would head to the movies if we weren't working the next day. You couldn't do this if you were picking the next morning, as you had to get up too early. So movie going was usually saved for those evenings when you didn't have to work the next day.

The theater not only ran current releases, but a genre of films that appealed to those working the bean fields, especially the older pickers. Such were especially drawn to movies like *Thunder Road*, *Tobacco Road*, *Of Mice and Men*, and *Grapes of Wrath*. I can understand the appeal they had for those who experienced the situations and circumstances depicted in these stories. While I would pay the ticket price and sit in the theater and view these movies, I found them depressing and hopeless. Like most of the pickers in the camp, I went to these same movies, year after year, especially Robert Mitchum in *Thunder Road*.

In retrospect, even as difficult as that lifestyle was, I see my time as a fruit picker being very special. We were involved at the tail-end of a transitory way of life that in the grand scheme of things, occupied but a short period of time (about thirty years); short even for the time-span of this great nation.

Some families that I knew in the fifties and early sixties seemed to be trapped in that lifestyle. Today, some members of those families might disagree with my choice of the word "trapped." They may be right, as I know that many of the second and even third generations that I worked, shivered, and sweated with in the strawberry and bean fields, were there by choice. There was a certain freedom they had in the lifestyle. Those who chose it didn't make a lot of demands on life, nor did they require much to get by. Their lives were simple, and they liked it that way.

I look upon that time and work with no regret or anger, but like I wrote earlier, there was a lingering embarrassment associated with it, probably because I felt that only those who could not hold full-time jobs would relegate themselves to the fruit-picker lifestyle. But, it provided necessary experiences and relationships that helped form and shape me. Many of the relationships I formed then are still a part of who I am today. Two of my sisters married sons of fruit-picker families. One is still married to the husband of her youth that she met in the Shumacher fruit camp in Stayton, Oregon. Another sister met and married the son of a fruit-picker, but that relationship has been long severed. Yet, all of us, sisters, husbands, nieces, and nephews, share this part of American history in our family tree.

The period of time we were on "the hill" spanned most of nine years, from the winter prior to my first grade until I graduated from the eighth grade. As I mentioned earlier, Dad's drinking precluded him from holding a steady job, therefore, as a family, we worked at whatever we could to make ends meet and to simply survive from day-to-day and from year-to-year.

Ironically, our stay on the hill ended at the time I introduced another family to this honest (but not prosperous) form of making a living.

During my seventh year, I had made friends with the Gallios twins, Harold and Howard. By the eighth grade, this relationship had become well established. I liked their dad and mom, too, and got along well with the entire family for that matter, eating in their home and spending the night with the boys on numerous occasions. They knew a little bit about my family history, but it never affected our friendship.

George was a millwright, and just prior to my eighth grade graduation, the twins informed me that their dad had been laid off from the sawmill in Dillard. Though the layoff was temporary, he was unemployed. Rather than just sit around and wait, George and his wife, Ada, decided to take the family berry picking at one of the camps in the Gresham/Sandy area and wanted to know if I'd come along to show them the ropes. Would I! But we needed Mom's permission. Dad was in jail following the beating where Mom had received the horrible black eye. Mom was yet to move us from the shack for the final time. George drove me home and asked Mom's permission to allow me to accompany them. She agreed. That was the last night I would spend in that house, for during my three-week absence, Mom moved off the hill, for good, into a house in Myrtle Creek.

The Gallioses and I had a great time. If my memory is correct, they had no idea where to go or how to go about landing a berry-picking job. I told them that if a farmer needed pickers, he'd have a sign out along the road by his farm or patch with the writing "Pickers Wanted." So we drove up Interstate 5 to the Portland Area, took a right at Oregon City, drove through Damascus and then on out toward Sandy. Sure enough, in no time we landed a job, somewhere in the Cascade foothills around Sandy.

George was quite a "do-it-your-selfer" and had built a small two-wheel camping trailer in which all the camping gear, cooking utensils, food, clothing, and miscellaneous stuff a person and family needed for a few weeks of camping was stored in special niches and cubicles. Everything seemed to have a designated space. So, while a picker's cabin was nice (and the farmer had one that he let George, Ada, and Carol, their daughter use), we boys "camped" in a tent.

Berry picking lasted about a week and a half. George decided that he didn't like picking strawberries. He didn't like the stooping; it hurt his back. So he packed us all up, hitched the camp trailer to the '52 Pontiac, and away we went to The Dalles for cherry picking. No cabins this time. We camped in the orchard, putting the features of the camp trailer to good use.

This orchard was on the crest of the bluff southwest of The Dalles, overlooking the city and The Dalles Dam.

We camped under the trees in the orchard. No commute was required in the morning or the evening. Eat all the cherries you wanted (and I wanted a lot), rest and eat lunch at noon, pick some more before it got too hot, then slack off for the rest of the day.

After a week or so, George made a call to the mill at Dillard. The mill had started again, and they wanted their millwright back. So we packed up all the gear, their dog Corky, the four Gallioses, kids and me. Away we went, this time heading south toward Bend on US 95. That's when I learned what a "vapor lock" was.

It seemed the carburetor on the Pontiac (which had a straight 8 in her) had a particularly annoying characteristic. When the engine got too warm it developed a pocket of "vapor" in the fuel line, and the fuel pump could not pump fuel into the carburetor. On the first hill out of The Dalles, just before we reached the top, the Pontiac quit running. There was nothing to do but open the hood and wait for the engine to cool down. Every few minutes, George would attempt to start the engine. On the final attempt, it started (otherwise we would still be there). That's the only time on the trip back home that we had one of those experiences. That taught me that I never wanted a vehicle that had a vapor lock problem.

I was in for a surprise when we pulled up to the shack. It was empty! No note anywhere. Nothing. Where were Mom and my sisters? They obviously had moved, and so I spent one more night with the Gallioses, helping them unpack the camp trailer. The next day I borrowed one of the boy's bikes and pedaled into town to find where Mom had hid herself.

Hmm, maybe she's trying to lose me, I thought.

The best place for news was Aunt Helen, Mom's sister. She knew. Mom had moved into a nice little three-bedroom a block off Main Street across from the Golden Rule department store.

So there I was, living in a real house, not a converted chicken coop either; but a house with electricity, running water, and an inside bathroom. She had obtained welfare assistance, some discarded but functional furniture; and finally, we were living like normal people.

It was at this time that I got my first newspaper delivery route delivering newspapers into the hilliest part of town. I still had my old beater RV bike that had been given to me by my third grade teacher, Mrs. Yokum, and so there I was, getting up at four-thirty every morning to make about seventy-five cents a day delivering forty or so newspapers; first uphill, then downhill, up another hill and down, until done; back to bed for another hour of sleep, up for school, and repeat it all the next day; seven days a week. This job proved that strawberry picking wasn't so bad after all. There were lessons I had to learn, and so I did.

I worked to buy my own clothes and other personal "stuff." Though Mom was being supported by welfare to pay rent, utilities, and food, there was little money for personal needs. Mom took in ironing to bring in a few dollars, and so we existed from month-to-month. This was how we lived through my freshman year. Even so, this was heaven compared to the old tarpaper shack on the hillside.

My second to last stint in the fruit-picking business was quite unusual, and it involved Harold Gallios in the late summer prior to my sophomore year. It had been at least a year since we'd seen Dad. Mom was dating on occasion, struggling to decide whether to divorce or not, eventually deciding not to. By this time, Mom had moved us again, into an older two-story home behind the *Myrtle Creek Tribune* print shop.

Now you have to understand how independent a lot of teens were back in the fifties. Harold and I were no exceptions. The Gallioses had some friends living in the Medford area, and for some reason Harold wouldn't let go of the idea that we should go down to Medford and pick pears. Harold was past his sixteenth birthday, had his driver's license, and wanted money for a car. His folks gave in. Now I had to get Mom to knuckle under. Mom was no match for my persistence, and so Harold and I got our way. Problem was, we had to make our own way to Medford.

The parents said, "If you're going to do it, you're going to be responsible for getting down there yourselves." We did; talk about independence. I guess we were simply flexing our wings, not quite ready to leave the nest, but close.

We each had a sleeping bag and some extra clothing and incidentals we carried in some surplus World War II army backpacks. George drove us out to the interstate and dropped us off at the US Highway 99 bridge junction to I-5. We hitchhiked the hundred or so miles to Medford, first riding in a logging truck that got us as far as Canyonville, ten miles. That wasn't too bad. Didn't take a whole lot of time; so far, so good. The driver, a young man in his twenties, was working hard to impress us as he shifted up through fifteen or so gears to reach cruisin' speed. It didn't impress either one of us much. It took him almost five miles to run through all the gears. He did the same thing shifting down when he dropped us off in Canyonville.

Our next ride was in a laundry delivery van with a driver who had some sort of problem with his right foot. He'd speed up to sixty, take his foot completely off the throttle, coast down to forty-five, then stomp on the throttle, building speed back up to sixty. This cycle went on until we reached Grants Pass. Over halfway there, and it was only mid-morning. By that time, I had a headache and wanted to throw up. I can't remember how we got to Medford after that ride; I can only remember walking real fast, then real slow as we made our way along the highway with our thumbs out looking for our next ride. The good news was that we only needed one more Good Samaritan to reach Medford.

The driver dropped us off on the north side of town. It was early afternoon and very hot. We located a market and bought some snacks and soft drinks. Harold had no exact address that we could use to direct us to these so-called friends of the Gallios family. He had some vague recollection that they lived around White City. That was north of where we were by several miles, and we had no idea what road it was on. We knew north, so we walked. It was early August and hot as all get out. So there we were, two teenagers over one hundred miles from home, attempting to locate some friends that Harold vaguely remembered lived somewhere north of town.

We walked, and we walked; then we walked some more. You know, at our new gait, first fast, and then slow, thanks to the laundry van driver. Harold and I had paused in our trek for a breather.

We were stupidly staring out over a weedy sort of pasture, each of us lost in our own thoughts. I think I fell asleep on my feet. Harold was sufficiently awake to notice a fluffy black and white tail weaving and bobbing through the weeds and tall grass on a trajectory toward us.

"What the heck's that?" he muttered.

"What the heck's what?" I repeated.

He pointed. We stood still, neither of us saying a word, as this apparition of a tail seemed to be closing in on where we were standing, right over a small culvert that went from one side of the road to the other. It soon became apparent that we were watching a momma skunk, a momma skunk that didn't seem to notice us when she broke out into the open a few feet in front of us. Momma skunk had her mind made up. She knew where she was going, and she disappeared under our feet into the culvert, over which we were standing. She was followed by three little baby skunks; just as the last baby skunk was about to disappear into the culvert under Harold's feet, he reached down and grabbed the little bugger by the tail and lifted it up to dangle in front of him.

I thought he must have a touch of heat stroke as he just held that little skunk right there in front of his face. It was the cutest thing, just hanging there kind of upside down with the softest set of brown eyes you ever hoped to see. Harold explains.

"Mom said she would like to have a pet skunk."

He then attempted to explain as he continued to hold the skunk by the tail.

"I also read somewhere that if you hold them by the tail, they can't spray."

My response was, "What're you going to do, hold his tail 'til it dies?"

That had to be the calmest wild critter either of us ever encountered. We decided that the only place of safekeeping was Harold's sleeping bag cover. At least it had a drawstring on it. That baby skunk let us put him in that bag, and he curled up in the bottom. Sufficiently rejuvenated by our skunk-capturing caper, off we went again.

There we were; two "homeless" kids, with a baby skunk in a sleeping bag cover, walking down a country road in southern Oregon, with our backpacks and sleeping bags under our arms. I didn't walk too close to Harold. I kept wondering when the little tyke was going to let loose with a good one. Eventually, we worked up the courage to check on our new travel companion. We set the bag down, carefully loosened the drawstring, and peeked in. You know, kind of at arm's length expecting to get sprayed in the process. But no, the little bugger was asleep in the bottom of the bag. Not even our jostling to open the bag had awakened him. So we carefully closed the opening with the drawstring and continued our walk.

We finally (accidentally, not by any intelligence exhibited thus far), worked our way into Central Point. Thirsty, we bummed some water from a woman hand-watering her front yard from a garden hose. By now, the sun was down, and we still had no idea where those friends were. Passing Central Point High School, we decided the football field would be as good a place as any to "camp" for the night. So we did. Ah, freedom.

Like I said, that skunk was the tamest little wild critter. Prior to spreading out our sleeping bags, Harold untied the drawstring on the sleeping bag cover and placed the bag on the ground. That cute little bugger slowly crawled out of the bag and just stood there, looking up at us with those soft brown eyes. We were able to hold the skunk in our hands and pet him just like one would a kitten. It had no desire to run, bite, or spray. Maybe it didn't have spray glands yet. What did we know about skunks, anyway? We played with it for a while, then tired, located some scraps of wood, and made a sort of box for it. We found a tin can and gave it some water from a handy spigot, then retired for the night on the green, freshly cut, Central Point High School football field. It just seemed to be a most natural place to spend the night. Good thing it wasn't scheduled for irrigation, or we'd have gotten a rude awakening.

The next morning, we knew we had to get serious about locating these "friends" who didn't even know we were coming. Neither of us wanted to hitchhike back to Myrtle Creek with the sob story that we couldn't locate them. So we hid our new pet in a more secure makeshift cage, leaving it plenty of water and a little bit of a candy bar. Maybe we left it a piece of a Twinkie, too. We planned to return for our new pet after we found who we were looking for, or gave up trying.

We traveled east and finally found the state road that lead to White City, which was still north of us. We hitched a ride, and it wasn't too long before Harold began to recognize landmarks. In an hour or so, we located the house. Wahoo!

The lady was home (I can't remember her name) with a boy and a mean little girl, both under ten. Imagine her consternation, and maybe unbelief, after Harold told her who he was and why we were there, two boys in their mid-teens on her doorstep. The lady didn't quite know what to make of the situation, telling us she would have to speak with her husband about us staying with them. Well, I should hope so. It's a wonder she didn't slam the door in our face and call the cops. We had told them we would pay some room and board. Maybe it was the fact we brought big bucks that won them over to our cause.

Miracles happen. They let us stay. The next day, we determined to land us a pear-picking job. The season was not quite ready. The good news was that there were several orchards within walking distance of the house. Within a few hours, we landed a job but still had to wait several days for picking to start.

The day we got to the house, Harold told the lady we needed to go back to Central Point to get his mom's skunk. Sheese! Even before a decision had been made to let us stay, we were making demands on her time. Harold had to explain that the skunk seemed to be relatively tame, and hadn't sprayed us, and had the softest brown eyes, and it was a gift for his mother. She was nice enough to do it. I remember the car she drove. It was a late '40s Henry J, a small car with a four-cylinder engine. It barely held us all; herself, two kids, Harold and me, and eventually the skunk. The skunk kitty was fine except a little thirsty and hungry. After we got back to the house in the White City area, she let us put the skunk in a rabbit hutch on the backside of the garage. We fed the little guy, and he was down right friendly until the little witch girl started poking it with sticks. She got what she deserved. He wasn't all that friendly to her, and when agitated, he let his instincts take over. She got a face full. We found out baby skunks do have baby odor glands.

We picked pears for about three weeks, each of us paying those good people a dollar a day room and board. Harold and I enjoyed the work. Days were hot in the Medford area in late summer, but we didn't seem to mind. We were making pretty good money, averaging around twelve bucks a day, liking that part real good.

We hadn't been picking much longer than a week when Harold had to get a car. "How else we gonna' get home," he quipped. And so, he located and purchased a '49 Dodge. Paid fifty dollars for it.

What in the world is it about boys and their first car? It doesn't seem to make any difference what kind of shape the car is in, what model it is, or how much one pays for it. The first thing a kid wants to do is see how fast it will go! Harold had a heavy foot and a rather brash way of treating this fine vehicle for one so new to the sport of "driving." The good news was that it was a relatively nice car. There was nothing wrong with it; that is, until Harold decided to give it its first "test."

Its transmission was one of those "fluid drives" that Chrysler came out with in the '40s, and it was sort of like an automatic, but then it really wasn't. Via experimentation, Harold determined he could downshift into first gear when going real fast, say, like fifty miles an hour. He decided to continue testing beyond the fifty mile-an-hour test. Wonders never cease. It passed the sixty-mile-an-hour test. It failed the seventy mile-and-hour test. Do you know what happens to a clutch plate in a '49 Dodge when you release the clutch pedal at seventy miles-an-hour with the transmission in first gear? You don't have a clutch any more. A shattering clutch plate makes a heck of a noise under one's feet, when it fails the "Down-Shift-Into-First-Gear-at-Seventy-Miles-an-Hour-Test. Otherwise known as "dsifgsmht."

Sitting in the car as the man of the house towed us home, Harold was testing several hair-brained excuses that would provide reasonable explanation as to why the clutch of a nice-running automobile would suddenly decide to self-destruct. He decided the best story was that the previous owner of the car sold him a lemon. He knew the clutch was going bad, and that's the reason he sold the car so cheap.

The fellow bought the story; yeah, right. Even so, we had to spend the next couple of nights swapping out the old clutch and pressure plate for the new clutch and pressure plate. So there we were, a hundred miles from home, rebuilding the clutch of that old Dodge. We did it, and we did it right. The only problem was that Harold wasn't too pleased in having to spend another thirty of his hard-earned dollars. In the meantime, my bank account was looking pretty good.

During this time, one of my cavity-ridden molars started to bother me. I had several teeth pulled prior to this time. I'm certain that preventative dental care, other than brushing our teeth occasionally with salt or baking soda, never occurred to Dad or Mom. When a tooth became rotten and abscessed, the cure was to simply have it pulled. Pulling this particular molar was not a simple, pain-free experience for me or the dentist. The tooth in question was cavity-ridden and literally cracked down the middle. The toothache it caused was one I call extreme. I asked the lady of the house if she'd drive me to the dentist, which she did. It was a tough extraction, as the roots had curved into my jawbone.

After four shots of Novocain, the dentist finally said, "Hang on, we've got to get 'er out." And he proceeded to do just that.

I almost passed out from pain, until, suddenly, the tooth let loose. Pliers, tooth, and dentist went flying across the room. During the extraction process, the dentist cut his thumb quite badly on a sharp edge of the tooth.

Good. He can suffer a little too, I thought. *Serves him right.*

My jaw was extremely sore for several days, so sore I could not open my mouth. All I could eat was soup sipped through a straw. But I didn't care. I could endure this. I was getting better day-by-day. Besides, I could still pick pears.

August was ending, and it was time to head back home and get ready for our sophomore years. Harold decided that the Dodge and he had to part ways. A four-door sedan with a flathead six-cylinder engine didn't fit the image he wanted when tooling around town. He sold the car for a slight profit. He called home, and his dad drove down in his brand-new 1958 Buick Special station wagon to pick us up. No more vapor lock problems for the Gallios family. The '52 Pontiac was history. We said our fond farewells to our new friends (which neither of us ever saw again), put the now fairly half-grown skunk in a small cage, and headed back to Myrtle Creek.

Harold's mother seemed genuinely pleased with her new pet, and the little fellow made himself right at home with their Siamese cat. The cat and skunk became good buddies and slept together in the same box beside their wood-heating stove. The skunk grew into an adult, and they never had it "fixed"; that is, until the "incident." On that day, the skunk was sleeping alone when the cat took a flying leap into the box, landing squarely on his back. When the Gallioses could get back in the house, they immediately took the skunk to the vet to have it "de-scented."

The skunk developed a mean streak over the next couple of years. It would suddenly, and without any seeming provocation, decide to take a bite out of the one who was handling it. It had developed a taste for Harold's fingers. They released it into the wild. I prefer house cats myself.

After getting back to Myrtle Creek from the pear-picking experience, I again had to locate Mom and my sis's. Imagine my frame of mind when I walked up to the front door, and it was locked. Not only locked, but there was no furniture in the house! Mom had moved again.

Sheese, I thought *This is the second time she's tried to lose me. I was beginning to wonder…*

The Good Dole

I had returned from the Oliver/Gallios pear picking sojourn to find Mom had moved once again; from our two-story home beside the *Myrtle Creek Tribune* print shop and office to the Cornutt rental. Dad had returned following his recuperation while living with his brother Arch, and during my absence, Mom had taken him back. This time, Dad didn't talk Mom into moving back to the shack. The Cornutt rental was definitely an improvement over the shack, even though it still had a wood-burning range and heater stoves. The good news, in this case, was that the range was used to heat water, and the house had an inside toilet and an old claw-foot bathtub. Wahoo; again, no outside facilities.

The hot water system was simple and efficient. One built a fire in the cooking range, and it heated the water using copper coils inside the firebox. It was heat-convection powered. It pulled cold water from the bottom of the tank through the heater coils, with the hot water flowing into the top of the tank.

Dad seemed to be off the hooch. He was quite enjoyable to be around. He was now the dad I choose to fondly remember. And, at this time, he took up studying with the Jehovah's Witnesses again, and listening to Herbert W. Armstrong's broadcast from a Medford station on Sunday mornings. I attended the Nazarene Church (when I felt like it), while Mom and my sisters attended the Assembly of God.

Dad got a job working for the owner of the wrecking yard in Tri City, thus we had a modicum of income; however, just barely enough to run the household. If my memory serves me correctly, for several months we continued to receive welfare assistance for rent and food. Then Mom received word that she was to receive a small inheritance.

Early in my sophomore year, Mom's uncle Victor (my grandmother's brother) died. By the rest of the family's standards, he died quite wealthy. I don't remember who died first, whether it was Uncle Victor or Aunt Rey. They died within a few months of one another, willing their assets to Grandma and the Backlund kids, their nephews and nieces. Because Mom was one of the nieces, she received several thousand dollars, which after taxes was more than a couple years' wages at that time. We were not rich, but for the first time in our lives, we had money.

Dad wanted to spend some of the inheritance on property north of town alongside the South Umpqua. He thought it could be used to grow produce, and I believe he was thinking about growing a truck garden and setting up a vegetable/fruit stand. Mom would have none of that kind of thinking. After all, it was her money, and she didn't want to spend it that way. To Dad's credit, he didn't argue with her and let her have her way. However, they did buy a fairly late model vehicle, a 1957 Studebaker pickup complete with an overdrive three-speed transmission, and a Trans-star rearend (another name for a "limited slip" differential).

One thing Dad liked about the truck was that "limited slip" differential. This was a fairly new innovation at that time and would enable the truck to get traction when most vehicles were stuck in the mud (so to speak). This was the nicest vehicle Dad ever owned, and Dad loved that Stude (pronounced "stew'dee"). He also bought a new McCullough chain saw and went into the woodcutting and fence post business that winter. He didn't make a whole lot of money in the venture, as it was late in the year, but when added to his income as a part time worker at the Tri-City Auto Wreckers, at least he was able to put food on the table and pay the rent. Of course, with Mom's inheritance, the welfare assistance went away.

Shortly after I turned fifteen (in my freshman year), I obtained my learner's driving permit. Much to my pleasure, and with a family vehicle, I became the designated driver. Being thus so designated, it provided me the benefit of riding in the cab with Mom and Dad. My sisters had to sit in the bed. Dad was safety-minded, having built some sideboards to keep the girls from flying out on the corners. I was warm, cozy, and comfortable in my new role, and loved it. And of course, I didn't mind being seen tooling around town in a fairly late model vehicle.

At one point, shortly after Dad got the truck, he had to drive to Grants Pass to pick up a part he had ordered. I believe it was for the pickup, but I cannot remember what it needed. He had me drive.

On our way down he turned to me and said, "Want a smoke?"

I said, "No thanks, Dad. I don't smoke." Funny, I was embarrassed in saying it.

He got a sort of twisted grin on his face and turning to look out the window retorted, "Well, if you ever decide to smoke, let me know. There is no need for you to go behind my back. I'll buy the smokes for you."

Gee, I thought. *That's sure nice of him.*

I never developed the habit though. Oh, I'd smoke a cigarette now and then. Some of my friends took up smoking about this time, and I would borrow a smoke when in the company of peers. I didn't have any strong desire for the weed, except for a short two-week period in my early Air Force career when I attempted to jump-start the habit. After coming to my senses, I threw my last pack in the wastebasket and gave up smoking forever.

When Harold Gallios turned sixteen, earlier in our freshman year, and prior to our pear-picking trip to Medford, he had passed his driver's test, receiving his license. I couldn't wait for mine. I got mine in December of 1959 as a sophomore. I was taking Driver's Ed at the time.

One school day, the DMV office at Roseburg sent an instructor down to Myrtle Creek to give driver's tests. I went along with two or three other boys to take the test. The instructor drove us to the location in the Driver's Ed car, a 1960 Chevrolet Impala two-door, with a bronze and cream two-tone paint job. Just before it was my turn, the instructor turned to me and apologized, telling me that I couldn't take the test because I had not yet completed the course. He explained that the school insurance would not cover me to drive the test car without the Driver's Ed instructor present in the car.

Of course I was disappointed, but suddenly I had an idea. "Can I go home and get my dad's truck?" I asked.

"Sure," he said, with a smile on his face.

I ran the few blocks home, got Dad to drive me back in the Stude, and when I returned, I was next in line. I seemed to be the butt of some jokes from the other kids who had attempted to pass their driver's test. None of them passed, and so they were kidding me about using a pickup to attempt to pass mine.

Now that Stude had an eight-foot bed, no power steering, and was a stick shift to boot, but I parallel parked flawlessly, shaking like a leaf in the process. Then we went for the drive test.

What is there about a driver's test? I barely passed. The major problem I had was getting that truck to move forward from a dead stop on a hill without moving backward. I finally did (after stalling out a couple times). The fellow testing me subtracted thirty points for the hillside problems, but I got my license, while the rest of the boys had to eat crow. That was one of the proudest moments of my life. All who have obtained their driver's license should be able to relate to that statement. Now I could drive anywhere by myself. *Freedom* is just another word for nothing left to lose...That's why I passed the test. I had nothing to lose.

This was back before the days when liability insurance was mandatory, and all I needed in order to drive was cash for gas. It was cheap, around thirty cents a gallon. Once in a while, Dad would let me take the truck to go visit friends or just take a drive. I didn't have a lot of extra money, and so while those opportunities were limited, they were most graciously received and appreciated. I'd work at odd jobs to get gas money.

Interestingly, I had been driving the pickup for some weeks around town on short trips to the store or other errands prior to me getting my license, but the day I got my license, I was pulled over.

"Oh, nothing wrong," the cop said, with a twinkle in his eye. "Just noticed a new driver in town and wanted to make sure you had a license."

Whew! Those who have ever been pulled over by a cop and didn't receive a ticket know the definition of "relief."

Around this time, George Gallios built the twins a broomstick mill.

The broomstick mill consisted of a three-horsepower 115 volt AC electric motor driving two 12-inch saw blades, separated the width of a broomstick cant. These "cants" were 1.25-inches square and five-feet long. We'd push the wood into the blades by hand, retrieve the wood from the other side, turn the wood 90 degrees, and run it back through the saw. This produced a perfectly squared 5-foot long, "raw" broomstick cant. We'd tie the cants with bailing twine twenty-five to a bundle, and when we got a truckload of bundles, haul them into Roseburg to the broom handle mill, where they were "turned" into broomsticks. We'd get ten cents for each cant. So while it wasn't a huge moneymaking concern, at least it was spending money, more for the twins than for me. I'd help them occasionally, when they felt generous, but for the most part, it was their operation. I appreciated the opportunities they provided and the new skills I learned.

The raw material for the broomstick mill was free, couldn't beat that price with a broomstick handle. George, the twin's dad, had bought an old '47 Chevrolet 1½ ton flatbed to use for hauling the finished product to the broom handle factory in Roseburg, and for hauling the raw material from its source. Once in a while, Harold or Howard allowed me to refine my driving skills by letting me drive the truck back to some blackberry bushes on the property they rented. That's where we dumped all the pieces of wood that didn't look like a broom handle cant. Come on. Give us a break. The tailings were out of sight, and nobody complained. Anyway, I was able to refine my "double-clutching" skills as the old Chevrolet truck had one of those four-speed non-synchronized transmissions.

The source of the raw material was the burner chute at the mill in Riddle, where George worked as millwright. The burner chute fed the slab waste from the head rig and re-saw into the burner. All we had to do was back the truck up to the chute, reach in, and pull out a slab that looked like it had sufficient wood left from which to make a broomstick.

That was the routine. Get a load of slab wood, haul it home, cut a broomstick cant or two from each slab, throw the waste into the back of the Chevrolet truck, haul the unused pieces out to the blackberries behind the house, tie the cants into bundles of twenty-five, load the truck, and haul the finished bundles to Roseburg. It was a lot of work; it was made more difficult when the saws would get dull and have to be sharpened (only George could do that). But we'd work even with dull teeth, forcing the wood into the blades, until the circuit breaker blew in the house, race to the house to reset the breaker, and then start all over again.

Howard was the frugal one. He saved his money and bought a nice-looking and nicer-running Mercury two-door coupe with a flat head V8 and a three-speed overdrive transmission.

Even then there was a mystique about a Mercury, a very unique body style with smooth flowing lines, and in my opinion, of the '49, '50, or '51 Mercs that are prized today, the '50 two-door is the most beautiful. Howard loved that car. Shucks, we all loved that car. But, most boys with their first "love" fail to appreciate it. In a couple of years, he was driving a 1949 Studebaker, flatbed pickup; but in pristine condition, that Mercury would be worth some bucks today. Rebuilt, those rods are going for many thousands of dollars.

From his share of the sale of the broomstick "cants," Harold purchased a '31 Chevy, old by even my standards at the time. It had a straight six engine that was not sufficiently powerful for Harold, and so he gets the idea to put a Ford flat head V8 in her. Yeah, boost that power. Give'r the ability to smoke the tires. Well, make'm chirp anyway. He wanted me to help him get the engine. Thing was, the engine was in a '47 Ford "abandoned" in a pasture in Tri City. Harold neither asked if it was for sale, nor did he ask if he could have it. He just took it, with my help. Whether it was a running engine or not seemed to be a moot point at the time.

It was after dark, and the temperature below freezing when we coasted down the dirt lane. A wire stock fence was between the road and our objective. Without making too much noise, we climbed over the fence, proceeding to work our way up to that "free-but-for-the-asking" old Ford. It was on its left side.

Like I said, Harold had no idea whether the engine was good or bad, but he wanted it. We worked by the light of the stars on that frosty evening. In what seemed like an eternity, we eventually had the bolts off the transmission, the motor mounts disconnected, and wires and hoses cut. We pushed the engine out of the engine compartment onto the frosty pasture grass and like the two crazy kids we were, proceeded to roll the complete engine back to the car. Somehow, we got it under the fence and positioned at the back of the car. We opened the trunk lid, lifted the engine into the trunk space, tied it down, and were out of there shaking and quaking in our boots; but relieved that we had not been caught during the most significant act of larceny in which I was ever involved. Now Harold had something to spend his broom handle money on.

While Harold did not excel in academics, he excelled at the mechanical. In a few weeks, he had the engine installed and running. He had purchased a three-speed Ford transmission, bell housing, and clutch assembly to mate up to the flathead, modifying the driveline to fit. But because the '31 Chevy had no steering column shift linkage, Harold had to come up with some other alternative for shifting gears.

This was the beginning era of the muscle cars. Ford, Chevrolet, and Dodge were starting to do the one-upmanship in cubic inches, horsepower, and lighter chassis and bodies. One of the options they were beginning to offer was the four-speed, synchronized transmission. The first passenger car I knew of that had a four-speed was a 1959 Pontiac Catalina two-door sedan. It also had a 389 cubic inch engine topped with three deuces for carburetion, with chrome-tipped dual exhaust pipes extending from under the rear bumper. Man could that car lay rubber; two long, smoking, black strips of rubber.

A poor man's version of the factory four-speed was a floor-mounted three-speed shifter. You could buy one of these kits at the auto supply store. Harold had other ideas. He would make his own, and he did. He studied the kit in the store window, and from memory designed his own, using high school auto shop equipment. It worked well, too.

Harold was gifted in mechanics, and in the years that followed, always seemed to be tinkering with one of his cars to make it more powerful and faster. Shoot, after high school, he inserted a Chrysler big block with two four-barrels into a '57 Ford two-door hardtop. Man, there's just something about cubic inches, carburetion, and horsepower.

I got my first car late winter or early spring of 1960. Dad surprised me; he bought it for me! He still had some of Mom's inheritance money left to spend.

He had spotted a 1952 Ford two-door coupe on Trout's used car lot between the Umpqua Bank and the Myrtle Creek Bakery. Dad paid a hundred dollars for this maroon and white two-tone beauty. I drove it home. But because the old flathead was a little tired and had an appetite for oil, Dad immediately spent another hundred dollars of Mom's inheritance to have the engine overhauled. Man, was I anxious to get that car out of the garage. I made myself a nuisance stopping at the shop on my way to and from school, anticipating when that engine would be done and I'd have my own wheels.

Finally the car was available, and as long as I earned my own gas money, the car was basically mine. But with the car came responsibilities. I was responsible for its maintenance. That's how I learned to change plugs and points, set the timing, replace hydraulic cylinders, u-joints, radiator hoses, brake shoes, and other nickel and dime stuff that seemed to always keep me broke. If I remember, there was also some muffler work that had to be done; Tires, tires, tires. None of the durable radials we have today, but the old bias ply, rayon tires that had a form of rubber that attracted every nail, screw, or tire-puncturing debris imaginable. Why, you could park the car and watch a nail fifteen feet away slowly roll its way under and into the tire. But regardless, I had a car of my own!

Of course, with a car, there's dating, and on a few occasions Harold and I would double date, going out for pizza, or to a drive-in movie. Being a red-blooded American male, I had certain urges; but being a "good boy," I kept them in check and treated my dates respectfully. I was always the consummate gentleman. Maybe the girls appreciated it, maybe they didn't; but that's who I was. I did not want to ever do anything that would shame my earthly dad, nor my heavenly Father, even at that age.

One of my gasoline moneymaking opportunities came from the benevolent owner of the Tri City Wrecking Yard, where Dad worked. His name was Bud. He was the stepfather of one of my classmates, Fern Reglingshaefer. All those who knew Fern affectionately referred to her as "Bossy Fern"; she liked to tell her classmates what they ought to be doing and how to do it; nice kid, though. Anyway, Bud asked Dad to inquire of me if I'd like to earn some cash stripping electrical wiring bundles out of old car carcasses before they were hauled off to the steel mill for melting; sounded like a good idea to me. So on an occasional Saturday, I'd be at the wrecking yard with Dad; but while he might be in the garage repairing an old clunker, I'd be out in the yard stacking up a pile of wire bundles. When I got a good pile built up, I'd start a fire under it, burn the rubber coating off the copper, and be left with nothing but wire. Bud would weigh it, and he'd pay me half the going rate for scrap copper. I'd make five or six bucks at a time doing this and have more than enough for my week's gasoline.

One day I walked into the garage, and Bud had Dad replacing a three-speed transmission on some old beater of a car. From under the car, Dad's muttering some barely discernable expletives deleted. Bud asks, "What's that you say, Tiny?"

Dad says, "I can't get this stupid, blinkety-blank shift linkage hooked up correctly. No matter what I do, I end up with everything backwards."

"Well," Bud quips. "Don't worry about it too much. The owner might be pleased that he has the only car in Douglas County with one speed forward and three in reverse."

Money was where I found it. On another occasion, I was walking the banks of the river. At the location where Myrtle Creek empties into the South Umpqua, the electric power company had discarded lots of copper electrical cable ends and pieces. There was probably a couple hundred pounds of the stuff pushed over the bank almost at the water's edge, just free for the taking. I made good use of the rest of the day, hauling my treasure home, making quite a pile in the back yard. It was heavy ten-gauge or larger electrical wiring and promised to pay me some good dividends when I got the outside coatings burned off. I lit the pile off with a few pieces of pitchy pine kindling, and once on fire, there was no stopping it. Boy did that insulation burn and smoke. Big, black, billowing clouds of smoke, laced with yellow, orange, and red flames.

I'm dead I thought. *The fire department's gonna come a' call'n and I'm gonna' be arrested for attempting to burn down the neighborhood.*

Man, it was like a house was going up in flames; you know, like when asphalt shingles burn. But luck was with me. No sirens and no complaints from the neighbors. They probably all looked out their windows, thought, *Ah, nothing to worry about. It's just the Oliver boy burning the house down.*

It was over quickly. The fire was out, my heart rate dropped back to normal, and I had a pile of clean copper ready for market. I let it cool, loaded it into the Studebaker, and hauled my loot to the wrecking yard. Of course, Bud asked me where I got the wire, and I had to do some fancy explaining, but he bought my story and paid me the going rate. I made over thirty dollars, which was about two day's wages at that time, and only for an afternoon's work! Was I pleased? You bet! (Dad was jealous).

During this time, I was also doing odd jobs for George McNaughton. I'd see him at Sunday school, where he'd then tell me that he had some things for me to do. (I talk about the McNaughtons in the chapter titled "Good Influences.")

And so I spent the winter and spring of 1960 of my sophomore year.

That summer, we picked strawberries and beans at the Schumacher fields in Stayton. Dad let me drive the '52 Ford, while he drove the Studebaker loaded with our camping gear and personal necessities. As with prior picking excursions, I paid Mom and Dad a buck a day "room and board," and that was the extent of my living expenses. They bought the groceries, and I got to keep the rest. I don't remember how much I made that year, but I must have made a reasonable amount. After buying all my school clothes and other necessities, I still had plenty left over. I can't recall needing to work at all through my junior year.

Late fall of my junior year I "harvested" my last doe off Dole Road; little did I know it would be so at the time.

I skipped school that day, packed a lunch and a canteen of water into an old army ruck sack (the same one I carried when Harold and I made our pear-picking trip to Medford), and told

Mom and Dad that I was going to hike over the top of Timber Butte onto the Blackard land on the north slope of the butte. This was the area that Dad had logged back in the early fifties. I was very familiar with the terrain. There was that small year-round creek fed by springs on the north side of the butte. I was thinking about catching some of the trout that hung out just for the taking in the lower reaches of the stream. I dug some worms and put them into an old Prince Albert tobacco can (these cans were like a small hip flask and worked absolutely perfect for holding worms until you could place them on a hook); put the worm can and some fishing line and hooks into the ruck sack; grabbed the .22, and headed out the back door for Timber Butte. Straight up I went, up the little draw that ran by the back of the house, up past the city water tank, and into the saddle overlooking the town on the south and the old shack on the north. From there, I turned right and hiked the ridge until I hit the top of Timber Butte; the same route I took some forty years later on "the trek" that I wrote about in the early pages of this book.

I had spent the better part of the morning hiking over the mountain. It was early afternoon when I dropped down into the fishing stream on the Blackard property. Darn if I didn't surprise a barren doe. I dropped her with a single shot, field dressed her, and left her hidden under some limbs and brush next to the old logging road that Dad had used years before, but which cars could still drive on; that is, if you didn't mind them getting a little muddy and scratched up.

I had come to do some fishing, and so after cutting a willow pole, I rigged up and fished the stream for the next couple of hours. I caught a good mess, cleaned, and wrapped them in leaves, and stuffed them into the rucksack. By this time, it was mid-afternoon, and I had a long walk back home. But I wasn't about to go back over Timber Butte. I continued down stream for a short distance until the stream crossed under Dole Road through a large concrete culvert before emptying into the South Umpqua about 50 yards from the road.

At this point, the road was running directly north and south, and I had to turn to my left and walk the road about three miles south to get home.

From where the fishing stream flows into a culvert under Dole Road, you will find that the railroad tracks lay between the road and the river. I decided to head back for town, and for a mile or so to walk the tracks instead of the road. The tracks were within a few feet of the road. I hadn't progressed even a quarter of a mile, and I was looking for something else to do. I decided to find some beer bottles, throw them in the river, and use them for target practice. I climbed the few feet from the railroad grade onto Dole Road and located about a dozen bottles, placing them in a collection pile on the riverside of the road. You have to picture in your mind that Dole Road, the railroad, and the river were all within jumping distance at this point. You could slide down the bank from off the road, step across the tracks, then slide down the bank another fifty feet or so and be in the water.

Where I was standing on the road gave me a good open view of some nice slack water over a deep hole. I threw the bottles over the tracks into the river and there they floated in that slack water, just waiting to be sunk. I proceeded to do just that, shooting a dozen or so rounds, killing one beer stubby after another. This was lots of fun, but as events began to unfold, I became acutely aware that this was not the place for target practice. It didn't enter my mind that across the river on the west side, and within .22 hollow-point range, was Interstate 5. By this time (1961), Interstate 5 was pretty well completed through this part of Oregon. There was a dense stand of maple, alder, and oaks between the river and the highway; but there was also an Oregon Department of Transportation weigh station slightly downstream, from where I had been shooting! Oops!

Little did I suspect that I had set the Oregon State Police into action. They had called out the cavalry, sending state patrol vehicles from both ends of Dole Road to converge on a certain spot (and person) who obviously was some kind of terrorist threat to all transportation on Interstate 5, if not also an open threat to national security. People do interesting things when they think they are being shot at, and I learned that the Oregon State Patrol was conditioned for response.

I became aware of their "response" when after walking about another quarter mile of tracks toward home, I glanced back north just in time to see an Oregon State Patrol pickup, with lights flashing, bounce over the crossing, heading in my direction. It was like a light went on. *They're after me!* I panicked. Instead of immediately climbing over the tracks, up the bank, and back up slope onto Timber Butte, all I could think of was, *Get those stupid fish out of my rucksack! I don't have a fishing license! It's not trout season! And I've skipped school! And I'm going to jail!* I slid off the track grade into some brush by the river, threw the fish into the water, and then walked along the river keeping the brush, trees, and railroad grade between me and the Oregon State Police.

I resigned myself to the fact that the jig was up when I spotted a second vehicle from the south converging on the spot where I had exited the tracks, and where the Oregon State Patrol pickup was. It dawned on me there was probably somebody at the weigh station who had binoculars on me the entire time! I decided to *give myself up*.

As I climbed up the bank from the railroad tracks to Dole Road, I had visions of what reform school was like. I reached the tracks and just sort of stood there looking up at those two patrolmen as they looked down at me from off the road.

"Looking for me?" I asked. They just stood up there on the bank of the road, arms folded across their chest, glaring down at me, not saying anything.

I stepped out on the road and continued walking toward them, preparing myself for what it would feel like to be spread-eagled, handcuffed, stuffed into a back seat, and carted off to jail.

You know what? They didn't even tell me to put my gun down. One of the officers, who turned out to be a game warden, told me to move in a little closer where he could talk to me. They both could obviously read the situation, and all they saw was a skinny teenager. They probably concluded, correctly, that I was simply a little careless choosing a location in which to engage in target practice. A teenager walking the streets of Myrtle Creek carrying a .22 was not an unusual sight at that time. I did it several times. Nobody stopped, asked me what I was doing, or called 911 (didn't have 911 back then anyway).

I received a lecture on public safety, with a few questions and comments regarding where my home was, my truancy, what in the world I was thinking, and things like that. All this time, I still held my rifle. They never inspected it, confiscated it as evidence, or asked if it was loaded, or *anything*! After a few minutes, the other patrolman left and the game warden told me to get in the pickup and he would drive me home.

When I climbed into the cab, it was then I noticed hair and blood from the doe I had killed on the front of my jeans! Maybe it wasn't as obvious as I thought it was, but I thought I had a neon sign around my neck that flashed *poacher! poacher!* If the warden had noticed, he didn't say a word, but just talked about boys, school, and "field dressing game," and "hunting"...things like that. He didn't even take me to the house, but dropped me off at the top of the grade where Dole road descends into Myrtle Creek, right at the point where the final trace of the Applegate trail merges with Dole Road. He told me to be careful and get on home, as it was getting late. I walked back to Mr. Stone's tarpaper shack; spent a little time shooting the breeze about the *River Incident*. He laughed.

I never told Dad or Mom about *the incident*. Nothing "happened," so there was nothing to tell…really.

It was late in the afternoon when I got home. Neither Dad nor Mom were concerned that I had been away almost ten hours. By this time in my life, I had developed a pretty good head on my shoulders and could be trusted in just about all situations and circumstances to do the right thing. Of course, their opinion about me being of sound mind may have changed if I had told them about being driven "home" in a state game warden's pickup. And it seemed that the right thing at the time was to tell Dad that we had to go get ourselves a deer that I had hidden alongside an old logging road on the north side of Timber Butte. Dad said he didn't need me and that he could find it. How in the world he located that doe off the old logging road well after dark I will never know. But he did, and we had fresh venison for breakfast the next morning; back strap it was. Mom fried it the way she always did. Good stuff, that venison, when it's dressed, prepared, and cooked right. I can still taste it on my mind's tongue.

So we hunkered down into the winter routine. Dad and I would cut firewood or fence posts to supplement Mom's dwindling inheritance. Late that winter, the money ran out and Dad told me he had to sell the car. I was a little disappointed, but appreciated that he asked me, and that he expected me not to make a stink about the whole thing. I didn't. I simply handed the keys over to him, and in a few days the '52 Ford was just a memory. I was back to pedaling my old English racer for transportation. It wasn't too bad that winter. I put on a wheel-powered generator for lights and a speedometer. I was pretty much in fashion that way. But here I was, now in my junior year, and without wheels; except for those times Dad would loan me the Stude. Humbled, yes, but very much appreciating that Dad was still off the bottle, until one day…

I came home and found that Dad and Mom had been drinking beer. I feared the cycle was going to start all over again, but it did not. Dad would have a beer on occasion throughout my junior year, but he never got drunk, nor did he ever speak in unpleasant words or tones to Mom or us kids. Dad seemed to have recovered sufficiently to at least live a somewhat normal life, and he did so for the next several years.

We continued to live my junior year in the Cornutt rental, and in late spring of 1961, we loaded the Stude pickup once again and headed for the Randall strawberry fields east of Estacada for the fourth and final time.

It was a most pleasant time for me. There were several boys and girls from different cabins about my age, and what with Eagle Creek being just "down the hill," there were many hot summer days spent in its waters swimming and fishing; teenage kids having fun, innocent and pastoral; at least, that is what is etched in my memory.

Dad had an agreement with the Randall family that it would be okay to stake himself out by the berry fields around dusk and pop off a doe now and then. Thus, he became the de facto meat supplier for the camp. Those so inclined would occasionally dine on venison and strawberry shortcake. We were truly living off the fruit of the land.

On one occasion, I asked Dad if I could take the truck and drive to Gaston to visit Floyd Barth, an old high school classmate who had moved from Myrtle Creek the year before. To my surprise Dad said, "Be back in a couple of days," and I was. I enjoyed my visit with Floyd and his family, too. We both were heading for our senior years.

We worked through the season and, because beans were not ready to pick, we drove to Sandy and located a raspberry grower who needed pickers. It was a warm, dry summer. We camped under some broad leaf maples on one end of the berry field, feasting on clean fresh raspberries whenever we wanted. But because the raspberry season pretty much parallels the strawberry season, picking was over quite quickly. It was time to pack up and hit the road south for the Shumacher farm in Stayton.

It was still too early for pole bean picking, which didn't start until the first week or so in August. There was work "stringing" pole beans wires for the later bean plantings. Automated stringers were just coming out, but many farmers were still manually stringing the bean wires.

A lot of labor was required to set up a pole bean field. First, the beans had to be planted in rows about four feet apart. Each row had two large anchor posts, one at each end. Depending on the size of the bean field, a row might be a couple hundred yards long. Between the anchor posts, "interim" posts were set every twenty feet or so. (The main anchor posts at each end of a row were more or less permanent.) These "interim" posts, if that's what one called them, were set by a machine on the end of a tractor that gripped a 10-foot interim post, and then "pressed" them into the ground. Once these interim posts were in place, a galvanized wire was strung from the top of one anchor post to the top of the other anchor post at the end of the row. The stringer wire was stretched (for tightness) and then stapled to the top of each interim post. A bailing-type twine was then attached to the bottom of each anchor post, pulled tight, and stapled to the bottom, a few inches above the ground. You now had two parallel stringers for each row; one on the top for carrying the weight of the beanstalks, and the other for holding the string in place until the stalks grew over the top of the wire. As such, the row was now prepped for "stringing."

Stringing consisted of "dispensing" white cotton string from off a conical-shaped spool. The dispensing tool was made from a piece of thick-gauged tempered wire, in sort of a rectangular shape, with one end fitting into a sort of hook on the other end. You released the wire from the hook, routed the non-hooked end through the spool, re-hooked the wire, and you were ready to string. It's not complicated, but if you can't picture all this, don't concern yourself. Just know that's how we did it.

You started by tying the exposed end of the string to either the lower or upper stringer, then moving up and down, up and down, bringing the wire spool under the lower stringer, then over the top stringer, changing hands top and bottom with the string rolling off the spool until completely dispensed in this fashion. Up-down, up-down, hundreds of times for each spool, thousands of times a day. No weak-backed person need apply. I think we earned fifty cents a spool, maybe less. It was hard work, yes, even more hard on one's back than picking strawberries. But, "stringing pole bean" was one of the ways to earn money between the strawberry- and bean-pick'n seasons.

Money earned stringing pole beans, when added to money earned picking strawberries (my poke was exceeding $200.00), was burning a hole in my pocket. It was time to think about buying my own car. I would be in my senior year starting that September, and I wanted transportation that could not be sold out from under me. I started looking. I was anxious...too anxious, which led me into making the worst decision of my car-buying experience ever. I had located a car in Turner. It was a 1952 Dodge two-door coupe that had some difficulty starting. Would I listen to Dad? No! I knew a good buy when I saw it, and I wanted that nice-looking '52 Dodge. Why with a little work on the engine, a split manifold, and dual exhaust, I'd be the talk of the school. So I paid the guy $150 for it.

Almost to the hour that I bought the car, we got word from Roseburg that Pat, my oldest sister, had lost one of her twins. She had married the year before, become pregnant, and had gone into labor, losing one of the babies. Well, being family and all, Dad and Mom thought we ought go down to console her and her husband, and I decided that I would drive us all down in the Dodge—another bad decision. Seems like I had some lessons to learn, and one was not to take an unproved vehicle with known problems on a trip like that.

Before too long into the trip, the engine started to overheat, but by keeping it under fifty, we inched down Interstate 5. South of Rice Hill, a rod started knocking. We crawled into Roseburg, engine steaming, clanking, and a'banging.

Pat and her husband, Hubert McGinnis, were living in a small two-bedroom apartment, not too far from Roseburg High School. Their apartment had an attached garage. Hubert let me put the car on blocks in the garage. We visited only that day and evening, and the next morning Hubert drove us back to Stayton. I left the car at their apartment, saying that I would be back after bean picking was over to take care of it. The proper care would have been a couple of sticks of dynamite; lesson learned. Listen to your dad; he does know a thing or two. I never did go back for that car. Besides, by that time, I had bought the "red beauty."

So without transportation once again, there was nothing to do but throw myself into the bean pick'n business, and did I! I wanted another car. But now I was out $150 of hard-earned berry pick'n and bean string'n money, and I wasn't about to ever again buy a "pig'n a poke." Now I wanted money and lots of it.

The early bean plantings were up and ready for harvest by late July. I worked from sunup to well into the hot afternoons, one of the first to start and the last to quit. In twenty-two days of bean picking, I averaged $22 each workday, making well over $400.00 for less than a month's work!

I worked through August, during which my next two oldest sisters met the fellows they were to marry. Both of them married children of dust bowl parents. As mentioned in an earlier chapter, my next to youngest sister, Carol, is still happily married to her husband, Richard. What a great couple the Richard Smiths are.

There were other characters in that last camp in the summer of '61 that linger in my memory. One was about my age and was the son of a Mennonite couple with three kids who lived out of a covered wagon. It wasn't like the old Conestogas, but more or less customized to modern covered wagon specifications. Ha! The family had parked it under some tall Maple trees down by the Santiam River. A couple of horses pulled their rig into camp one day, and they were told that they could make camp on the river. Their oldest son, who was slightly older than I, sported a full face of whiskers, and he loved to box. Shoot, I was shaving a few sparse whiskers maybe once a week, and here was this "kid" who looked like Grizzly Adams. For some reason or other, Dad thought I was a pretty good boxer, and one evening when the boy had come into camp looking for takers, Dad encouraged me to take him on. I held my own, not that I was that good a boxer, but I simply did not want to get hit. So I sparred with him sufficiently to convince Dad I was no Mamma's Boy, and exited gracefully.

Meanwhile, I still had my heart set on my next car, whatever it would be.

A few days before bean picking was over for the year, Dad sprung the biggest surprise—*ever*! I think we went into shock over what he had in mind. He had decided to move from Myrtle Creek to North Plains. Here's how it came about.

The "straw boss" at the Shumacher camp was a toothless old coot we called "Old Joe." He was well into his eighties, at least it seemed to me he was. He lived in his own "executive-style" mobile home that was parked in the middle of the camp. Well, at one time, his mobile home could have been classified "executive." It was pretty well abused, but at least it was better than any of the cabins in which the pickers lived. It seemed that Old Joe needed to have that trailer towed to North Plains where he parked it for the winter on his son Dewey's property. Now I'm assuming some sort of agreement was reached between Dad and Old Joe. Joe knew that Dad had a pickup, and I'm assuming that the agreement reached was stated something like, "...Tiny, you tow my trailer to North Plains for me, and I'll let you live in it rent free for the winter."

So that's what we did. After bean picking was over, we piled all our "camping gear" into the truck, loaded the girls in back with Penny the dog, and with Mom and Dad riding shotgun, we pulled out of camp. I was the designated driver hoping to keep a fully loaded, half-ton, underpowered Studebaker pickup from careening off the back roads. I drove to Newberg, over Chehalem Mountain, through Hillsboro, then into North Plains. We made it with no problems. However, if I remember correctly, the truck never got into overdrive, even going downhill. That was quite an experience for a fairly inexperienced driver. We had no sway bars, nothing but a ball hitch mounted to a custom wrap around bumper. Shoot, while the bumper was connected to the frame, it was really no more than decoration. It's a wonder that trailer didn't start waggling and swaying and throwing us all off the road. I think sometimes God sends angels to protect the ignorant.

By the time we got settled into our new "home," it was only a few days before the start of school. We still had to return to Myrtle Creek to pick up our stuff. Our "stuff" consisted of what few clothes and personal effects we wanted to keep with us in our new "home." What we had done before leaving Myrtle Creek was move out of the Cornutt rental. Mom had some friends who had a building on their property off Clark's Branch Road where we could store what few things we wanted to keep, and then we took off for the summer. So we drove back to Myrtle Creek to retrieve our "stuff." Driving back north on Interstate 5, it suddenly occurred to me that we had left Myrtle Creek for good. We were out'a there.

Back in North Plains, I prepared to attend Hillsboro Union High School. I bought school clothes, just as I usually did, using the money earned in the fields. My heart was still set on getting some wheels. After all, I was now a senior and after buying all the necessary school clothes and supplies, I still had money burning a hole in my pocket.

One day just before school started, some of our berry and bean-picking friends stopped by. Jim Belk was married to one of Richard Smith's sisters, Alice. Jim told Dad there was this nice-looking '50 Ford two-door sedan on a lot in Forest Grove, and the dealer only wanted $150.00.

After Jim left, Dad drove me out to look at the car, and I fell in love. She was a beautiful brilliant red head, decked out with a new set of white-wall shoes and the most beautiful body I had ever seen…for a two-door sedan. The interior was immaculate; no rips or tears, looking as if it had just come from the factory. It had the original tool kit and the owner's manual; she had the standard flat head V8, with three on the tree and overdrive. And she purred like a kitten. The dealer gave us the previous owner's name to affirm that the engine had been overhauled, and so I bought my first love. Complete with dual exhaust, she was indeed a head-turner and a thing of beauty.

This is how I remember leaving Myrtle Creek. Life continued to be good. Dad was not drinking. Later in my senior year, we moved from the trailer into an old log cabin, just south of Main Street in North Plains. It was a good year. I did well in my senior year, making new friends, dating, attending church, and living what one would call a "normal life."

Good Influences

(Reasons Why I Will Never Live Like This)

Before I close this book, it is fitting and proper to mention those who influenced my life for the better during my early years on Dole Road. I'm certain those whom I mention will downplay the role they played in my life then, and in the impact they had on who I became as an adult.

Mom had an older sister, Helen. Aunt Helen, her husband Glen Thackery, and my two cousins, Karen and Marilyn, lived in Myrtle Creek and attended the Assembly of God church. Mom attended church off and on, and occasionally, she'd have times of regular week-to-week attendance. As youngsters, my sisters and I had no choice in the matter and attended with her. Of course we'd put on our Sunday best, which probably was more like most peoples' Sunday worst. But at least it was clean and ironed.

It was at the Assembly of God Church where I was introduced to God. Pastor Gordon Hadley founded the church in 1948. In the process of writing this book, to my great surprise and pleasure, I was to discover that he was alive and well (his wife had died some years earlier), and obviously able to communicate quite well. I then sent Pastor Hadley a manuscript copy asking his permission to use his name, so that I could share, in a small way, the part he played in my early life. He graciously granted permission in his own clearly-legible handwriting. At the time of his letter (May 18, 2010), Pastor Hadley was a healthy 102 years old, still living in Myrtle Creek, and still attending the Myrtle Creek First Assembly of God. Those who know him call him "Pastor," and rightly so. Thank you Pastor Hadley for the part you played in forming me into an instrument of God's amazing grace.

It seemed to me that Pentecostals were into defining one's relationship with God by what one did. And the better you were at doing whatever was accepted decorum, the more pleased God was with you. Well, I dearly wanted to please God, but had a difficult time understanding why it was so difficult. Even so, I came to believe there was a God, and in the Sunday School Bible classes, the rudiments of my faith were laid. Thus, at a fairly young age, I began thinking of myself as a Christian and regulated my ways accordingly, as in the back of my mind I did not want to incur the wrath of God.

Because of "my faith," I was tagged by my peers as being "religious." It wasn't that I was preachy or anything like that. I actually enjoyed going to Sunday school and learning about the Bible and about God. Overall, the people at the "Assembly" accepted the Oliver family, and Mom enjoyed the fellowship as well. And so, at the Myrtle Creek Assembly of God, the foundation was laid in me for belief in God, His Son, and salvation.

Occasionally in his sober stages, Dad attended church with us. Mom, a few years before she died, told me that Dad had accepted Christ and was baptized in the baptismal in the Assembly of God Church. When Mom told me that, it stirred a faint memory of the event. Of course, Dad did not maintain any regular church attendance, and by church definition, was tagged a "backslider."

As I mentioned in another chapter, sometime between 1953 and 1955, Dad became acquainted with the Jehovah's Witnesses. I can see now why Dad would have been drawn to them. They had a sort of pragmatism in their view of Scripture, and I believe that Dad looked at the world and life through pragmatic lenses.

Thus interested, Dad began attending their fellowship in Myrtle Creek, and of course the family went along.

Dad's association with the Witnesses didn't last but a few years, off and on. But later, in my tenth or eleventh grade, Dad began studying their material once again. A couple of the local men would meet with Dad in our home in the Cornutt rental.

Dad had a falling out with the organization over some doctrinal differences and asked the two men to leave the house during one of the in-home Bible studies.

It was shortly after Dad's falling out with the Witnesses that he began listening to the Herbert W. Armstrong Sunday radio broadcast, "The World Tomorrow," from a Medford station. Subsequently, Dad sent for Armstrong's free publication, the *Plain Truth* magazine, and I too, as an older teen, began reading their Bible-based articles.

Armstrong and his organization, *The Radio Church of God* (later to become the *World Wide Church of God*), pulled no punches. Armstrong (also a pragmatist, in my opinion), in his doctrine and in his speaking ability, appealed to Dad, and was probably why I would read the magazine. Armstrong had a certain "I know what I'm talking about" swagger to his presentation, and he presented the Bible as he saw it, and it seemed to have God's plan and purpose for creation all tied up in a nice sounding package. Little did I know how that brief introduction would affect my life for years to come. The next chapter provides some brief but interesting details regarding this subject.

Let me give you some details about the Gallios family. In the seventh grade, I met Harold and Howard Gallios. This relationship continues to the present. Not that we have kept much in contact since our first marriages, but I still count these two fellows as a very special part of my early years; and later, too. When I married in 1965, Harold was my best man. Interesting, too, is the fact that Grant Olds, who later was having Bible studies with Dad, was their uncle. Grant's wife, Eldora, and the twin's mother, Ada, were sisters. They were good people. Thus, more ties with the Jehovah's Witnesses. In any event, the twins and I hit it off right from our first introduction, and in no time I had another set of close friends. As a matter of fact, I liked the whole family. Just being who they were provided another stabilizing influence for me.

The Gallios family played a big role in my teens, providing a place where I was accepted and appreciated for who I was. I guess you might say they "adopted" me. I spent a lot of time at their home and doing what boys that age do; walking the railroad tracks, swimming, and talking about girls and cars. The twins were into sports, Howard into baseball and Harold wrestling. Harold was one of those gifted with natural strength, coupled with a gift for wrestling. His strength was pretty phenomenal. As a sixteen-year old, he was able to grip, with both hands, more than 300 pounds on a set of bathroom scales. I could manage around 180 or 200 pounds, and I wasn't exactly a weakling. Skinny yes, but my "training" in an assortment of physically demanding work provided me a reasonable amount of strength. But no way could I match Harold. I attempted to wrestle with him, but gave up after being beaten fair and square about 10,000 times.

Harold struggled in school, found it boring, except for high school shop classes in which he excelled; especially auto mechanics class. I always thought him gifted in many related areas, but after eleven years of trying to cut the grade academically, he dropped out of high school in our junior year. He wanted me to drop out with him, but my heart was into finishing school, and so I said no.

Harold and Howard were paternal twins and just about as opposite in every respect, including appearance. Where Harold was outgoing, spontaneous, and impetuous, Howard was quiet, studious, methodical, and, in addition, an artist. Somehow, the three of us got along quite well. Both Howard and Harold were popular with the girls, just the opposite of me. I was shy and reserved, thinking myself too poor, and often would go out of my way to avoid them. This changed after I got my first car. Suddenly I was more in demand, not only as a taxi for my friends who didn't have transportation, but the girls were now available for dates now and then. I wasn't too serious about girls until my junior year anyway, so they took a "back seat" to my other interests, which were mostly hunting, fishing, and passing time along the river; either with friends, family, or simply by myself.

As I said, the Gallioses played a significant role in my later teens, providing a place where I was accepted and appreciated for who I was. I can't remember attending a Witness meeting with the Gallioses. Their dad, George, and the kids didn't seem to attend church regularly, but their mom, Ada, and grandmother, Mrs. Plum, did. How well I remember the "Pistol Packing Mama" incident on the Plum place up South Myrtle Road.

The Plum "ranch" was located at the point where the road from the Super Y Market and South Myrtle Road intersected about a mile south of town. The "ranch" consisted of about five acres of land and was on the creek side of the road, extending from the road to the bank of South Myrtle Creek. There were three domiciles on the property, the main home in which the Olds family lived, a smaller home in which Mr. and Mrs. Plum (the grandparents) lived, and an empty home next to the creek. George Gallios had constructed the home along the creek some years earlier, moving his family into it, but left when work demanded. There was electricity wired to the home, and it was being used for storage. One of the things stored was a phonograph player.

The Jehovah's Witness fellowship had arranged to use the Plum property for a picnic and BBQ, and a few days prior, Harold and I were conscripted to mow the pasture for the event; you know, for softball and games like that. The field we cut was between the two occupied homes and the now empty home down by the creek. We cut grass all afternoon using power mowers to sling grass and cow manure until the pasture became sufficiently "manicured" for respectable folks. Other work was being done by church volunteers. A small amplifier with an outside speaker was set up at the empty home for public address purposes during the BBQ.

During our work on the property leading up to the event, Harold and I had discovered some old '78s; one of them being, "Pistol Packing Mama." We played these inside the home alongside the creek during our breaks. But for the event the next day, we thought it would be great fun to hook the phonograph up to a microphone and broadcast this great music for the benefit and enjoyment of all, even though Harold's Aunt Eldora said she didn't like the song. But we actually thought it would not only be funny but would be enjoyed by many in attendance. When events were well in progress, we sneaked off to get the ball rolling. Didn't take us no time to place the microphone in front of the phonograph speaker, and we were in business. The turntable was spinning, the volume was cranked up, and the public address speakers were "speaking." Little did we know that Harold's Aunt Eldora had had her fill of that song in the days leading up to this event.

She came storming into the house.

"I told you not to play that song," she yelled at us (obviously in order to be heard over the speaker volume), and in a controlled slow-motion move lifted the record from the still spinning turntable, and broke the vinyl across her knee.

No, she told us *she didn't like the song*. She did not tell us *don't play the song*. For some reason, she took exception to lines such as, "...drinking beer in a cabaret, and was I having fun. Till somebody shot out the lights and now I'm on the run. O lay that pistol down, Babe. Lay that pistol down. Pistol packing Mama, lay that pistol down..."

As she stomped through the door, Harold looked at me with a silly grin on his face, and says, "Good thing she wasn't packing a pistol."

About the same time I met the Gallios family, I made a break from the Assembly of God church to the Nazarene church that was across from the elementary school. For some reason, one Sunday in my seventh or eighth grade, my sisters and I walked right past the Assembly of God church and down the street several blocks to the Nazarene Church, and for the rest of my time in Myrtle Creek, that's where I attended church, when I attended.

This wasn't my first visit to the Nazarene church, as my good buddy Gordon Simmons and his family attended the fellowship. Over the years, I had attended from time-to-time with Gordon. I was acquainted with several others in the fellowship as well; Mr. Kinney of Kinney's Variety store for one. Also, my sixth grade teacher, Mr. Misner, was a member, and that's where I discovered that he had a fine voice, as he would be scheduled to sing special music during the worship service. I'd listen to him sing and think, *Man, I sure wish I could sing like that someday*. Little did I know then how God would go about granting that wish.

At some point in my attending the Nazarene church, I met the McNaughton family.

George McNaughton was the son of Scottish immigrant parents. George and his family lived at the end of Norton Lane, a rather gnarly lane about a mile and a half mile long, off Highway 99, and only in as good condition as the neighbors along its length were inspired to keep it. George's dad and mom lived in a rather Scottish-looking cottage, located at the head of a small valley between two hills. Scottie raised sheep. As far as I know, they were his sole source of income.

George entered the Marine Corp as a seventeen-year-old, physically surviving the horrors of the South Pacific. He was proud, and rightly so, of his service to our country. But his service was not without latent emotional scars that would, in the '70s, be labeled "Delayed Stress Syndrome." In visits I had with George in the years preceding his death, he would reminisce about the mopping up operations on Iwo Jima and having to go into the caves that pockmarked the island to burn out the Japanese soldiers. I cannot imagine the horrors. He was especially proud of the fact that he was an eyewitness to the raising of the American flag on Mt. Seribachi.

George, his wife Arlene, and three kids, Kathy, Chris, and Allen, had a small farm about a half-mile past his dad's place at the end of Norton Lane. George had a cow or two, a few steers, homing pigeons, and dogs. That was about the extent of his farm, as he had a full-time job as a lathe operator for Nordic Veneers on East Diamond Lake Boulevard five or so miles east of Roseburg. Six months after graduating from high school, George put in a good word for me, and I landed a job pulling veneer off the greenbelt. For the six months or so that I held the job, I roomed and boarded with the McNaughtons.

George had become acquainted with my dad when both of them were working for the same logging outfit after the war. For some reason (maybe because he knew Dad), George took an interest in me. After church one Sunday, he asked if I'd be interested in working for him discing some acreage using his Caterpiller-10

George was one of those men who simply did things as his heart moved him, and in this way befriended and mentored several of the local lads. He had a good heart, and I benefited from it. Of course, at the time, I had no idea what he was doing. I thought he just needed to get some work done and needed a good worker, so I said, "Sure."

So one weekend in late spring of my sixteenth year, I found myself behind the clutch levers of a Cat-10 pulling a disc plow across one of his pastures. And boy, did I think I was something. Shoot man, I'm a cat skinner. So for several evenings and weekends, I could be proudly seen sitting in the seat of that Cat-10 pulling that disc plow to turn under the weeds.

I guess I must have been acting a little uppity about the whole matter. One day I rode my bike into his yard expecting to be running the Cat, but it was already at work in the pasture. Kathy was operating it. Now Kathy was George and Arlene's eldest daughter, but she still was no more than twelve or thirteen at the time, and she was doing what I had been doing. That took the starch out of my chauvinistic feathers. The only consolation was in the fact she got the Cat stuck in a seep that George had told her to stay away from.

George and Arlene didn't preach to me at all. They simply lived their Christian lives by example, and I was taking subconscious notes; notes that I have read over and over in my mind down through the years. They were what I call "down to earth but heavenly minded people." Their friendship and quiet example provided an anchor for a young man. They were both living examples of what a real Christian is, and should be. And so their examples played a major role in directing the course of my life.

If only we could truly appreciate the power of "words fitly spoken." I thank God for George's comments one cold and rainy night on our way home from work.

Our conversation was lagging as we descended the south side of Robert's Mountain. The rain was falling, windshield wipers were slapping, and the lights of his Chevy three-quarter ton flatbed reflected off the wet pavement of Interstate 5. George broke the silence asking, "Dan, what are you going to do with your life?"

I didn't answer immediately. I needed to think. *Well, I was a high school graduate, had a decent paying job in a veneer mill, and was saving money for the first time in my life. I was rooming and boarding with George and his family at that time.* Prior to George's question, I had not given the subject much thought.

I felt I had to give a serious answer to this serious question, so after some contemplation I astutely replied, "Well, I don't know exactly, George. Get married, buy a house, have some kids, I guess."

The answer didn't satisfy George, so he probed a little deeper. He then asked, "Dan, how much do you think I get paid an hour at the mill as a lathe operator?"

At the time he asked the question, I failed to see its relevance to our conversation. I retorted without thinking, "I don't know. How much do you make?"

With a serious kind of chuckle he said, "Dan, I make $2.72 an hour. That's thirty cents more an hour than you make. I run the lathe, and that's the third highest paying job in the mill. The millwright, and then the foreman, make the most money. Now, if you stay in this valley, this is about all you can ever expect to earn, 'cause I've been at this job for fifteen years and I'm only making thirty cents more an hour than you, and you're pulling on the green chain! If you are going to make something of yourself, you need to get out of this valley. Go to college. Join the Army, the Air Force; some branch of the military. I don't care, but get out of this valley, or in another fifteen years, you are going to be right where I am."

Well, that got my attention. I didn't have anything to say. Nobody had ever been so open and frank with me regarding my future, and so the wheels started turning. Which, I think, is exactly the response George wanted me to have. For the first time, I began to think seriously about what I wanted to do with my life.

Again, I think about what it is that influences our decisions. Certainly, George's conversation played a big part in directing the course of my life from that point on. But I also think about another friend I had in my late teens, Richard Sowersbery. Because he was my friend, and because of what he did, he influenced my decision to leave Myrtle Creek and join the United States Air Force.

Though brief, Richard's friendship was based on a common respect we had for each other and the joint relationship we both were building with Jesus Christ.

Richard and I became acquainted late in my junior year at Myrtle Creek High School. He was a senior. We both attended the Nazarene church. He had a jewel of a personality, kind and outgoing; the kind of person you liked being around. Our friendship was just beginning to develop when Dad moved us from Myrtle Creek to North Plains the summer of 1961. Even so, Richard and I stayed in touch, occasionally writing one another.

Just prior to my graduation in 1962, Richard enlisted in the Air Force, and shortly after basic training, sent me a picture from Kirkland AFB, New Mexico (you know the kind of staged photos one can have taken in a leather flight jacket and with full dress headgear). Sometime thereafter, probably early 1963, he sent me a letter telling me he had just been diagnosed with lymphoma. *Cancer!* He was coming home.

All who knew Richard were in shock, including me. To this day, my reaction puzzles and shames me. I withdrew from Richard. I remember seeing him once after he returned to Myrtle Creek. He had been discharged within a few weeks following the diagnosis that his cancer was terminal. While the Veteran's Administration continued to treat him at the hospital in Portland, not once did I visit him during his stays. He died at home about three months or so following his discharge.

I cannot provide an explanation for my actions at that time. Like the death of Bobby Hulie, I simply could not bear to attend Richard's funeral. I was rooming and boarding with the McNaughtons, and I know that my actions puzzled both George and Arlene. For whatever reasons, I still cannot explain why I reacted as I did. I know that though our time together in the flesh was short, Richard, too, was used to fashion me into an instrument of God's eternal peace.

Because of what George said on that cold and stormy night as we drove over Boomer Hill from Roseburg to Myrtle Creek, and because of who Richard was and what he did, a seed was planted. Forces were operating in me, of which I was unaware. I became increasing uncomfortable with my job as a green chain laborer at Nordic Veneer adjacent to the Diamond Lake Highway east of Roseburg. While the money was good and I was able to purchase a fairly nice car (a '55 Pontiac two-door hardtop), the benefits did not prevent me quitting the job. I moved back to North Plains. It had been a year since I had graduated.

I spent a few days off and on that summer picking berries with my folks for one last stint in Schumacher's field in Stayton. I picked some cucumbers north of Forest Grove with Harold Gallios, who connected up with me that summer, then in October of that year, with George McNaughton's comments ringing in my ears, I joined the United States Air Force.

Did all these people I write about leave their mark on me? Did George have an impact on my life? Did Richard Sowersbery? You bet they did. They all did. While I personally never told most of them about the impact they had on me, aside from what is written herein, I told George several times in the years prior to his death in 2005. Yes, all mentioned herein played their assigned role in instilling a burning desire for something better. In their own way, each contributed to stoke the embers of change into a burning flame; a flame fanned by a couple of probing questions in a '49 Chevy flat-bed truck that cold early spring night in 1963.

In the later years of George's life, especially the last two or so, I visited as often as I could, as he was dying of cancer and its ensuing medical complications. I had several opportunities to let George know that he played a huge role in my teenage years, and that I appreciated and loved him for who he was. And my feelings are the same for Arlene. My hope is that these words are but a small token of the appreciation I have for the impact both these people had on me in my childhood years.

The McNaughton family presented me the honor of officiating at George's funeral in February of 2005.

I have learned to reflect on, and thus appreciate, all the people God brings into my life as he forms and shapes me into who he desires me to be.

Some six years prior to my enlistment in the Air Force, in the summer between my seventh and eighth grades, my cousin, Denny Sjorgren, caused me to consider the fact that I did not have to live the way my dad lived. I remember the time and the circumstances in which I expressed my heart's desire; that time and those words were etched on plates of stainless steel in my memory. *(And, yes, Denny, you also played a role in who I have become.)* Let me tell you about that time.

I had spent a week or so visiting Denny at my Aunt Edna's and Uncle Stanley's home at Elgarose, west of Roseburg. Denny's older brother, Dick, drove me home in the back seat of his little MG sports car. Dick and Denny stayed for a short visit. Denny and I went to play on a swing on the limb of a large oak in a clearing a couple hundred feet from the house. Dick was visiting with Mom and Dad. Denny and I grew tired of the swing and were walking back toward the house, and yes, the "shack" and the overall environment were not a pretty picture.

Denny, with a tone of disgust (for which I cannot blame him) was looking at all this and said, "Dan, how in the world can you live like this?" He wasn't being mean, just honest in asking a question. It deserved an answer.

Of course I was ashamed. But I knew the answer and said, "I will never live like this."

I believe God put that thought in me, and as it smoldered it eventually burst into flame, becoming a light that has guided me to this day. I would like to think that if I went back to the old home site today, and if I listened hard, I would hear the same words echo off the canyon walls of Timber Butte, *I will never live like this...I will never live like this...I will never live like this...I will never live like this.*

Peace

I believe that from my first breath, in all the dismal and seemingly hopeless periods of my childhood, and in all life's situations and circumstances that followed, my heavenly Father has tenderly formed me into an instrument of His eternal peace. His patient grace was the key that opened my heart to understanding. This peace is the sequel to all the evil, suffering, and labor of my childhood experience.

In the angry times, I would fantasize about taking matters into my own hands and putting an end to Dad's troubled existence. As an alternative, I would pray that God would cause him to drive his car off Dole Road, through the opening in the cliff overlooking the Highway 99 bridge over the South Umpqua.

Yes, there was anger. And there was fear so deep and dark I imagined I could taste it. But the anger and fear were not so much against the man who triggered the depths of my emotions as they were against the helplessness and hopelessness of the circumstances. I see in all life's sorrows and evil, a primitive grace at work; a grace that created a yearning for well being, as well as rest and peace. Such were the latent yearnings that directed my path over the years. I have come to see that it is fruitless to think what might have been if my environment had been different, for I now see that every factor was necessary for me to be placed where I am today, and for the role God desires I play as one whom he chose, called, and educated. Therefore, as I pursue God's purpose for me, I believe that every factor in my life, every situation (good and evil), every acquaintance, every friend, contributed to making me who I am.

As I stated in the introduction, even before I began life's journey from Dole Road, God saved me. Oh, I knew little about what happened to me the day I first believed; but since that time, and especially since standing in grace, I believe He has guided and directed my steps for my learning. Of course, it is only as I look back from the vantage point of time, that I am able to see reason and purpose in the path God destined I walk. Strangely enough, and mysterious though it seems, as I ponder that path, I see all experiences embedded with a dignity I cannot adequately explain. Not only do I see the dignity of God's grace at work in the events and circumstances, I laud His name that by them, and especially in my later years, He brought my life full circle—back to those whom He appointed to play roles in my life during that troubled period.

I cannot deny the shame I felt that resulted from my childhood environment of poverty, alcoholism, and domestic violence. That caustic environment coupled with early life experiences in the grit and gravel of Dole Road embedded a desire to never live as I lived then. I also came to understand that in order to maintain a modicum of peace in that environment, Mom and us kids had to continually placate the abusive anger of a drunk. It was a constant but unconscious force that imprinted on me a need to please others, and to seek their approbation. In retrospect, I see that these forces played a role in all I chose to do and with whom I chose to associate; whether in the secular or in the religious arenas of my adult life. In a sense, I desired to be normal. But "normal" for me was not normal for God. My assumptions about lessons from the past were that I had to work hard to make something of myself—to better myself above the stigma and shame of Dole Road. He desired something better, and thus He laid out a curriculum in secular and religious "hard knocks" that would teach me about love unconditional, and would bring me into a love relationship with Him.

He began the process by pulling me from the familiar and transporting me into the unknown.

Within a year and a half after leaving Myrtle Creek, I enlisted in the United States Air Force. It was October 12, 1963. College was not a choice for me, but military service was. There, I received an intensive education in avionics electronics that set the foundation for my life's avocation as an electronic technician and technical writer. First, basic training at Lackland AFB, San Antonio, Texas, followed by electronics fundamentals at Keesler AFB, Boloxi, Mississippi, and then advanced electronics at Lowry AFB, Denver, Colorado. At Denver I met Ruth, my wife to be. We were married in Portland, Oregon August 22, 1965, and after a short honeymoon drove to Minot AFB, North Dakota, where I was stationed until 1968. Our daughter, Sally, and son, Edward, were born during that assignment.

During my time in Minot I began an intense study into the doctrines promoted by the Radio Church of God, pastored by Herbert W. Armstrong, and shortly after my re-enlistment in 1967, Ruth and I began attending their fellowship in Bismarck, North Dakota. Just before my new assignment to Camp Douglas, Wisconsin, both my wife and I were baptized as members into that denomination.

Because of the denomination's teachings regarding military service, I applied for a discharge as a conscientious objector, and was honorably discharged in November 1969.

In the years immediately following my discharge, Dad and Mom were both alive. All my sisters had married, and were working to raise their families. Between the five of us kids, we gave them twenty-two grandchildren.

Dad and Mom had moved several times since our initial move to North Plains, Oregon in 1961, and in the late '60s, they purchased a small lot and home along Oregon Highway 47 between Birkenfeld and Jewell, Oregon. Dad received a Social Security stipend, and a military disability retirement, and while not financially well-off, Dad and Mom at least had sufficient for the necessities.

Dad never completely quit drinking, and in the latter months prior to his death, he was drinking constantly and heavily. Just a few months before he died, Mom phoned and asked me to drive him to the Veteran's Hospital in Vancouver, Washington, for detox. But upon release, he immediately went back to the bottle. Within a few weeks, just prior to his 67th birthday in February 1974, he died of a stroke. His grave is in a small community cemetery in Mist, Oregon.

Within a year following Dad's death, Mom married Jack Hogg. Seems like Mom liked older men, because, like Dad, Jack was about fifteen years her senior. She settled into his home in Winston, Oregon, and for the first time in her life was financially secure. She no longer had to "watch her pennies." While the sudden remarriage was a surprise to family and friends, an even greater surprise was her desire to learn to drive. After repeated failures through Jack's instructions (his well-kept 1965 Rambler being much worse in appearance for his efforts), I advised her to take lessons from a private instructor. She took my advice, and after three lessons, passed her driver's test. She wasn't shy about showing off her hard won skills and freedom, and rightly so. All who knew her were proud of her accomplishment. She used every excuse to get behind the wheel; even trips to the Pacific Coast and to the Portland area.

After Jack's death in March, 1997, Mom lived by herself in Winston, continuing to give of herself to family and friends until suffering a massive stroke in June, 2003. The stroke left her paralyzed from the neck down, though with all her mental faculties in place. I would travel regularly to Roseburg to visit her (usually playing guitar and singing the old songs) in the Rose Lodge Nursing Home, where she was being lovingly doted on by my sisters, Patsy, Ellen, and Linda. I love my sisters. They daily provided a witness to all in their unconditional love and care for Mom's needs until her death in September, 2004. She was laid to rest among family and friends who had preceded her in death, in the Elgarose Cemetery, west of Roseburg, Oregon.

Following my discharge in November of 1969, my wife and I moved back to the Portland, Oregon area. There I obtained employment as an electronic technician with Tektronix, Inc. of Beaverton, Oregon, and we moved into a rental in Hillsboro. Within a year I obtained a position as a technical writer, which was my principle avocation; both as a full time employee, and in my latter employment, as a contract technical writer. In June 1971 my wife and I were blessed with a second son, David; and in January 1975, a second daughter, Julie. And so with gainful employment and with shared domestic responsibilities, Ruth and I were committed to raising a family and to our church life.

In February 1972, we purchased a new home in a development in Aloha, Oregon. We were "in heaven," so to speak; especially for me as I pondered events and circumstances over the previous decade that had moved me from a canvas-sided shack to a new, four-bedroom home in Aloha, Oregon. It was indeed a testament to the power of my will that had set itself to never live as I had lived as a child. And I set my sights higher. Within three short years, we sold our home, purchasing a daylight basement home on two-acres in the country between Canby and Hubbard, Oregon.

By this time in my life I had much to be thankful for, and I was feeling pretty good about myself. I had a nice home, a wonderful family, and my job was going well. I advanced quickly in levels of responsibility; eventually managing several groups of technical writers. Additionally, I was teaching the trade in company classes, and I was working as a consultant to local community colleges and undergraduate schools to help establish technical writing curriculums. In my final two years of employment at Tektronix, I obtained a program marketing manager position. And, I was becoming somebody in the church; where I gladly took all jobs assigned, from sound technician to teen ministry; eventually receiving ordinations as a deacon, then lay minister. I had arrived, so to speak; a testament to perseverance and the human will. I was confident in my abilities, and appreciated for them. Hard work had paid off.

But winds of change were beginning to blow. Shortly following my promotion to a program marketing manager, Tektronix began down-sizing. My position was eliminated, but I was offered a choice. Take a manufacturing management position or a severance bonus. I took the severance bonus and using some of the monies set up Technical Communication Services, a contract technical writing company. Thus, in '86, I opened a company office in Beaverton. The business immediately prospered.

At the time I classified myself as one who had "pulled himself up by his own bootstraps." While my achievements were not the stuff of legends, my high opinion of myself was fostered by the compliments and "pats on the back" received from family and friends. In retrospect, I truly did desire to be known as somebody who had pulled himself from the pit and mire of life, and by application of specific principles was able to achieve a modicum of success by the world's and the church's standards. In a worldly sense we were not rich; still, those whose care for which I was responsible did not go without. We had sufficient for extensive vacations to fun spots and resorts around the Midwest and Western United States, including two trips to Hawaii. These were yearly events done as part of holy day observances of the church to which we belonged. In time, Ed and David became college graduates, and my two daughters were happily married. So even family-wise I had something in which to boast. But forces were working in both the secular and the religious arenas of my life to teach me that pride comes before a fall.

By the late '80's I had created a comfortable nest for myself and family and was settled in its softness and warmth. I had responsibility, I had self-worth, and I felt I was appreciated and loved for who I was—both in the secular world of business and entrepreneurship, and in the church. My life had meaning, and I could measure how well I played my role by exponential increases in responsibility. Pride in self kept pace, and this is what my past imprinted on me. Pride! I am somebody; I am appreciated; my life has value; and would continue so if I just kept my nose to the grindstone.

Sadly, since entering the Air Force, my association with those outside my immediate family played second fiddle to my church "family." Ironically, the church's exclusive doctrines (some have termed them cultic) appealed to me, providing the identity that soothed my shameful past; I felt special, being convinced I had found the true way, and had been called into it by God Himself. Like in my secular work, I applied myself to learn all about this "new way." But, because of the strong doctrinal position, most of my spare time was allotted to church responsibilities and functions. Oh, there were the occasional reunions with aunts, uncles, cousins, nephews and nieces, over the ensuing years, but there was never a close familial relationship. Fellowship and friendships were pretty much tempered through the church's teachings and thus I held at arms length all who did not believe and act as I did. Thus, it was with my old friends of the past. As I stated, there were occasional visits, but too often, such visits were years and even decades, apart. Even this arena of my life was due for a drastic change. Changes in all areas of my life seemed to have been precipitated by changes in my occupation and in the church; which, both, interestingly, began in 1986.

Following the death of the church's founder, Herbert Armstrong, in 1986, certain senior ministers began to question some of the doctrines, such as Sabbath keeping, food laws, and so on. The change process was lengthy, and in time, the subject of grace was introduced and taught. But human nature being what it is, there's always two sides—those who embrace the "new" and those who resist the "new." I began to embrace the new—grace. Not only were doctrinal teachings questioned, but I began to see how the old doctrinal teachings had tempered friendships and relationships. Light slowly dawned on me that the foundation upon which I had based friendship and fellowship was built on sifting sand. Eventually the factions within the church became too great and in the spring of 1995 the church split, divided right down the middle over doctrinal differences. My family also became divided; my wife and two eldest children remained with the old teachings.

I take no credit for any of the changes that occurred in me. I give all credit and glory to Almighty God for the events and circumstances that transpired in the late '80s to mid '90's; for indeed they precipitated my transformation from one whose identity was based on what I did, to an identity based on who I was in Christ. Of course there are two sides to the story, and there are those who disagree with my assessment of what transpired. But as I look back, I can only conclude that God was not through with me, as He began to tear down the pillars that supported the plateau of prestige upon which I based my life and future. Sadly, I must also relate that my marriage, just shy of forty years, fell victim to the forces that rocked my life at that time.

As Corporate America would label it, somebody "moved my cheese"—I was thrust from the nest! At the time I would not have described my change as "thrust" upon me, for the verb implies action by an outside force. At the time, I thought the change was channeled by my hand, not another's. But as light began to shine in shadows cast by fear, doubt, and ambiguity, faith illumined God's grace. I was being transformed.

In May 1995, through no seeming difficulties or effort on my own, I obtained full-time employment as Director of Corporate Communications with Marin Telecommunications Incorporated

(MTC) in Petaluma, California, where I had worked for several months prior as a contract writer. Within a few months I was also assigned responsibilities as Director of International Sales. In fulfilling these responsibilities I had to travel; primarily to train new sales associates in London, Amsterdam, and Buenos Aires. In each of these places, God orchestrated situations and circumstances in which he validated me as one of His sons.

Because of what I experienced during employment with MTC, and because of the changes that had divided the church, I felt compelled to write and submit letters of resignation as an employee of MTC, and as a minister of the World Wide Church of God. My wife and I loaded up the moving van again and returned to our home (which had remained empty during our absence), in Amity, Oregon. Now, I was unemployed. My contract technical writing business had been neglected and was lying in the ditch, and I had stepped away from thirty years of corporate religion. And, to make matters worse, friends and associates on both sides of the church split viewed me with suspicion, and pretty much treated me as a pariah whenever I would visit their fellowships. Truly I was out of the nest.

I rolled up my sleeves and went back to work, seizing what I thought was a new opportunity and direction.

Our home in Amity was situated on an acre and a quarter lot. My wife and I decided to divide the property into three lots, and place a new manufactured home on the largest parcel. I did all the lot development and site prep and within six months we were comfortably settled in our new home, which included a twenty-four by forty garage. This experience was so gratifying that I decided to take the Oregon State General Contractor's test. Lo! I passed. I became a general contractor. My eldest son was a college graduate by this time, and he and I, working together, never worked so hard to starve to death. I hung up my general contractor's license after a year or so, and took a full-time job as a technical writer with Flight Dynamics, Inc. of Tigard, Oregon, remaining employed until January 2002.

For thirty years my denominational affiliation with the World Wide Church of God worked to teach me lessons that law was not dead, and that one could earn God's approval by works. But, as I matured in grace, I joyously came to understand that all one has to do to receive salvation's gift is believe in Christ's death, burial and resurrection (I Corinthians 5:1–3). No works, no effort, no sacraments. Just faith. I was beside myself with joy, and was convinced I had reached the pinnacle of learning, and so I wrote, and sung, and taught; even having a weekly live radio program on a Portland radio station. And yet, what I gained in all this new learning and experience was not the end—it was just the beginning, the first of many plateaus. Each step, each lesson, required time to digest. It had to be reviewed in my mind again and again and validated by His Word. And so it was in grace that I began to discover what it meant to be free. Free from the chains of my past, and free from the chains of working to become somebody for God.

Initially I did not welcome the liberation. Its immediate effect was separation. And the transition required painful incidents in order that learning could occur from the old to the new. My views of reality required an adjustment that without pain could never occur.

I had to learn what it meant to rely on God. By January of 2002, I knew my marriage was in trouble, and because of debts accumulated due to faulty "investment" decisions, I was now not only facing nuptial bankruptcy, but financial bankruptcy as well! Truly, all I had built by my own efforts was disintegrating around me. First, financial bankruptcy, then eighteen months of unemployment, followed by marital separation. The lovely new home I had built for our retirement was sold and assets divided equally. I moved into a seniors' mobile home park in Newburg, Oregon, and shortly thereafter, obtained a technical writing job with AEC, Inc. in Sandy, Oregon; one month before my unemployment benefits ran out. I not only was learning lessons about being one of God's sons, but was learning that He also cares for His own.

During my separation, I met, Chloe, my future wife to be. We were married in May 2005. I then relocated to Chloe's home in Vancouver, Washington. For some reason she did not want to live in my 1973, fourteen- by fifty-foot single-wide mobile home in an over 55 retirement park. Living in Vancouver, I had to put on another hat. Chloe had custody of a five-year old grandson, and so at age 62, I stepped into a father-role again.

As I look back on where I was on Dole Road, I know I came far by human standards, but not without cost. But regardless, I shall never lose sight of the lessons the journey provided, for the journey brought me from poverty, to an interim comfortable nest, and then finally into His enduring rest. I can say with confidence, that I am now anchored. At one time I was a stranger to the Land of Grace, I was rootless, a transient, adrift in life's sea salted with pride. But now He has anchored me in Him, in the knowing I am one of His beloved sons, never more to be cast adrift, but forever anchored in the Rock of Ages and in the arms of love.

....

But even these plateaus of learning and blessing were not the destination. It was just part of the journey, and so in the past few years, I have been reconnected with family and old friends in a new way—the way of love. We maintain contact by phone, emails, occasional visits, and the social network sites. The circle of relationships that began during my childhood on Dole Road is becoming more complete with each passing year.

Interestingly, during almost all those times that I have narrated in this story, I played the guitar; and sang the old country songs for friends whenever and wherever invited. And I would sing special music in church, sing for funerals, and sing for weddings. But, much as I had enjoyed using my talent, and as much joy and pleasure it seemed to provide those who listened, I had never written a song until I began a love relationship with my Lord and Savior, Christ Jesus. Prior to that time, I was always singing somebody else's music. But when grace entered I became somewhat "picky," searching for songs that, at least to me, appropriately heralded the subject. But, as I obtained higher plateaus of understanding of God's grace and His love, even these songs began to lose their appeal. And then the music came.

In late 1999, I wrote the song, *Alive in Him*. Since then, I have completed over sixty songs, not through my effort, but due to the simple fact that I believe God uses me, as His instrument, to compose His music. Besides, all is for His glory and not mine. Starting in late 2005, through the encouragement of my wife, Chloe, I began to record the music. I have just completed my fourth CD, *Love Transcendent*, through Tate Music Group, Inc., studios of Oklahoma City. Interestingly, the music is often the vehicle that initiates the reconnection with "friends on the hill."

I leave you with these two final things. First, the words of the Apostle Paul who writes, "By the grace of God I am who I am" (1 Corinthians 15:10). Like Paul, I too am who I am, and it is all a result of His work. Thus, I am at peace with my heavenly Father. Further, His conciliatory work on Golgotha's Hill has allowed me to be at peace with all those within my sphere here on earth—including my earthly father. I do not hate him. I love him for who he was; not only my fleshly father, but also a vessel God used to form me into an instrument of His eternal peace.

Second, I leave you with the words to one of the songs I composed to honor a dear friend whose grandson was killed in Iraq. I find no other words adequately express who I am today by God's grace.

Peace, Peace, Wonderful Peace

(verse 1) As we struggle in life's trials, against the weakness of the flesh,
We find they're just the fiery darts of the unseen foe.
Worries and anxieties, seem to crush us to the ground
And in our pain and agony we cry for peace.

(chorus) Peace, peace, wonderful peace.
Flowing down from God's celestial throne above.
Peace, peace, wonderful peace.
Peace we have in the Beloved Son of His Love.

(verse 2) We endure on-and-on, in this battle from day-by-day
Though our life appears to be spinning out of control,
But this life's a stage where we learn, that no matter how the pages turn,
That He's finished it all and we can rest in what He's done.

(verse 3) This peace of mind we seek, we find the Word clearly does speak,
It says, "We've been justified by His enduring faith.
Not by our strength we find, this blessed peace of mind,
But in knowing He's holding us up in His loving embrace.

(verse 4) So let's live each day He gives, and walk by faith and not by sight.
And lift up holy hands to praise His holy name.
Praying always in faith, we grow in knowledge of His will
And every breath we take we grown in grace until…we have…

This is where I am today. This is where God led me as He wove, and continues to weave, the threads of my life. He knew me before I was born. He knew what I needed in the way of situations and circumstances, and in family and friends to bring me to Him in love and not in fear. Yes, in all that has transpired from the day of my first knowing, there was this desire for peace. And over time, I see that God has orchestrated events for my learning so that I could eventually come to know the very peace of God. It has been slowly draped over me, until today my fevered agitation and fretting are gone. His love has brought me to where I see Him as my all in all, and so I worship and praise Him for the work He is yet to complete in me.